THE PACIFIC RIM CONFERENCE ON
CHILDREN'S LITERATURE
from Scarecrow Press

One Ocean Touching: Papers from the First Pacific Rim Conference on Children's Literature, University of British Columbia, 1976. Edited by Sheila A. Egoff. 1979.

A Track to Unknown Water: Proceedings of the Second Pacific Rim Conference on Children's Literature, Melbourne
State College, 1979. Edited by Stella Lees. 1987. (First
published by Department of Librarianship, Melbourne State
College, 1980.)

A Sea of Upturned Faces: Proceedings of the Third Pacific
Rim Conference on Children's Literature, University of California at Los Angeles, 1986. Edited by Winifred Ragsdale.
1989.

A SEA OF UPTURNED FACES

Proceedings of the Third Pacific Rim Conference on Children's Literature

edited by
WINIFRED RAGSDALE

The Scarecrow Press, Inc.
Metuchen, N.J., & London
1989

Z1037.A1P25   1986

Grateful acknowledgment is made to the following writers and publishers for permission to reprint their material:

Excerpts from "The Owl and the Wind" by Madeline A. Chafee and from "Mr Owl" by Edna Hamilton. Reprinted with permission from Poetry Place Anthology. Copyright © 1983 by Instructor Books, Inc. Cleveland, Ohio 44130.

"Song of the Owl," published in Songs of the Dream People (Atheneum, 197 is quoted by permission of the author, James Houston. Copyright © 1972 b James Houston.

Conrad Aiken, "Owl," from Cats and Bats and Things with Wings. Copyright © 1965 by Conrad Aiken. Reprinted with the permission of Atheneum Publishers, an imprint of Macmillan Publishing Company, and of Brandt & Brandt, Literary Agents, Inc.

"Owls Talking" (1952) and "Blessed Lord, what it is to be young" (1961), from One at a Time, by David McCord. Copyright © 1952, 1961 by David McCord. By permission of Little, Brown and Company.

"The Bird of Night," ("A shadow is floating..."). Reprinted with permission of Macmillan Publishing Company from The Bat-Poet, by Randall Jarrell. Copyright © Macmillan Publishing Company 1963, 1964; reproduced by permission of Penguin Books Ltd.

Quotes from E. S. Craighill Handy, The Hawaiian Planter. Vol. 1: His Plants, Methods and Areas of Cultivation. 1940. Reprinted, by permission of the Editor, from Bishop Museum Bulletin 161 (Kraus reprint 1971).

British Cataloguing-in-Publication data available

Library of Congress Cataloging-in-Publication Data

Pacific Rim Conference on Children's Literature (3rd : 1986 : University of California at Los Angeles)
    A sea of upturned faces : proceedings of the Third Pacific Rim Conference on Children's Literature / edited by Winifred Ragsdale.
       p.   cm.
   Includes bibliographical references and index.
   ISBN 0-8108-2108-7
    1. Children--Pacific Area--Books and reading--Congresses. 2. Libraries, Children's--Pacific Area--Congresses. 3. Children's literature--Pacific Area--History and criticism--Congresses. 4. Pacific Area in literature--Congresses. 5. Pacific Area--Literatures--History and criticism--Congresses. I. Ragsdale, Winifred. II. Title.
Z1037.A1P25 1986
028.5'5--dc19   88-26534

CONTENTS

FOREWORD

In her keynote address at the Third Pacific Rim Conference on Children's Literature, Mildred Batchelder quoted
an Australian newspaper article predicting the possibility that
the Asia-Pacific area would play the same central role in the
21st century as the Mediterranean Sea in the Elizabethan Age
or the Atlantic Ocean throughout the Industrial Revolution.
How prescient, therefore, was Sheila Egoff's establishment
of the Pacific Rim Conferences on Children's Literature in
1976. Whenever people of this vast area come together to
share their successes and problems, whether in agriculture,
trade policies, or children's literature, they gain understanding. And it is in the spirit of helping the Pacific Rim area
to assume its importance in a harmonious way that advocates
of fine literature for children have met three times so far--
first in Vancouver, then in Melbourne in 1979 under the
guidance of Stella Lees, and most recently in Los Angeles.

The Third Pacific Rim Conference on Children's Literature was held August 24-29, 1986, on the campus of the University of California, Los Angeles. Its theme was "A Sea of
Upturned Faces: How We Share Our Literature and Related
Traditions with Our Children." Each meeting day carried a
subtheme: State of the Art of Children's Literature; Aspects
of Writing, Publishing, Marketing--Availability of Children's
Literature to Children; Forms of Children's Literature and
Their Transmittal to Children; and Individuality and Universality in Native Literature for Children of All Countries.

The papers in this volume speak for themselves as im-
passioned and committed views from the world of the poet,

ix

fiction writer, illustrator, editor, critic, storyteller, librarian, and teacher of children's literature. The reading of these papers at the conference was supplemented with traditional music, puppetry, magic, and book-related films, as well as an evening's storytelling festival. A centerpiece of the week was, perhaps, the presentation of nine fairly brief talks, some accompanied by audiovisual materials and each given twice to small groups for maximum exposure and discussion. They described practical problems in the field of children's literature common to Pacific Rim cultures: the preservation, study, and translation of traditional stories; the development of a literature reflecting minority children; and the provision of strong library service to young people.

Here is the gathering of the papers from the Third Pacific Rim Conference, dedicated to a greater understanding among Pacific Rim peoples and to helping children "share in the great common pool of story that belongs to all their kind; to find their own worries and feelings and wonderings there, defined and shared with others ... to extend life."*

> Winifred Ragsdale
> former Director
> George G. Stone Center for
>   Children's Books
> Claremont Graduate School in
>   Southern California

---

*Patricia Wrightson, "The Geranium Leaf," The Horn Book 62 (March/April 1986): 182.

PART I:

A WELCOME

The California State Librarian expresses his concern with
children's literature on an international scale as he greets the
conference participants.

Chapter 1

REMARKS

Gary E. Strong

It is an honor for me to bring greetings to this conference on behalf of the State of California and the California
State Library. I am pleased that we have been able in some
small way to provide support to your efforts and to be supportive of this incredible undertaking. Please allow me to
add my personal best wishes for the conference and the hope
and expectation that the acquaintances and friendships that
you forge here will last.

The benefits of developing cooperative service arrange-
ments among the librarians, authors, illustrators, and per-
formers of the Pacific Rim are apparent. Extremely important
is the identification of and access to materials and human resources, as well as an improved cultural understanding of all
the varied populations living on the Rim.

An understanding of our cultures is extremely important
in developing an understanding of the information needs of
this area. Through our children, we can achieve an international understanding and appreciation that will help us address
the issues of business and government, health information,
and communication. The better we are as information providers
and the better we understand and are made aware of these
needs, the better our role as library service providers will
be.

Our nations function as cultural, economic, political, and social gateways across the Pacific. A successful library service program that promotes the free flow of information could be a model for the world. What can we achieve together in the areas of technical training, staff exchange, and development of data-based information about our respective resources?

The problem of illiteracy must be a concern for us all. Our efforts here in California are only scratching the surface. We must work to teach adults to read in order to set good examples for our children. We must make 1987 truly the Year of the Reader!* How can we work to encourage the active creation of great children's literature as we look to the year 2000?

As the State Librarian of California, I remain committed to the continuing process of exploring these and other common interests. Members of my staff stand ready to continue to work with you and to contribute toward our common objectives. We share the common goal of excellence of service for our children and youth, and also the goal that they grow toward international understanding and lasting peace in the Pacific.

As you reflect upon these values, keep in mind a short chapter entitled, "At the Public Library," from The Human Comedy by the late William Saroyan. Ulysses Macauley, a pre schooler, and his good friend Lionel Cabot, an older boy whose limited mental capacity has prevented his learning to read, venture into the public library and are bedazzled by what they find.

> A little frightened at what he was doing, Lionel lifted a book out of the shelf, held it in his hands a moment and then opened it.
> "There, Ulysses," he said. "A book! There it is! See? They're saying something in here.... There's an A," he said. "That's an A right there. There's another letter of some sort. I don't know what one that is. Every letter's different, Ulysses, and every word's different...."

---

*Designation initiated in the Center of the Book, U.S. Library of Congress.

He closed the book slowly, put it back in its place, and together the two friends tiptoed out of the library. Outside, Ulysses kicked up his heels, because he felt good, and because it seemed he had learned something new.

The Lionels and Ulysses of tomorrow are going to miss a lot if we are not able to adequately support our libraries. Your commitment to children's literature at this conference is a significant assurance that library service is indeed vital to the maintenance of our common international goals.

My hope is for a bright and productive conference. My very best wishes and those of the State of California go with you.

PART II:

BEGINNINGS

Long years of observation and participation, together with
careful research, have resulted in Mildred Batchelder's presentation of the development of an international awareness in
the field of children's literature.

Chapter 2

LEARNING ABOUT SHARING--CHILDREN'S BOOKS
IN THE INTERNATIONAL SCENE

Mildred Batchelder

For a long time I have been thinking about the use of
books to promote world friendship and international understanding, about the use in the United States of children's books
in foreign languages and the use of translated children's books
in this country and elsewhere. I should like to review some
of the efforts toward these ends which I have observed in
this century.

As schools in the United States improved in the first
quarter of the century, teachers and librarians were seeking
more books, written for children, with information about other countries. Publishers responded with several series.
Among them were Peeps at Many Lands, Children of Other
Lands, The Little Schoolmate series, and the Twin books by
Lucy Fitch Perkins. Some were written by natives of the
particular country. Others, like the Twin books, were all
by one author. Of course the libraries already had a number
of stories from other countries, Heidi, Pinocchio, the Jungle
Books, Kim, Hans Brinker and DuChaillu's African adventure
stories among them.

By the 1920s publishing books for children in the
United States was becoming much more important than before.
Editors of children's books were added to publishing houses

9

for the first time. This became a trend and inaugurated what was called the golden age of children's books. To help librarians choose books wisely a children's librarian, Jessie Gay Van Cleve, was added in 1922 to the staff of the American Library Association monthly, The Booklist. In 1922 the Newbery Medal was established by the American Library Association to recognize and encourage new authors in the field. These changes, and others, brought with them more good books about countries, more fine picture books, story books, and information books.

In 1924 Clara W. Hunt, head of the children's department of the Brooklyn Public Library, wrote a small folder for the New York League of Nations Non-Partisan Association entitled International Friendship through Children's Books.[1] Over the years many articles and library programs in small and large libraries alike developed this theme and promoted books for use in achieving international understanding. Jella Lepman, founder of the International Youth Library in Munich described the characteristics that must be kept in mind in choosing books to increase understanding between peoples.

> Children's books worthy to create international understanding should never carry a missionary note. They should be free of nationalism and racialism and carry the message of true tolerance. They should be completely sincere, showing life in its broader aspects, portraying landscapes and customs of the diverse countries. Children's books should never be made the instruments of political propaganda. They should dwell on the human side of life.... They should be written with art and imagination and with hope. They should show the good and the bad sides of life quite realistically but also the wonders that courage and faith can create.[2]

For a period after World War II, few children's books were published in several European countries. American children's librarians, then and later, wanted publishers in other countries to know of U.S. books which they might like to consider for translation. The American Library Association children's librarians' section made annual lists of children's books it recommended for translation beginning in 1930 and for 35 years sent them to librarians in other countries to pass on to publishers. There was no easy way for foreign

publishers to see U.S. books of interest; they probably waited
until a reader or literary agent who knew their needs recommended a book to them. In 1972 the lists were replaced by
the American Library Association publication, Children's Books
of International Interest,[3] with a second edition in 1978 and
a third in 1984. The last edition no longer focused on books
which might be considered for translation but suggested to
teachers and librarians, here and abroad, children's books
published in the United States which could "help children
realize their place as world citizens."[4]

By 1984, publishers were enjoying several opportunities
to see many children's books from countries throughout the
world at the annual Frankfurt and Bologna book fairs; in
Bologna children's books are shown exclusively. More U.S.
publishers and editors, and a few librarians, have begun to
attend the fairs. Here books are easily seen, publication
rights can be negotiated, and first steps may be taken toward
sharing a wide variety of children's books internationally.
Also, ever since its founding in 1949, the International Youth
Library in Munich has been building a collection of children's
books from all over the world, and it provides a place where
publishers and others can see and consider children's books
for possible translation.

Long before libraries generally adopted policies of including books in foreign languages in response to the diversity of cultures within our country, children's librarians
felt it was important to have children's books in other lan-
guages--and for several reasons. One of the most important
was that English-speaking children would have the experience
of seeing children's books in other tongues than their own.
In addition, many beautiful books in European languages provided a pleasure and a valuable experience for children speaking any language. Some were the originals of classics already
on library shelves in English. Poring over these was for
some children their beginning realization of the diversity of
the world.

The first list by the American Library Association chil-
dren's librarians' section to help choose foreign language
books for libraries appeared in 1930 as Children's Books in
Twelve Countries.[5] In 1954 the same group compiled a list,
Foreign Children's Books Available in the United States.[6]
The committee preparing it was chaired by Helen Masten of

the New York Public Library, and it was published by that
library. Supplements were published in 1955, 1957, 1958,
and 1965, with Maria Cimino as chairman, in Top of the News,
the quarterly of the association's school and children's library divisions.[7,8]

Large libraries could cope with finding channels to buy
foreign children's books, but sources for purchasing them
were not accessible to small libraries and schools. The
American Library Association children's librarians' section,
again with Helen Masten as chairman, developed a plan for
selecting children's books in several languages and making
them available in packages to all libraries throughout the
country.[9] Lists were announced and widely circulated, and
the price for each package was shown. Frequent supplements
were added. A New York book dealer was persuaded to
handle the not inconsiderable logistics. At last, here was a
simple way to purchase well-selected foreign children's books.
Money to buy them came from library budgets and gifts. At
first there were three mixed-language packages, from $25
to $65, and nine single-language packages for about $15 each.
The program began in 1954, and by 1964 the Package Library
of Foreign Children's Books program was taking to many U.S.
libraries about 100 titles in Spanish and French, nearly that
many in German, about 25 in Italian and Russian, and somewhat fewer in Swedish and Hebrew.[10] Any library could now
easily select and buy one or many packages.

The ALA Booklist became an occasional source for selecting foreign books in the sixties, and by January 1985 it
had included 48 such lists.[11] Since then the lists, always
selected by a committee of U.S. children's librarians, have
appeared once a month. None is published unless U.S.
sources to buy the books can be listed.[12] To date, these
bibliographies have included books from 21 countries. The
language with the greatest representation is Spanish, with
18 lists. From 1973 to the present, lists in four Asian languages have been included--five in Chinese, four in Japanese,
one in Korean, and one in Russian.

Throughout this century urban public libraries have
traditionally provided books in the languages of any substantial part of the population. There is an interesting story of
how a collection of books in Japanese began in one U.S. library.[13] Mitsue Ishitake, a Japanese teacher interested in

storytelling, visited the Westchester Library System in suburban New York. Anne Izard, the children's consultant, showed Mrs. Ishitake her film, The Pleasure is Mutual, which demonstrates how to conduct a picture book hour. A few years later Mrs. Ishitake returned to the library. By then, with the help of the film, she had established a storytelling caravan funded by an advertising company. Within the next 14 years she was to develop 23 such storytelling caravans.

A local mother, Mrs. Sayaka Konishi,[14] attended the reception honoring Mrs. Ishitake on her return visit. The result was a plan to develop a collection of children's books to serve the large Japanese-speaking population in Westchester County. Mrs. Konishi herself purchased the first 350 books on behalf of the system during a visit to Japan. Mothers cataloged the books in English; core collections were established in three localities, with lists of books placed in all 38 libraries to facilitate prompt interlibrary loan. The Westchester Library System then began regularly to include an item for Japanese books in its annual budget.[15]

The American Library Association had an impressive exhibit at the 1962 Seattle World's Fair which included a children's library room and storytelling center called The Children's World. The library contained a large collection of outstanding American children's books and books from other English-speaking countries. The American Library Association children's services division, however, wished to include children's books in other languages than English. To accomplish this, invitations went to children's librarians in European countries asking them to approach publishers in their countries to see whether a selection of children's books might be sent to the exhibit. The response was generous: more than 200 books came from 15 countries. Titles were translated, and all the books were arranged by category on the shelves--historical stories, home stories, picture books, etc.--and the foreign books in each category were interfiled with the English-language books.[16]

The director of the Children's World for the duration of the Fair was Mrs. Elizabeth Margulis, a former president of the National Congress of Parents and Teachers and a trained children's librarian. Two members of the exhibit's volunteer staff were Dorothy Anderson and Spencer Shaw, both participants in this conference.

But to share books of other countries effectively, U.S. children must have them in translation. Translations of children's books into English from European languages and the reverse have been successful over the years when the book is a good choice for the receiving country. Similarities of culture, of education, of customs increase the chances of success. But children's books translated from Asian or African languages into English, or in the opposite direction, have faced the problem of making very dissimilar backgrounds and cultures understandable and interesting to children.

There are some exceptions. Japan during the later half of this century has produced many translations of American as well as English and other European children's books. In checking the 1986 catalog of just one Japanese publisher of children's books, I found 60 translated American books, including many of our outstanding picture books, all the Wilder Little House books, Minarik's Little Bear books, and others. The same company has translated a similar number of books from England and other European countries.[17] Beatrix Potter's little books had been available in Japan in large size but without her illustrations. In the early 1970s Momoko Ishii, an outstanding Japanese author of children's books, insisted that Japan should have Potter's books with Potter illustrations; fifteen of the books in the original small format, with the traditional illustrations and translation by Miss Ishii, were published.[18] Reciprocally, U.S. and European countries have translated and published Mitsumasa Anno's fascinating and ingenious picture books; and several Japanese authors have been translated.

In India, especially in the Bengali language, there have been magazines and books for children for a century, but I know only of a small selection from Tagore's poems translated for children here, and the book I remember must be long out of print. U.S. children, however, can learn of many of the traditional epics and hero stories of India, China, or Japan through selections and adaptations for children from those classics.

In our country too few of us are skilled in languages other than our own, so publishers and editors must depend on literary agents and other secondhand knowledge of books before choosing them. The decision whether to translate and publish a book begins with a reader's recommendation. In

addition to the normal costs of publication are numerous extra costs including payments for rights to the publisher, author, and translator. The quality of the book in its new
form depends on the translator. Translators of children's
books need special skills and experience. Only a dedicated
and inspired translator can produce an excellent translation
which transmits the author's style and tone and carries the
author's story with integrity to children.

Assuming that the translator's native language is the
language into which a book is to be translated--and this is
of first importance--he or she also needs an intimate knowledge of the language of the original book. In addition, as
one translator of many children's books into English says,

> Any conscientious translator will of course stay as
> close to both letter and spirit of the original as pos-
> sible, but especially in translating for children ...
> if a clash should arise, then the spirit of the work
> must take precedence.... Any necessity for adapta-
> tion may vary from book to book, and from age
> group to age group, but I would rather--with the
> author's permission, needless to say--adapt than lum-
> ber a text with footnotes.[19]

In the early years of the century children's libraries
not only in the United States but in Canada, England, France,
Scandinavia, and Germany had translations, some of them
very popular. These were engrossing stories wherever they
came from--Pinocchio, Andersen's Fairy Tales, Heidi, Twenty
Thousand Leagues Under the Sea, and many more. At the
same time American books for children were translated and
published in European countries--Mark Twain's Tom Sawyer,
Cooper's Leatherstocking Tales, and Harriet Beecher Stowe's
Uncle Tom's Cabin among them. The last title and the books
by Cooper were originally published for adults but became
young people's books abroad. All these translations were
read avidly in numerous countries. Translated books could
be a means of better understanding children, families, and
life in other countries.

Over the years, however, objections to some translations have been raised by librarians and others in the countries of the original book, whether from other languages into
English or in reverse. Swiss Family Robinson, by Johann

David Wyss, is one such book. It was not published until twenty years after the gifted and imaginative father had written down talks he gave to his four sons on Sunday walks. Trying to make information about nature, about other countries and about all manner of things interesting, he framed the stories in a desert-island, Robinson-Crusoe kind of tale. Later his son edited these stories somewhat, and the book was first published in Switzerland in 1812. Swiss Family Robinson was translated and published in England in 1814 and appeared for the first time in the U.S. in 1832. But Bettina Hürlimann, the Swiss author and specialist in children's literature, was not happy about a later U.S. edition. She wrote in her Three Centuries of Children's Books in Europe, "Even though the affection in which it is held in Europe may be declining, it still today (1959) enjoys an amazing success in English-speaking countries, and above all, in America." She adds parenthetically, "In saying this, it is perhaps worth recalling that the Americans do not take too pedantic a view of translations. The fact that this European book is still so much a favorite today on the other side of the Atlantic is probably connected to the fact that American editors, for the sake of liveliness, have treated this original, respected for 150 years, with considerably less reverence than (Europeans) would have done."[20]

A book for which the translations have been questioned by Americans is Uncle Tom's Cabin, by Harriet Beecher Stowe. It was published in the United States in 1852 as a political novel for adults. An English edition came out in the same year and another in 1853. The book has been translated into at least 24 languages, and I have seen a number of these. They are all short--not more than 75 pages long--although the original had 450 pages. Mrs. Hürlimann commented that "Uncle Tom's Cabin appealed to children and adults alike, and when at the end of the century, it had accomplished its task, it continued to live indestructibly as a book for children."[21] That it is still common in European school and public libraries for children is both puzzling and upsetting to me. In Germany I was told in the sixties that of course it was our most outstanding children's book.

In my many years of association with libraries for children in this country I had never considered it a children's book. It did not appear in the several classic public library lists of children's books published between 1900 and 1910.

The Children's Catalog, published periodically from 1909 to date, includes Uncle Tom's Cabin only in the 1916, 1917, and 1925 editions. The archives of Houghton Mifflin Company do reveal, however, that the 1905-1906 and 1911 catalogs advertised numerous editions of the book in the Riverside Literature Series, Riverside School Library, and other editions. Apparently these were the full length books. [22]

I have never found the source of those shortened versions appearing so frequently in children's libraries in several European countries. Mrs. Hürlimann stated that "[Mrs. Stowe] herself adapted [it] in a children's edition soon after its first appearance." [23] The research library at the Stowe-Day Foundation in Hartford, Connecticut, however, has not been able to establish whether Mrs. Stowe ever did--or did not--adapt a juvenile edition. [24] At any rate, I regret seeing this book in translation so frequently in Europe.

Another translation problem is created when a story is considered for publication in a country in which the story takes place but whose author is not a native or resident of that country. A Swedish publisher told me in 1961 that although her company did many translations from English, they never did a Swedish translation of such a book about Swedish life.

Similarly, Hans Brinker, Or, The Silver Skates was written by Mary Mapes Dodge, who had never been in Holland. It is questioned in the Netherlands. It was adapted when published in Dutch in 1867, only two years after it was published here. The adaptation was necessary, a Netherlands librarian writes me, because in order to use it in that country "all sorts of curiosities were dropped out, and [this] left an exciting book for boys." [25]

Translations into English for U.S. children are very desirable, but the number is not large and they are not kept in print very long. The American Library Association Batchelder Award was developed in order to recognize U.S. publishers which select, translate, and publish outstanding children's books from countries using languages other than English. First given in 1968, the citation has gone to 17 U.S. publishers, three of which received it a second time. These translated books give U.S. children an experience of good books already read and known by children in one or more non-English speaking countries. Most are worthy books that should long be continued in print, but I am sad to say that ten of the 17 are now out of print, two are available solely in paperback editions, and only seven remain in print as published.[26]

Today, libraries in this country must buy books quite soon after publication. This especially handicaps purchase of translations for they may not be discovered by librarians and bought soon enough to avoid the report that they are already out of print. It is not like buying children's books in the late twenties and thirties, when U.S. publishers had wonderful backlists. If you were slow in recognizing an outstanding book you could get it at a later date, even several years later.

So far I have been talking about translations to and from the languages of the developed, industrialized countries. Many of these translations were and are successful and make up an important part of literature for children. In developing countries good, well-chosen translations have a role to play, but as these are made available, local publishing and locally written materials for children must also be developed.

In the U.S. in the fifties the Franklin Books Program began to assist in the selection, translation and publishing of books in developing countries. In the first eight years, Franklin Books made it possible for local Asian companies to publish 1,000 U.S. books, 350 of them children's books. This meant more than one million children's books by 1962 translated from American English into Arabic, Persian, Urdu, Bengali, and Indonesian.[27] The procedure was that Asian countries requested books on a subject. The requests were for serious adult books or for children's books. Franklin Books then obtained, from selected lists or from cooperating librarians, the names of several of the best books on the subject. Requests for children's books were mostly for basic science pamphlets and other simple information books. Books were obtained from publishers by Franklin Books and shipped to the requesting country, and the books were examined by local people and publishers. If a publisher decided it would be economically possible to publish one of the books, Franklin Books would obtain the translation rights, would get an excellent translation made locally and would in part subsidize the publishing. The economics of the project, even with

Franklin's help, were very difficult.[28] Even when subsidized, translated books were expensive for the local purchaser. In addition, the size of the market for some languages was not large enough to make publishing practical.[29]

The lower one goes on the literary scale the more difficult it is to make a translation faithful to the original and at the same time understandable and interesting to children. For each book one must decide how literal the translation can be and still convey the author's meaning to the appropriate audience. But, as the president of the Franklin Books Program pointed out, both conscience and intelligence must be involved in considering any adaptation.

If children are to read, their books must be in the language they speak. Not surprisingly, until literacy is relatively common and there are education and books in the local language, reading is not possible for children. A church-related group was early to recognize the need for locally written children's stories in the indigenous language. The Committee on Christian Literature for Women and Children, an independent incorporated body with a link to the National Council of Churches' Division of Overseas Ministries, was established in 1912. It was concerned in its earlier years with grants to publish material for women and children translated from publications originating abroad. By mid-century, though, it was evident that the greatest need was for locally written material. Third world countries had few trained writers. To contribute to the discovery and training of writers in their native languages, Marion Van Horne of the committee staff organized workshops to discover and train local writers.[30] Miss Van Horne visited the American Library Association office at the time she was working on a doctoral study of the Newbery Medal books, which she went on to use in her workshops as outstanding examples of good writing for children.

In 1959 the first workshop in Thailand prepared family life materials for Southeast Asia. The same year in Korea she led a workshop which prepared material for a paperback series aimed at people who were newly literate. The need for material for children to read in their own language became so evident that it was decided future workshops should be directed chiefly toward good stories for children--stories of all kinds, not limited to Christian reading materials. The first workshop focusing on writing for children met in Fiji in

1963 for the purpose of preparing stories for a church school curriculum. The first on writing general stories for children was held in Alexandria, Egypt, in 1965. During the next twenty years Miss Van Horne led workshops on writing for children in more than 25 countries--in Asia, Africa, Latin America, and the South Pacific.

The workshops were the first step in a long process to develop authors. When writers were found who had talent they were offered opportunities for advanced training in colleges in their own countries. A very few were granted scholarships for study in England and the United States.

Publishing the stories in magazines and books was done at first by the church publishing houses, but as government recognized some of these works with prizes and as the state purchased them for school libraries, secular publishers began to be more active in producing children's books. One story from a workshop in India won a government prize and was translated and published in half a dozen of the Indian languages. In Indonesia several books which got their start in workshops won government prizes and were subsidized for distribution to schools. In Egypt the first workshop story about a retarded child was written.

To promote indigenous writing, the committee held several regional conferences and in the early eighties held an international conference in Aiya Napa, Cyprus, with representatives from more than 40 countries.

In 1963 Marion Van Horne's Write the Vision, a manual on how to write, was published for those who teach in writer workshops. This year it was translated and published in th Indonesian language. In 1970 her Give Children Wings, a manual on how to write for children, was published by the committee.[31] The author's examples of types of good writing are drawn from various Newbery Medal books. This book enables local writers to lead workshops similar to those she had conducted. Miss Van Horne's latest book, Training Teachers of Writing, is to be published by the David C. Coc Foundation late in 1986.

Internationally, information about children's literature and libraries became much more accessible with the appearan in 1968 of The World of Children's Literature, by Anne

Pellowski, published by R. R. Bowker. It abstracts articles and books, reporting on children's literature, libraries, and book-related activities in 87 countries, some fifteen of them Asian. The introduction to the international section of this bibliography ends with three recommendations. I want to mention and comment on a few of her salient points. Her first recommendation states that "one of the rights of children is the right to identity--personal and national." This makes it evident that books and materials for children, especially for young children, should reflect the environment they know and should be in their native language, the one they speak. Further, when there are no native writers to write such books there should be training courses and assistance to potential writers. She notes that existing oral literature should be translated into written and pictured form.

The second recommendation states that "simultaneously with the development of an indigenous literature, the introduction of the best and most suitable materials from other countries should begin. Translations should be made of some of the best of current production in other countries, as well as from the more recognized classics." The third states, "It is unlikely that children's books will ever be completely free of nationalistic bias (as distinct from national identity), but it is not too impossible to hope for the elimination of exaggerated stereotypes, especially those derogatory to race, color or creed which are most offensive to a given race or people."[32] In addition to the introduction I have just mentioned each region or country entered has an introduction which summarizes progress represented by the literature of that area. The book is a gold mine of information.

This spring I read a quotation from a Sydney, Australia, newspaper which makes me look at the future in a way new to me: "Increasing numbers of farsighted people see the [Asia Pacific region] playing the same central role in the 21st century as the Mediterranean in the Elizabethan Age or the Atlantic throughout the Industrial Revolution. Already its tensions and opportunities are signaling a major tilt in the balance of global power."[33] Obviously the organizers of the Pacific Rim Conferences on Children's Literature were among those "farsighted people." Literacy has increased remarkably between 1960 and 1980, especially in those Asian countries which have had fast growing economies. By 1980 in Korea, Taiwan, and Hong Kong it had reached more than 90 percent and in

Sri Lanka, Thailand, and Singapore to more than 84 percent
The figures on literacy in developing countries come from th
Resource Systems Institute of the East West Center in Hawaii
The Center is itself an indication of Pacific Basin growth and
importance. Started in 1960 by the U.S. government, the
Center now also receives support from Asian countries, cor-
porations and private agencies.

The growth in literacy makes necessary an increase in
printed materials and books, especially of children's books.
In a number of countries this means books in several lan-
guages--for example, there are four official languages in Sin
pore and fourteen languages in India. In the latter, howeve
children's book publishing might be limited to no more than
five or six! For most of us in the United States these are
complications almost too difficult to imagine.

Children's books have been widely published during
this century in the western and industrialized countries and
also in Japan and the Soviet Union, and they have been
available in bookstores, schools and libraries. Children's be
vary in quality, some excellent and many mediocre. Third
World countries are moving toward writing and publishing
books--not only textbooks, but also story and information
books for children at different levels of reading experience.

In developing countries, national libraries may take ar
active role in the distribution of children's books. Some ha
branches from which children's books can be obtained. But
since the more traditional libraries are not available to many
children, especially in rural areas, ingenious and new ways
of getting books to children are being tried. The proceedir
of the first two Pacific Rim Conferences on Children's Litera
ture gave me a fascinating view of children's books and libraries in a number of developed and developing countries a
well as about some aboriginal civilizations. The proceedings
of the first of these, the Vancouver, Canada, conference in
1976, One Ocean Touching,[34] were published in 1979. Thos
of the second conference in Melbourne, Australia in 1979,
A Track to Unknown Water,[35] were published in 1980. Together they make up a significant record. These proceedin
are splendidly supplemented by the proceedings of the IFLA
UNESCO pre-session seminar before the IFLA 1981 conferenc
in Leipzig, Library Work for Children and Young Adults in
the Developing Countries, published in 1984.[36] Chairman o

the preparatory committee for the seminar and one of the editors of the proceedings was Geneviève Patte, librarian of a very special model children's library, La Joie par les Livres in Clamart, near Paris. I wish all these proceedings were widely available in library schools and libraries. Especially since the seminar Mrs. Patte has been frequently sought by developing countries to advise them on ways to work out appropriate library plans.

All three volumes demonstrate that essential to the existence of satisfactory books for children are books in the native language written by local authors with training in writing provided when that is needed. These are fundamental to the children's literature of a country. Well-chosen translations should supplement indigenous literature, but the base must be an adequate supply of books written in the native language. All three proceedings make clear the importance of library distribution plans based on an analysis of children's book needs worked out by groups involving local parents and teachers as well as librarians. Unusual and ingenious ways to reach children with books should be welcomed and tried. Copying foreign models is frequently irrelevant to local needs, and adapting them may delay starting more practical and promising methods.

Sharing memories is one of the delights of being connected for a long time--say 60 years--with one field, one profession. It is equally rewarding to be pushed this year to look beyond what has long been observed and worked with; and for that I have the conference planners to thank.

NOTES

1. Clara W. Hunt, International Friendship Through Children's Books (New York: League of Nations Non Partisan Association, 1924). Also in Publishers Weekly 106 (27 December 1924): 1967-70.
2. Jella Lepman, "Utopia or Reality--International Understanding Through Children's Books," Top of the News 21 (June 1965): 323-25.
3. Virginia Haviland, Children's Books of International Interest (Chicago: American Library Association, 1972).
4. Barbara Elleman, ed., Children's Books of International

Interest, 3d ed. (Chicago: American Library Association, 1972).

5. Children's Library Association. International Committee Children's Books in Twelve Countries. (Chicago: American Library Association, 1930).

6. Children's Library Association. International Committee Foreign Children's Books Available in the United States. (New York: New York Public Library, 1954).

7. Children's Library Association. International Committee "Foreign Children's Books Available in the United States," Top of the News 11 (May 1955): 47-50; 13 (May 1957): 37-41; 14 (May 1958): 34-39.

8. Children's Services Division. Committee on the Selection of Foreign Children's Books, "Foreign Children's Books Available in the United States," Top of the News 21 (June 1965): 325-28.

9. Children's Services Division. Package Library of Foreign Children's Books Committee, "Report," Top of the News 16 (October 1959): 64.

10. Package Library of Foreign Children's Books, General Catalog (New York: by the program, 119 Fifth Ave. 10003, 1964).

11. Barbara Elleman (children's books editor of Booklist) to Mildred Batchelder, June 1986.

12. "Distributors of Children's Foreign Language Books Update," Booklist (1 January, 1986): 670-71.

13. Anne R. Izard, "An Everyday Miracle," Friends of IBB Newsletter (Winter/Spring 1984): 34.

14. Sayaka Konishi, "Excerpt from The Children of Two Countries," Friends of IBBY Newsletter (Winter/Spring 1984): 4-6.

15. Anne R. Izard to Mildred Batchelder, August 1986.

16. Information from the American Library Association Archives (Batchelder file), University of Illinois Library, Urbana. Courtesy of Selma Richardson.

17. Fukuinkan Shoten Publisher, Books for Children, Complete Catalog (Tokyo: Fukuinkan Shoten, 1986).

18. Momoko Ishii to Mildred Batchelder, 1973 and 1974.

19. Anthea Bell, "Children's Books in Translation," Signal No. 28 (January 1979). (Stroud, Gloucester, England: Thimble Press).

20. Bettina Hürlimann, Three Centuries of Children's Books in Europe, tr. and ed. by Brian W. Alderson (Cleveland: World Publishing Co., 1968), p. 106.

21. Ibid., p. 174.
22. Mary Lee Donovan to Mildred Batchelder, 14 August 1986, quoting Houghton Mifflin Co. Catalogues, 1905-06 and 1911.
23. Helen Canfield to Mildred Batchelder, 8 August 1986, quoting her research in the files of the Stowe-Day Foundation, Hartford, Connecticut.
24. Hürlimann, p. 174.
25. Annie Moerkercken van der Meulen (Voorburg, The Netherlands) to Mildred Batchelder, July and August 1986.
26. Batchelder Award books out of print in 1986 checked by Cooperative Children's Book Center, Madison, Wisconsin.
27. Datus C. Smith, Jr., "American Children's Books Chosen for Publication in Asian Languages," Top of the News 18 (December 1961): 11-14.
28. Datus C. Smith, Jr., "Translating Books for Newly Developing Countries," Publishers Weekly 190 (1 August 1966): 22-26.
29. Datus C. Smith, Jr., "The Economics of Children's Books in Developing Countries," Children's Book Council Calendar, 1978.
30. Marion Van Horne to Mildred Batchelder, January through July, 1986; and folders and lists of the Committee on Christian Literature for Women and Children, 1963-1986.
31. Marion Van Horne, Give Children Wings; a Manual on How to Write for Children. (New York: Committee on Literacy and Christian Literature, 1970).
32. Anne Pellowski, World of Children's Literature (New York: R. R. Bowker, 1968).
33. World Press Review 32 (March 1986): 6.
34. Egoff, Sheila A., ed., One Ocean Touching: Papers from the First Pacific Rim Conference on Children's Literature (Metuchen, N.J.: Scarecrow Press, 1979).
35. Lees, Stella, ed., A Track to Unknown Water: Proceedings of the Second Pacific Rim Conference on Children's Literature (Carlton, Victoria, Australia: Melbourne State College, Department of Librarianship, 1980; Metuchen, N.J.: Scarecrow Press, Inc., 1987).
36. Library Work for Children and Young Adults in the Developing Countries: Proceedings of the IFLA/UNESCO Pre-session Seminar in Leipzig, GDR 10-15 August, 1981, IFLA Publication 28 (Munich and New York: K. G. Saur, 1984).

AUTHOR'S ADDED NOTE

American Library Association sections or divisions are referred to in the text in general terms to simplify reading. For those interested, the precise names were as follows:

1901   ALA Section for Library Work with Children established

1941   The section became the ALA Children's Services Division, one of three parts (with Young Adult Services Division and American Association of School Librarians) of the ALA Division of Libraries for Children and Young People.

1956   The ALA Children's Services Division became a separate division.

1977   The Children's Services Division changed its name to ALA-Association for Library Service to Children.

PART III:

WHAT IS HAPPENING TODAY?
THE STATE OF THE ART OF CHILDREN'S LITERATURE

Experienced representatives of four nations touch upon the
writing, publishing, marketing, and accessibility of books for
children in their countries. Margaret Bush then looks at
present trends and possible future forms which children's
books will take.

Chapter 3

CHILDREN'S LITERATURE:
STATE OF THE ART IN CANADA

Sheila Egoff

I would first of all like to congratulate the organizer, or organizers, of the panel for the direction they have given to it by their title. What we want to know about other countries is what is going on now. When you say to a person, "How are you," you really do not want a resume of his health problems for the past ten years. Still, I think that about a minute or two of background is in order here so that you may better understand our not inconsiderable accomplishments in the field of children's literature since the middle of the 1970s.

The most important economic and cultural challenge that we Canadians face is that we live next door to the United States with an area larger than it and with a population smaller than that of the State of California. Our situation, vis-à-vis the United States, was perhaps best expressed by one of our Prime Ministers, Pierre Elliott Trudeau, when he said: "Living next to the Americans is in some way like sleeping with an elephant; no matter how friendly and even-tempered is the beast, if I may call it that, one is affected by every twitch and grunt. Even a friendly nuzzling can sometimes lead to frightening consequences." Those of you who have followed the recent acid rain or "shakes and shingles" controversies between our two countries and who are interested in the concept of free trade will know exactly what Mr.

Trudeau meant, although I hasten to point out that we Canadians realize that our economic health is largely dependent upon that of the United States.

In terms of publishing, the greatest difference between Canada and the United States, and indeed between ourselves and most other countries of the Western world, is that Canada imports more than it publishes internally. Indeed, it is the greatest book-importing area in the world despite its small population. The Canadian market is just large enough to be attractive to foreign publishers, so all large English and American firms have long had branch distribution outlets in Canada. Thus it can be readily appreciated that our local products face, right at home, enormous competition from abroad. Specifically in terms of children's books, this means that fewer than two hundred Canadian titles published annually in English must vie with close to three thousand from the United States and about another three thousand from other English-speaking countries.

Other factors put constraints upon our publishing industry. With a small local market, publishers cannot afford to take risks, especially with a new, unknown writer. Few have a popular or impressive backlist, the bread and butter of any major firm. The publishers of Winnie-the-Pooh or Charlotte's Web, for example, will continue to rake in a tidy sum each year indefinitely, with little or no effort. No Canadian publisher has a book in this kind of commercial league.

The existence of our two official languages--with a serious lack of translation from one to the other--compounds the economic ailment by reducing the profit margin for books in either English or French. The list goes on. There is our regionalism (far more pervasive in Canada than in the United States); our policy of actively encouraging multiculturalism (which further fragments both publishing policies and the readership); and our huge distances and empty spaces which make the distribution of books difficult (90 percent of the population is spread in a thin band along our four-thousand-mile boundary with the United States).

It would seem that if pure laissez-faire economics governed the publishing of Canadian children's books, there would hardly be any publishing. But a fairly rich and individualistic society cannot tolerate a situation in which foreign imports totally govern the cultural development of its children, and so government has had to intervene. Both the Canada Council and variations of arts councils at the provincial level provide grants to authors, illustrators, and publishers to keep the system afloat--barely. The government has recently announced an influx of $13 million into the publishing industry, from which books for children will benefit greatly. It need hardly be said that this injection of public money has both good and bad points, but there is no doubt that it is indispensable.

However, I hasten to point out that with all this government support, and it is not endemic, we do operate on the free enterprise system unlike countries of the Eastern Bloc such as East Germany and Czechoslovakia (which are the two I know about), where children's books are channeled through one government-vetted publisher, giving rise to the answer, when you ask the question, "How many of your books are first rate?"--"They all are."

It has always been taken for granted that the more books produced, the greater the chances of getting a few excellent ones. It is a case where Canada has beaten the odds as we have so often done in our history--such as, for example, keeping the country together from east to west when the economic tug has always been between north and south. From our past with only, say, thirty such titles published in a given year, we have inherited some very fine children's books. But since the middle of the 1970s there has been a tremendous upsurge in the production of our children's books--publishers now give us more than two hundred titles each year in the English language--with a commensurate rise in excellence. The axiom is proving itself to be correct.

As is usual in history, there is no one reason for the events; they just all seemed to come together. Much has been attributed to a rise in nationalism, and probably there is a cause-and-effect relationship here. Even more, I think, can be attributed to the children of the baby boom who flocked to our universities in the 1960s--like those in the United States they are our best-educated generation in terms of opportunity--and who found there burgeoning courses in Canadian literature. I can remember that in the late sixties and seventies so many students applied for such courses that not all of them could be accommodated. This coincided with a flourishing of the Canadian novel. Some of our modern adult novelists are deemed by international critics to be among the best in the world--Alice Munro, Margaret Lawrence, and Robertson Davies, to name only several--and I think that children's literature tends to follow adult literature about a generation later. But back to the baby boom children. They in turn demanded Canadian books for their children, especially their young children. This demand coincided with a publishing phenomenon, the rise of small and regional presses, many of which are devoted exclusively to the publishing of picture books. Before the mid-seventies our libraries were filled with American and British picture books, which I hasten to say we still do not want to be without. We take pride in the internationalism of our libraries.

I would now like to say just a few words about children's literature in general. Common to most children's fiction are a primacy of narrative, child protagonists, emphasis on dialogue and action, and a clarity of style and issues. The best of children's fiction worldwide possesses in addition the creative tension of a strong plot, deft characterization, vitality of language and emotional depth. A good story is a good story wherever it is told, whatever the nationality of the storyteller. I think that in books from other countries we look first for the universal accent of the author and only secondarily for resonances of a cultural accent. If we consider the books from cultures other than our own that have broken the barriers of both place and time--Swiss Family Robinson, Heidi, Pinocchio, Bambi, Emil and the Detectives, Pippi Longstocking--we see that the universality of theme and the child characters take precedence over a strong national background or a cultural voice.

It is true that some books, like some wines, do not travel well, and certainly most Canadian books of the past have not done well in the international market. But that situation is changing due partly to the recognition of Canadian adult literature, partly to the more aggressive practices of our publishers, but chiefly because many of our recent writers have achieved that quality of universality while hewing to their Canadian roots. I shall have time to mention only a few of them.

Brian Doyle's Angel Square is one of the most brilliant

and fascinating children's books I have read in a long time. What it has, most of all, is a strong plot, unlike many modern novels for children. The young boy, Tommy, identifies with "The Shadow" of the 1940s radio program and sets out as a detective to solve the mystery of the anti-Semitic attack upon the father of his best friend. What Tommy discovers is, in the words of the radio Shadow, "the evil that lurks in the hearts of men." There are many charming scenes in the book, especially one recounting Christmas in Tommy's rather poor, single-parent home with an eccentric aunt and a retarded sister. But the story does depend a lot on local background (our capital city of Ottawa at the end of World War II), local knowledge, and, most of all, on an understanding of parody. The French-Canadian, Protestant, and Jewish children who cross Angel Square every day on their way to their various schools are not really pummelling one another to death. The boys are actually fast friends and the violence is to be taken as symbolic of the adult world, not the child world. It is a story on two levels, and although very Canadian it has the universal themes of both racial prejudice and family love. Although I do not think that Angel Square will have a wide appeal, it will be an unforgettable experience for those readers who want something besides a formula book. It has been published in the United States.

Kit Pearson's The Daring Game has been such a success in Canada that Viking Press is distributing it in the United States, and a paperback edition is also available. It is set in modern-day Vancouver in a girls' private boarding school and is loosely based on its author's own experiences. Of course, The Girls Own Annual, that bastion of the British school story, has long since disappeared from the reading of modern young females. Yet I think that the popularity of The Daring Game demonstrates that the appeal of the boarding school story still lingers, even if that appeal is only an exotic one. Unlike the stereotypical pattern of the past, however, Kit Pearson provides fine writing, believable characters, and a delicate sense of morality.

Surprisingly enough, few writers in Canada have built on the tradition of L. M. Montgomery's Anne of Green Gables. An exception is Bernice Thurman Hunter with her Booky series. These consist of three episodic novels, That Scatterbrain Booky, With Love from Booky and As Ever, Booky, all published in the 1980s. Like the Anne books, these have no real plot other than the chronicling of a feisty, disaster-prone child toward a sensitive maturity. The background is that of the Depression era, which is lightly sketched in with moments of poignant humour such as Booky's loss of her baby-sitting job for eating forbidden oranges.

Many of you, I am sure, will know the books of the Canadian writer Jean Little. Her latest one, Mama's Going to Buy You a Mockingbird, is by far her best. Her story of the reactions of a young adolescent boy to his father's death is as emotionally charged as Katherine Paterson's Bridge to Terabithia, as well written, and as resonant with symbols that do not impede its meaning on a primary level.

I am also sure that most of you know of Monica Hughes as the author of the Isis trilogy. But since many of her books have been published both in Canada and the United States, you may not realize that she is Canadian, having emigrated well over twenty years ago. I have found much recent science fiction for children rather gloomy and pessimistic, and I rejoice in all of her works for their practical optimism and ultimate faith in the generosity of the human spirit.

In much of modern fantasy we find young protagonists whose emotional turmoil plunges them into another era in which they experience a distancing from and so a resolution of their own personal problems. Playing Beatie Bow, by the Australian writer Ruth Park, is perhaps the one we know the best. But Janet Lunn's The Root Cellar should have a special appeal for American readers since the historical section of the fantasy is set in the American Civil War. The protagonist in our time is a twelve-year-old American girl who is already lonely and alienated when she is sent to live with a large, boisterous Canadian family close to the American border in Ontario. Her loneliness leads her through the root cellar of the old farmhouse where she sees a land as divided as her own heart and where the suffering makes her misery seem miniscule.

Jan Truss's Jasmin is akin to many protagonists in modern realistic fiction (such as Tree in Virginia Hamilton's Sweet Whispers, Brother Rush) in that they have too much responsibility for their age. (My cousin from Trinidad tells me that in the West Indies such children who, in effect, have no childhood, are referred to as having "no boy" or "no girl,"

an apt but sad way of putting things.) Jasmin is forced to
have an old head on young shoulders in her large, chaotic,
demanding family with the additional care of a retarded brother. She also feels that she is going to fail grade six; and
when her brother ruins her science project, she runs away.
She tries to make a place for herself in the northern Alberta
bush (escape to the wilderness is a strong metaphor in both
American and Canadian literature), but it fairly soon defeats
her. The ending has been criticized for being a bit too pat
and happy, but I have often noticed that such endings are
not criticized by child readers.

I indicated earlier that we have had a phenomenal rise
in the publication of picture books, and I mentioned some of
the reasons such as the output of the small presses. Another reason is, I think, largely societal: this is the inci-
dence of single-parent families or two working parents with
the concomitant necessity of placing children in day-care
centers, nursery schools, and so on. These institutions make
good use of picture books. One could say that there is a
ready-made audience, both of adults and children, for almost
anything publishable. We now have published in Canada almost everything we need: ABC books, counting books, board
books, pop-up books, bilingual books, inexpensive books, and
some that could be in competition for excellence with the best
from England or the United States. Of these latter, I have
time to mention only three.

Ian Wallace's Chin Chiang and the Dragon Dance is
based on Vancouver's Chinese community, but it could be
any Chinatown outside of China. In pictures that move from
action to mood, we see a young Canadian-Chinese boy come
to terms with his culture and his fears by joining his grandfather in the dragon dance of the Chinese New Year's celebration. Tim Wynne-Jones's Zoom at Sea is an original and marvelous quest fantasy about an extraordinary kitten who wants
to go to sea. This is a very unusual picture book, and it
is kept firmly grounded in reality by the matter-of-fact black-
and-white illustrations. In Brenda and Edward, Maryann
Kovalski tells a tender fable of animal friendship in the tradition of Arnold Lobel's Frog and Toad or James Marshall's
George and Martha. Kovalski's anthropomorphic dog characters love and lose each other only to be reunited in their
old age.

I hope that I have given you some indication of the present state of Canadian children's literature. In considering the all-over international theme of this conference, I have one final thought to offer. I can only speak for Vancouver, and some of my colleagues even there could well disagree with me, but I sense that our children's reading is getting very narrow--chiefly popular American or popular Canadian. You and I know the value of the finest of children's literature from all cultures. I think that if we really believe in and want the best for our children, we all have to strive harder both in our educational systems and in our libraries to make sure that they are at least introduced to the best.

BOOKS MENTIONED

Doyle, Bryan. Angel Square. New York: Bradbury, 1986.

Hamilton, Virginia. Sweet Whispers, Brother Rush. New York: Putnam Publishing Group, 1982.

Hughes, Monica. Isis Trilogy. New York: Macmillan, 1981-1983.

Hunter, Bernice. Booky Trilogy. Richmond Hill, Ontario: Scholastic TAB, 1981- .

Kovalski, Maryann. Brenda and Edward. Toronto: Kids Car Press, 1984.

Little, Jean. Mama's Going to Buy You a Mockingbird. New York: Viking Kestrel, 1985.

Lobel, Arnold. Frog and Toad. New York: Harper Jr. Books, 1970.

Lunn, Janet. The Root Cellar. New York: Macmillan, 1983.

Marshall, James. George and Martha. Boston: Houghton, 1972.

Montgomery, Lucy Maud. Anne of Green Gables. Originally published in 1908. Now available in numerous hardcover and paperback eds.

Park, Ruth. <u>Playing Beatie Bow</u>. New York: Macmillan, 1980.

Paterson, Katherine. <u>Bridge to Terabithia</u>. New York: Crowell, 1977.

Pearson, Kit. <u>The Daring Game</u>. New York: Viking Kestrel, 1986.

Truss, Jan. <u>Jasmin</u>. New York: Atheneum, 1982 (A Margaret McElderry Book).

Wallace, Ian. <u>Chin Chiang and the Dragon's Dance</u>. New York: Macmillan, 1984.

Wynne-Jones, Tim. <u>Zoom at Sea</u>. Boston: Merrimack Publishers Circle, 1986.

Chapter 4

CHILDREN'S LITERATURE:
STATE OF THE ART IN JAPAN

Okiko Miyake

For me, presenting a paper at UCLA means that events have come full circle. When I was a student, I wrote to Frances Clarke Sayers asking for an interview. She praised me much when I arrived at her office at UCLA exactly at the appointed time. You cannot imagine how difficult it was for a foreigner to get to this campus using public transportation in 1964. Talking with her was a precious initiation into the teaching of children's literature at the college level.

Describing the present state of Japanese children's literature in a short time is difficult. I shall limit my paper to the subject of the status of literary books in Japan.

Until about 1960, children's books were of very poor quality and quantity in Japan, and consisted mainly of retold classics. They were mostly given as presents, like toys. Adults themselves could not enjoy children's books, because the literature was not mature enough. Very few high-quality books were placed by parents or teachers into the hands of children. Before World War II, contemporary Japanese children's literature was all short stories, similar to art fairy tales such as Hans Christian Andersen's.

In the 1960s many longer stories began to be published

in book form--the golden age. By then, however, a simul-
taneous development was occurring: Japan was becoming a
highly technological country, with its well known accompany-
ing problems. Television, which permeated instantly the lives
of children, combined with Japan's diminishing recreational
areas and multi-polluted regions and, at the same time, its
bureaucratic, strict system of education. Children have lost
their skill in imaginative power because of television, exciting
and violent animated films, terrible comics, noisy, garishly-
colored plastic toys, and self-indulgent computer games.
They have lost the chance to be in touch with nature. And
mass-produced culture has awful power.

It is said that, as a result, many young people cannot
read high-quality books any more. An often-used phrase reflects today's situation: "Kei-haku-tan-sho." That means,
"light-thin-short-small." Contents of books are becoming di-
luted, the numbers of words are diminishing, and text is
spread out. As an example, I can compare an anthology of
children's short stories published in 1963 with the revised
edition of 1985. Inside each is the same story, which required
only 12 pages in the first edition, but 16 in the new one.
The presentation of the story is now completely different, because the publisher has to endeavor to challenge children less
through print size and embellishments.

In Japan, the biggest products in publishing are comics, especially weekly comic magazines. The record is held
by Shonen Jump magazine: the December 21, 1984, issue
sold 4,070,000 copies. It continues selling about 4 million
copies each week. It might surprise others to learn that the
ages of readers are widely spread, from seven or eight to 24
or 25 years of age. From these magazines, million-seller comic books are born constantly. Comics accounted for 17 percent of the annual total publishing sales figures in 1985. In
contrast, the number of new children's trade titles in 1985
was 2,310. Perhaps only one out of ten is worthy of a book
review. The publishers do not usually report their sales
figures, but it is presumed that the volume of sales per title
is not more than 10,000.

There are several recent trends in children's publishing.
First, the life cycle of formerly long-term sellers has become
short. Second, paperback editions have become very popular.
(We have five competing publishing brands, Iwanami Shonen

Bunko, Kodansha Aoitori Bunko, Kaiseisha Bunko, Popurasha Bunko, and Four Bunko; the last is a cooperative arrangement of four small publishers to protect their properties.) Third, fiction emphasizes entertainment values, like the "Zukkoke" series by Nasu Masamiki. And fourth, many histories, biographies, or popular classics are being turned into comic books. Until the 1980s, comics were generally regarded as a low, popular form of entertainment, not worthy of the attention of the serious-minded; but now some of them have risen above that low opinion to the status of a serious art form. This is one point where mass culture and mini-culture meet between both extremes.

Adults suddenly realized a few years ago that children' literature is the medium of anti-mass cultures, and that as a mini-culture it has a very great importance. Is the literary book, then, completely emaciated? No is the answer. As par of the commodity market, sales figures of literature have been falling off considerably, but its standards have never been lowered. Even as literature has been driven into a tight corner financially, it has realized its great raison d'etre more urgently than before. The more literature is isolated from mass cultures, the more its critical power becomes sharpened and deepened. Now in the 1980s many adults enjoy children's books as an art--they search for a point of view about life, want to see truth represented simply, and try to comprehend their highly complicated society. Children's literature has re ceived wide acceptance among adults. Big newspapers have children's literature review columns, and some universities, like my own college, have children's literature classes or even whole departments for its study.

A few words about accessibility of children's literature and young people's reading preferences are in order. In 1984 the number of children's rooms in public libraries was 1,241. About 4,000 Private Home Libraries, called Bunko, cover this deficiency. The Bunko movement is one source of pride in modern Japanese children's culture--it is the product of volunteer work, with small, informal libraries situated mostly in private homes, open one day a week, a service for children supported by mothers.

A 1984 reading poll by the Mainichi newspaper tells us that the number of books a young person read per month tha year was 7.4 among the elementary school children, 2.1 by

junior high schoolers, and 1.6 by high school students.
During the elementary school years pupils have time to enjoy
books, and the numbers and contents of books read have remained almost the same during the past 30 years--mainly
classics like "Sherlock Holmes" and "Little Women." In the
case of junior high and high school students, however, reading trends have been changed completely. The latter read
only light books or topical books for relaxation from entrance
exam preparation.

Japanese authors of children's books, meanwhile, fight
desperately to identify fundamental themes. They try to write
about affairs from various angles, three dimensionally and with
many stratifications. It is a truth universally accepted that
writers write only for themselves. Literature is essentially
the medium of self-expression. In Thorny Paradise most
writers say they don't consciously intend to write for children,
but it results as a necessary consequence. "When I started
to write it never occurred to me to write for children. I
wrote about them, for adults ...," says Nina Bawden. And C.
Walter Hodges says, "I am writing in every sense for myself.
I suggest we are all writing for ourselves. For if in every
child there is an adult trying to get out, equally in every
adult there is a child trying to get back. On the overlapping
of the two, there is common ground."

In Japan, one typical theme of self-expression is the
Second World War, for the war experience is vivid in our
memory. Inner, unavoidable needs push the authors' experiences up from the bottom of their hearts. Most Japanese
adults have a strong need to tell their children the sad and
miserable memories of their experiences. Through children's
books we continue to send peaceful messages. But it has required a long time for authors to get to the point of holding
their heavy pens.

At the beginning, requiem-type works appeared, like
The Harp of Burma by Takeyama Michio (1947) and Twenty-
four Eyes by Tsuboi Sakae (1952). Fantasies came later. In
1959 Inui Tomiko published Little People Lived in the House
Under the Shade of the Tree. (Ms. Inui was the editor of
Iwanami Shonen Bunko, the paperback classics series, both Western and Japanese.) She tried to write a Japanese fantasy like
The Borrowers from Britain. In this story, an English teacher
left her hereditary Little Family to a Japanese family when she

was forced to leave Japan during the war. Ms. Inui's intention is very clear--even during the war the Japanese family
protected the British Little People from every harm. Nobody
Knows Little Nation by Sato Satoru (1959) is also set under
the influence of the war. That two writers created full-length
fantasies at the same time was not an accident. The Little
People and Little Nation were both symbols of survival, peace,
and the continuing of life and nation.

Gradually, people were able to apply their strong memories to the writing of realistic stories. Black Rain, published in 1966 by Ibuse Masuji, is about the atomic bombing
of Hiroshima. It is told in the form of diaries of ordinary
people, and it has a quiet power to appeal to generations who
did not experience the war. Children's Battlefield by Okuda
Tsuguo (1968) is based on his real evacuation experience.
Bon-Bon by Imae Yoshitomo (1973) is based on his experience
of air raids in Osaka. Then came Barefoot Gen by Nakazawa
Kenji in 1975. It first appeared in the weekly comic magazine,
Shonen Jump, proving that comic books can also treat serious
events like Hiroshima and that both extremes can meet at one
point.

There have also been picture books with a World War II
setting. In 1973 Only the Cat Family Could Survive by Saotome Katsumoto, illustrated by Tashima Seizo, told of the terrible air raids over Tokyo in picture book form. I know that
when Hiroshima No Pika by Maruki Toshi (1980) was translated in the States in 1982, it was recommended only for in-
termediate or older children; in Japan it was recommended for
all ages. The heroine, Me-chan, is seven years old. Younger
children can recognize the sincerity of the writer. If authors
tell the truth, then books are perfectly suitable for all ages;
especially in learning about war, the sooner the better. We
believe that the value of a picture book is its imaginative
power. We cannot teach or explain about the whole war, but
we can show an image. A picture book can sow an imaginative
seed in the impressionable brain of a small child, and some
day the plant will begin to bud. One famous picture book
creator, Takeichi Yasoo, of the Shikosha Publishing Company,
says in Ehon Mangekyo, "Picture books are now not merely
articles of consumption, nor the instruments for temporary
amusement. They are compansions through life even after
the child grows up, and the relationship continues to the end
of his life." And Indian author A. Ramachandran tells us,

"Throughout the world of the children's book, literature has the quality of make believe, but strangely enough not the illustrations. I may call these illustrations translations of verbal imageries into pictures, because the pictures themselves fail to create imageries of their own. This is perhaps due to the western tradition which has developed a pictorial expression near to the visual world and which is accepted by many as the basis for illustrations of children's books." Imagery is the most important point to criticize in picture books. Maruki Toshi holds out hers to every human being.

Many adults misunderstand the ability of children. Children don't necessarily express their ideas using language, but they can feel more strongly than adults. That is why picture books can attract public attention and why artists choose that medium for self-expression. The field flourishes remarkably in Japan.

It is a pity I do not have space to write about other highly active genres in Japan like school stories, young adult literature, collections of pseudo-folktales, and family stories. The art of literature does not have big power in Japan, but I trust its small power can reach the deeper place in human beings there and in other parts of the world.

BIBLIOGRAPHY

Blishen, Edward, ed., The Thorny Paradise. England: Kestrel Books, 1975.

Ramachandran, A., "Giving an Eye," from Imae Yoshitomo, ed.: Ehon-no-Jidai. Kyoto: Sekai-Shiso-sha, 1979.

Takeichi Yasoo, Ehon Mangekyo. Tokyo: Iwasaki Shoten, 1986.

BOOK LIST

Ibuse Masuji, Black Rain, trans. by John Bester. Tokyo: Kodansha International Ltd., 1969.

Imae Yoshitomo, Bon-Bon. Tokyo: Riron-sha, 1973.

Inui Tomiko, Kokage-no-Ie-No-Kobitotachi (Little People Lived in the House Under the Shade of the Tree). Tokyo: Fukuinkan Shoten, 1967.

Maruki Toshi, Hiroshima No Pika. New York: Lothrop, 1982.

Nakazawa Kenji, Barefoot Gen, vol. 1. Tokyo: Sankusha, 1978.

Nasu Masamiki, Zukkoke Sanningumi series. Tokyo: Popura-sha, 1978- .

Okuda Tuguo, Bokuchan no Senjyo (Children's Battlefield). Tokyo: Riron-sha, 1968.

Saotome Katsumoto, Neko wa Ikiteiru (Only the Cat Family Could Survive), illust. by Tashima Seizo. Tokyo: Riron-sha, 1973.

Sato Satoru, Daremo Shiranai Chiisana Kuni (Nobody Knows Little Nation). Tokyo: Kodansha, 1961.

Takeyama Michio, Harp of Burma, trans. by Howard Hibbett. Rutland, Vt.: Charles E. Tuttle Co., 1966.

Tsuboi Sakae, Twenty-Four Eyes, trans. by Miura Akira. Rutland, Vt.: Charles E. Tuttle Co., 1983.

Chapter 5

CHILDREN'S LITERATURE:
STATE OF THE ART IN MEXICO

Carmen Garcia-Moreno

First I must tell you why I became involved with books
and children. It was years ago, and my very first job was
in the Benjamin Franklin Library children's room, a room that
was later closed. A lady there who later went to the First
Pacific Rim Conference was Toni Gerez, and she was crucial
in getting me involved. If I'm at this conference, it's because
she led me to books and children.

I shall go into the past for just a little bit, for when
I write about books for children, I am writing about the
1980s. In Mexico we had very little before. Nevertheless,
Mexican culture and folklore are rich and varied and colorful, as are its legends, folktales, and oral tradition. We
have great writers, poets, and many painters. One can really
speak of the literary tradition and the pictorial tradition. We
also have good publishers--there's a good and strong publishing industry. With all this talent and capacity, however,
very little has been used for children. Very few writers and
artists in the past have dedicated their talents to writing and
illustrating children's books, and no publisher was dedicated
to the art of making good books for children. It is a well-
known fact that almost half of the population of Mexico is under 18 years of age. This means we are speaking of 40 million youngsters. Seven million alone are under six years of

45

age. Nonetheless, the importance of providing good material for the young has not been fully recognized or met--not until very recently. There has been no real reading tradition, no inherited sense of the importance of books at an early stage in life, no reading at home or at school, no school libraries; therefore, no books for children. This is not the moment to go into the reason, except very briefly. We're going to look at the present, primarily, and into the future. If anyone is interested, however, I do recommend the various studies on Mexico and its literature for children by Isabel Schon that investigate why there were no books for children.

As I have said, then, very few authors wrote books for children. During the nineteenth century and the first half of this century there were almost no authors and no illustrators. We find not more than twenty titles before 1900 and about seventy titles from 1900 to the late 1970s. When the Mexican Chapter of the International Board on Books for Young People (IBBY) was founded in 1979, we were asked how many books for children were published a year. In that year we found only three. Some or most of the books that had been published at that time were published by the authors themselves and then sold or given away to relatives and friends, some schools, some bookstores. Others were published by the Public Education Secretariat, which had had, since its creation in 1921, a department of publications. It did publish books for children from 1921 to 1924 when José Vasconcelos was Minister of Education, a set of very beautiful editions of the classics with illustrations by well-known artists. That was it. In a rather scattered manner a few books were published in the 1920s and 1930s and not much in the three decades that followed.

Obviously, then, no serious efforts existed in the country to write or publish books for children, not even to keep or make known the few that were published. It is hard in our day to find any of these editions. Only a few libraries, and perhaps a few private collections, have copies of them. And the books published during the first eighty years of this century were not extraordinary. They were not written with children in mind; they were few; and I don't think they formed a very important contribution in content. We cannot consider them, therefore, as part of a children's literary tradition. There was never a national children's hero or a well-known character whom children could identify with or recognize, unless one mentions Cri Cri el Grillo Cantor, the well-known singer and writer of stories put to music, whose work has not been published in book form.

The books of this period were not attractive to a child. Usually they were didactic and moralistic and rather dull. This was probably one reason children did not like to read and also the reason, when I asked in later years, "Why don't you publish books for children?" more than one publisher answered, "We don't and we won't publish books for children because Mexican children don't read." Now I know differently, because in that old Benjamin Franklin Library children's room, which was very tiny, kids from all over the city came and literally fought over the books. These were sent from the American Library Association and they were in English. The kids did not read English, so what we used to do was to translate them, type the translations, and paste them into the books. Years later we were doing the same thing. So I know the children read, I know that they like to read, but we'd never given them anything to read.

Fortunately the situation has changed. Some of us did not believe that Mexican children did not like to read because we had seen them devour books. Besides, the situation nowadays is quite different from what I have briefly described-- it is certainly much brighter. The year 1978 was an important one, for then things began to turn in another direction. Within the Public Education Secretariat a new division of publications and libraries was created and given much more influence than it had ever had. The Library Department made a plan to create and develop a nationwide public library system; but what concerns us here today is that for the first time the public libraries, both the new ones and those already in existence, would have children's sections. While the Department of Libraries planned, developed, and implemented this first library service for children, the Publications Department developed a program for children's publications. When the first children's room opened its doors to the City of Mexico in 1979 and when this was followed by other children's rooms within Mexico City and other cities and towns around the country, the need for more and better children's books published in Mexico became obvious. Before then our libraries were full of books from Spain and Argentina.

Before proceeding, I must mention other libraries that

once existed but had closed over the years. The Biblioteca Cervantes, which was founded in 1923 also by Vasconcelos, had a very good children's collection. These books disappeared when the library closed down. The children's room in the Biblioteca de Mexico was a place where one would go to do homework. It was very strictly regimented, like part of the school; that was the one transformed in 1979. And I have already mentioned the children's room in the Benjamin Franklin Library, which closed its doors because of a new USIS policy. Eventually, then, Mexico had no children's libraries left. I must mention the children's library at the Universidad Iberoamericana because I was the director of that library--a university library. My colleagues thought I was rather mad when I opened a children's room there. It opened in 1975 to serve a large community of children from areas surrounding the university. All these libraries, too, had on their shelves books from Spain, Argentina, and Venezuela--very little from Mexico.

Also about 1979 and 1980 thousands and thousands of children finished, for the first time, six years of primary instruction. They had learned how to read and write, and many would go on to high school, but for most this was the end of their education. It was therefore necessary to have books for them so that they wouldn't forget how to read and write, books both for information and for recreation. The Ministry of Education was aware of this.

Something else interesting happened in 1979. We founded the Mexican Section of IBBY, which later became the Mexican Association for the Promotion of Children's Books. We had to leave IBBY and call it the Mexican Association because we were told that IBBY had a very foreign influence and our organization should be more Mexican. The officials didn't know that what we were fighting for was to have Mexican authors and Mexican illustrators and books published in Mexico. We changed our name and converted it into a nonprofit organization whose purpose was to encourage new and young writers and illustrators to create for children, and to encourage publishers to publish those books. We wanted both indigenous writing and translated versions of good books from other countries. We worked very hard; we lectured in schools, to parents and teachers and children; we organized book exhibits and book fairs; and we did everything we could do to move the publishers.

Then we decided we had to do something more--to develop an international book fair. We wanted to do this in order to prove that an unexplored, huge market for children's books existed in Mexico. We wanted to arouse interest in good quality, attractive books among publishers, teachers, parents, and children, bringing to Mexico the best of children's books from other countries. IBBY-Mexico, therefore, conceived and organized in November 1981 Mexico's first International Children's Book Fair, sponsored by the Secretariat of Public Education. I'm happy to say that it's still alive. We're going to present the sixth book fair this coming November, and this fact is important because the idea comes from the previous administration. In Mexico, when we change our president every sixth year, everything stops. Everyone forgets what has been done before. But the book fair is continuing. It has become somewhat different from what we originally intended. We had planned that its major purpose would be the buying and selling of publishing and translating rights, but it has become a selling book fair. Mexican publishers sell every book they have in stock in November, so their publishing program is geared to the dates of the fair. It's also very difficult to find children's books in the bookstores in Mexico, so all the parents, librarians, and teachers save money for this event and do their buying then. We don't approve of this completely--we wish buying could be a year-round program--but this is better than nothing. We had nothing before. The fair's major success is that it has continued for five consecutive years. We are now preparing for a longer Sixth International Book Fair, lasting two weeks instead of one week. The number of books sold each year is overwhelming. In spite of devaluation and inflation and an earthquake, children's books sell. After last year's earthquake, we were sure we wouldn't attract too many people, but the exhibit was packed and more books than ever were sold.

Another of IBBY-Mexico's aims has been to prove that there are many authors and illustrators among us who merely need the opportunity to display their talents. For this purpose, during the first book fair in 1981 we sponsored the Antoniorrobles Prize for unpublished material. Most of the prizewinning texts and illustrations get published. In the beginning, we really had to take our prizes around and beg the publishers to consider them; now they beg us and fight among themselves for the prizes. We feel this prize is a real accomplishment.

The efforts of the Asociacion Mexicana/IBBY-Mexico to promote children's literature in Mexico have had an enormous impact. The number of titles translated into Spanish and published in Mexico has reached 400 within the past five years as well as about 250 original contributions by Mexican authors and illustrators. That means 650 titles printed and made available in Mexico quite recently. Of course the contributing factors I mentioned earlier are in force: the public library with its newly-developed children's departments; all those children graduating from the sixth grade for the first time; the foundation of IBBY-Mexico; and the book fair. This is no small feat, considering that recent times have been, and still are, very hard for the country.

Prior to 1980, only two publishers printed children's books in Mexico. After the events mentioned previously, several new publishing houses dealing exclusively with children's books have opened their doors, and several others have become interested enough to open sections for children's book publishing. Distributors of imported books for children-- and I'm speaking basically of distributors of books from Spain-- have increased in number. Throughout the country libraries and reading rooms have proliferated, while various magazines for children and a radio station exclusively for children have appeared within the past few years.

Many authors and illustrators have participated in events related to children's books on an international level, thanks to IBBY-Mexico's interest and belief in the international, universal appeal of good children's books. For instance, both in 1984 and 1986 Mexico participated successfully in the International Children's Book Fair in Bologna, Italy. There was strong interest, especially on the part of the Scandinavian countries, in translating some of these books into other languages. In addition, some Mexican books have received international recognition, such as Julieta y Su Caja de Colores, by a well-known artist called Carlos Pellicer, which also received a plaque at the BIB (Bienniale of Illustrations Bratislava). We're very proud that our Mexican illustrator, Felipe Davalos, was the winner of the first Ezra Jack Keats Award. (The U.S. Board of IBBY and UNICEF established this biennial award, honoring the memory of one of the United States' most widely known illustrators, to encourage talented illustrators to continue working in the field of children's books. Eligible persons must have published at least one book but not more

than three. Nominations were solicited for the 1986 award
from Canada, the United States, and Mexico.) Davalos' work
includes, I must mention, the illustration of a book written
by a young lady who had published it herself and distributed
it herself. Davalos is also the author-illustrator of Las Tor-
tugas de Mar (National Conference for the Promotion of Education) and Un Asalto Mayuscula (Vicky Nizri). Davalos'
work was recognized by the Keats Award jury "for graphic
and technical prowess, relationship of illustration and text,
storytelling quality, and appeal to children."

As we have seen--or should I say, as I believe--the
Book Fair was a turning point when things began to change.
But I must mention a few of the most important publishers
and what has happened to them since, because the scene is
not so hopeful as it sounds. The first is Ediciones Oceano.
Oceano, headquartered in Spain with a publishing branch in
Mexico, published twelve of our Antoniorrobles prizes in co-
edition with the Ministry of Education. The books are out of
print, and Oceano will not go into children's book publication
again. Organización Editorial Novaro, which was a large publisher of Walt Disney, did eighteen beautiful books. The
first six had been published in English in the United States
by Little, Brown and in Great Britain by Methuen, I believe;
the second six were centered around the Mexican Revolution;
and the last six presented ecological themes of Mexico. Editorial Novaro has now closed down. Another publisher, Pro-
mexa, after 1981 published a fine collection of 24 classics for
children, beautifully illustrated modern editions of such tales
as Snow White and Mercer Mayer's Sleeping Beauty plus two
Mexican legends. These 24 books are out of print, and the
publisher is not going to reprint them in Mexico. This publishing house also did the Benjamin Series, having purchased
the rights from Gallimard in France, which in turn had translated the books mostly from English. The books cost about
20¢ American money, including such titles as Rosemary Wells'
Noisy Nora and The Enormous Crocodile by Roald Dahl. The
children loved them. Once more, two Mexican titles were
added. No more. This series is not published in Mexico any
more; they're published in Spain. So we import them and
pay hundreds of pesos for them.

The news continues to be mixed. Editorial Patria, which
was very famous as a school book publisher, has launched
Coleccion Piñata, which presents informational rather than
fictional material. They have published a beautiful series on

such subjects as chocolate, silk, sugar, and paper--about ten
or twelve titles--and they are continuing to do about three
titles a year. On the other hand we have Editores Salvat
de México, which did a co-edition with the Ministry of Education of a children's encyclopedia, very Mexican in flavor and
content. Editores Salvat does not publish for children any
more. Fernández Editores, the oldest publisher of children's
books, has made all the Walt Disneys, too, and not very good
translations of the classics, school books, and coloring books.
But they have started to do something else: they have published several stories which have won the Premio Juan de la
Cabada, the prize offered by the National Institutes of Fine
Arts. They are also planning a new series by two talented
young women, a writer and an illustrator. Then Compania
Editorial Continental, a publisher of science and technology
texts for universities has begun to produce science books for
children. This company translates British series, and it
finds doing this less expensive, even if they have to buy the
rights, than getting national talent to write them. SITESA,
also science and technology publishers, are now translating
U.S. science series and producing new science series by
Mexican writers and illustrators.

On the positive side, one publisher has published a
series of portraits of Mexicans as well as some Latin-American
stories. Editorial Trillas is probably the strongest publisher
of children's books, and they have published most of our
Antoniorrobles prizes. From 1981 to 1986 they have published
250 titles, most of them original, as well as a few good, well-
selected translations. Trillas does most of its books for very
young children, and their price is very reasonable so that
every Mexican family can afford them. The books cost 50¢
to $1.00 and they are usually new stories by young authors
and illustrators. We also have Editorial CIDCLI (Centro de
Informacion y Desarrollo de la Comunicación y la Literatura
Infantiles), which is devoted entirely to children's books. It
is quite new and has published several collections of well-
made books, rich in Mexican flavor, some written by well-
known Mexican writers who had never before written for children. CIDCLI also does co-editions with the Ministry of Education and other large publishers. The Education Bureau has
done some very good books centered around Mexican historical
episodes, and it, too, is preparing for the next book fair.
They have the means, but so far not a very well-defined outline of what they want to do or what kind of collection they
want to build.

In 1982 our border was closed to all imports, including books. This was our golden moment; we could have published original books as easily as we had been importing them. But the moment passed. Once again we can buy books from Spain, Argentina, or Venezuela. But we need to combine books from other countries with a strong publishing program of our own. The present state of our economy and the rising cost of paper and printing have slowed down the publication process except in a few isolated cases--when, for example, a publisher does a co-edition with the Public Education Bureau. So once more it is easier and less expensive to import than to produce books of our own. Many publishers have therefore become distributors of Spanish books. This in itself is not bad; it's good, if only it could be balanced by local production.

Now we are standing at the threshhold, looking at the production of Mexico's first children's books. It has been a long, hard road, and we have walked a long way in a short time. We still have a long, long way to go. Much needs still to be done in the areas of writing, illustrating, producing, and distributing books. We need to work even harder, but I do think we're on our way. I hope that in spite of adverse circumstances we're standing now at a point of no return when we can only go ahead. Mexico's children need good books, and they are still waiting for them. They do read; they do like to read. Notwithstanding its dark moods and deep social and economic problems, Mexico must keep working to improve the quality of its children's books in order to satisfy the reading needs of its young population. The children of Mexico need good books today to be better-informed citizens tomorrow, to nourish and enrich their daily lives, to keep in touch with the world of dreams and fantasy as well as with their own cultural heritage, and to have acquaintance with the language and the cultural heritage and traditions of children in all the other parts of the world.

Chapter 6

CHILDREN'S LITERATURE:
STATE OF THE ART IN THE UNITED STATES

Dorothy Anderson

I can't begin this paper unless I make a confession.
I said yes to this marvelous assignment not because I'm an
expert on the state of children's literature in the United
States, but because it was such a thrill to imagine myself
being the United States' representative of something! I told
everybody. I told my mother, "Well, I have this paper to
write; I'm the United States representative...." She said;
"United States?! Not just UCLA? The United States?!" And
me a Canadian....

Nonetheless, I am perfect for the task, because you
wouldn't want to hear the biased opinion of one person, even
an expert. But I am an excellent reporter, so I immediately
turned to a panel of real experts, and I report my findings
to you today.

My informed sources, those I interviewed for this repor
are the following: Mary Purucker, my wise and witty col-
league who teaches children's literature in our graduate schoo
at UCLA and also an actual, functioning librarian--a rare
thing among educators, publishers, authors, and so forth;
Paula Quint, with the Children's Book Council in New York,
a very wise observer indeed; Barbara Karlin, a local advocate
of children's books whose reviews many of you have read in

54

Publishers Weekly, the Los Angeles Herald-Examiner, and the Los Angeles Times; and Susan Hirschman, president of Green-willow Books, publisher, editor, seasoned observer.

These are my infomed sources. I thank these professional colleagues for their candid opinions. Each of them assured me that I must say that these are but opinions from them. Who would ever dare, in fact, to be the U.S. representative? Here's our report, gathered under five headings.

I.

Children's literature in the United States is healthy. And by that I think Mary Purucker means that it feels alive and growing and changing in a very healthy way. For example, look at the work of Cynthia Voigt. She's chosen a very unusual and fresh form in which to present her thinking. She's not writing sequels as other people have done in the past. She's using her own exciting form; she herself is growing and changing.

Look at the growth in the work of Chris Van Allsburg. Sendak. Cynthia Rylant. Virginia Hamilton. Individual authors are growing and changing, as is the profile of the whole literature.

II.

Children's literature in these United States is diverse. About diversity Paula Quint says the following: our field, because it's not market-driven as is adult literature, demands diversity just because of the children themselves. She mentions how you can truly distinguish between the literature of the 1960s and the literature of the 1980s. She feels we're no longer so parochial--we're more international, and we have more diversity both thematically and by type of book.

For example, books for pre-schoolers. Think of Rosemary Wells, or Helen Oxenbury, who comes from England. And Japan's Shigeo Watanabe. Beautiful, wordless concept books--international. This diversity, as Mary Purucker points out, is reflected in the very funny works of M. E. Kerr. Cynthia Voigt stands by herself. Virginia Hamilton isn't afraid, as Mary says, to be literary. She doesn't compromise for popularity's sake, and she freely moves from folktale to science fiction to young adult books with a fresh approach in each case.

In the area of diversity, more subjects have opened up I think there's been a lot of discussion in the literature abou how there are no holds barred in our literature. I feel quite excited about that. I always bring in a friend, Sonia Anderson, a librarian in these parts, to my children's course; and she brings a load of controversial books. She scares the young people in that class. The kinds of provocative and previously controversial subjects are almost endless; and very often the treatment these days is quite skillful. These are not moralistic tales. Whether they're fiction or nonfiction, these subjects are treated very well in many cases.

Paula Quint says we're finally aware that childhood is not such an innocent time. Maybe it never was, but I think Meyrowitz's article, "Where Have the Children Gone?" In it h talked about how adults have become more childlike, running around in little playclothes, and how children have become more adult, wearing makeup when they're seven. And how you can't fool the children anymore because they watch on television parents discussing children, handling the problems. So they think, "Oh! That's why they did that!" One can't say to a child, "You're not old enough," because even if he doesn't comprehend the nuance of the subject, he surely knows what it is generally all about. That innocence--I'm not here to lament it; nonetheless the books reflect its loss.

Paula Quint sees three factors shaping the state of children's literature in this country: first, the marketplace (and even though she's said that publishing for children isn't market-driven I think I know what she means); second, society's current perception of childhood; and third, the versatile and often brilliant minds of the editors. One person at one house might love a book, the very same book another editor might hate. But each has a thoughtful and informed reason for the judgment. This allows for a great deal of inte esting diversity in publication.

III.

The third characteristic of children's literature in this

country is its generally high quality. It's a wonderful time.
There are more best books than ever before. There seems
to be a high level of writing, and the characters are strong.
Children's librarians seem to get quite engaged by the characters not in just one or two good books but in lots of them.
The themes, as Mary Purucker notes, are unafraid and yet
subtly developed--a nice touch. The authors are not simply
rolling over us with a steam roller, they are writing strong and
yet subtle stories. They don't moralize and yet they do show
psychological growth and insight. Mary asks, "Isn't it great
that children's literature didn't end with E. B. White or Made-
leine L'Engle or Robert McCloskey?" The good stuff is still
coming.

Now, lest this sound like a Pollyanna-type report, we
do admit that there were lots of mediocre things published,
say, in the 1960s. And I suppose a few slip through yet.
In fact, Barbara Karlin will add a realistic note about that
in a minute. But it still is true that we have a harder time
than ever giving awards because there are so many best books.
In fact, Susan Hirschman believes that we ought to move
away from trying to give one best book award and instead
celebrate all the best books. She even thinks that Frederic
Melcher would agree with her. She is a one-woman crusade
for not limiting our celebration to one title each year.

I promised you a little negative tone, a touch of reality. Barbara Karlin, for one, is disappointed; even though
she sees many beautiful books for older children--sensitive,
wonderful books--she thinks that there's too much gadgetry
and gimmickry in books for younger people these days. She
says, "We've got books that are toys, books that are purses,
books that are wheels, books that float, books that talk...."
And she for one is bored with that.

IV.

I think children's literature in this country has become
increasingly authentic. There's authenticity in the portrayal
of people's lives, in their language, in the emotions that are
reflected, and in the environments presented. I remember
how touched and impressed I was by Where the Lilies Bloom
when it came out in 1969. I remember how clear that un-
familiar environment became to me. I don't know that kind of

family tradition, or even that kind of courage, but the book gives a fine presentation of an environment and of lives and even of language.

In keeping with the notion of authenticity, characters seem to be less predictable than ever. There are fewer stereo types; even adults are flawed. The latter situation has been creeping up on us for decades, but now adults are really flawed. The kids must love it! Mary Purucker notes that fathers have taken on a new role in literature. They've become more visible and more real. Realism is a synonym of authenticity. As an example of a book with fully realized characters and few taboos, Mary mentions <u>Prairie Songs</u> by Pam Conrad.

V.

Children's literature in these United States currently is focused on the younger child. I heard this from every one of my consultants. Susan Hirschman, Paula Quint, Barbara Karlin, all say there's an overwhelming, enormous increase of books for the very young. And they note the new emphasis on parenting. People are older when they have children. They want their infants to get off to a good start. We've had the "baby boomlet," and since the 1960s we've noticed a rise-- really a spectacular rise--in books for the very young child. Remember in 1968 <u>Rosie's Walk</u>? In 1978 Don Crews' <u>Freight Train</u>? And Molly Bang's <u>Ten-Nine-Eight</u> in 1983?

There's more buying and translating of foreign children books for the very young; not so much as you probably have noted in older children's books, for many of the reasons that Miss Batchelder has already spoken of. But Quint and Hirsch man both credit the Bologna Book Fair for accelerating the trend of exchanging younger children's books. Think of imports like <u>Anno's Alphabet</u> from Japan, <u>Ernest and Celestine</u> from France, and even <u>Peter Rabbit</u> from England.

* * *

The first time I traveled to Europe I went with a very American young woman who thought the bicycle, the typewriter--everything important to living--had been developed in the United States. As I pointed out this and that invention throughout Europe, I realized how parochial many American

attitudes were. The titles we now have which have been published internationally indicate that our nation has really grown
up in its recognition of literary values existing abroad.

A related topic is the growth of bookstores and a fabu-
lous growth in the numbers of children's books being sold.
Paula Quint says that in California, for example, a wonderful
association of booksellers for children exists, with a membership of nearly 200 persons. Publishers are very much encouraged by this. Formerly, publishers thought that about
80 to 85 percent of their sales were to public libraries and
schools. Now the bookstores are sharing nicely in making
books accessible to children. I grew up, of course, at the
feet of Mildred Batchelder, and I remember hearing her always
promote and believe in <u>all</u> access points. Whether she was
talking about school libraries or public libraries or bookstores,
her belief was that "the more they read the more they read"
and that we should support and encourage all access points.
It seems to be happening here. Even as the funding for public libraries and school libraries is in jeopardy, children with
enough money can still find what they need in the bookstores.

Barbara Karlin also notes the paperback phenomenon.
Can you remember when we thought paperbacks were evil
things? Well, at least in the bookstores they're not, and old
favorites--inexpensive paperback editions of quality books--
are being brought back into the bookstores. That means
more affordability, and more children can get more books.

And now I'm going to add a postscript, a sort of sixth
heading. None of my informed sources characterized the state
of children's literature in this country as <u>representative</u>,
that is, representative of the population in this country.
This is a particularly burning issue with me. I live in a city
that is now 53 percent so-called minorities. I'm living in a
community where the population of this university, for example, represents a whole new wave of immigration to this
country. Los Angeles has become the port of entry for
thousands of people, as New York was at the turn of the
century.

At the turn of the century library ladies went out to
perform moral, uplifting duties. I know that some authors,
like Dee Garrison in her wonderful book <u>The Apostles of Cul-
ture</u>, somewhat discount this kind of activity because of its

missionary orientation. Nonetheless, those professionals performed a service for the new immigrants that is not being equaled in this day. Library directors are hard pressed to find children's librarians with that kind of motive for service. Indeed, without the missionary imperative I'm not sure that we're going to get children's librarians to perform those services anymore.

What I am concerned about in connection with this paper however, is that our literature begin to embrace the experience of these new children, that they have something even more than wonderful literature that is universal. They should have something that reflects their own experiences. I say it selfishly, because I think those of us who have been here for a while need to understand the new immigrants, need to know of their cultural heritage, and need to know them. I know there's always a time lag before good authors emerge from different cultures and before the publishers catch on, but I await eagerly the time when the Hispanic immigrants, the Oriental immigrants, and all the people who are enriching our society here will find their way into the literature that we are proud to call our own.

I suppose the consensus, then, is that we feel children's literature in the United States enjoys a healthy climate on the whole, is diverse, of high quality, and authentic, and that we're proud of it. And this in spite of political and intellectual, sometimes even spiritual, constraints that we see in society.

People still seem to believe that the child is the future, and they seem to not limit activity in the child's behalf. Susan Hirschman argues that there's still room for a committed author to write an honest book in this country, and publishers can still publish what they believe in. The field is wide open, she says, for creativity and excellence.

And I like that.

BOOKS MENTIONED

Anno, Mitsumasa. <u>Anno's Alphabet</u>. New York: Crowell, 1975.

Bang, Molly. _Ten-Nine-Eight_. New York: Greenwillow, 1983.

Cleaver, Vera, and Bill Cleaver. _Where the Lilies Bloom_. Philadelphia: Lippincott, 1969.

Conrad, Pamela. _Prairie Songs_. New York: Harper Junior Books, 1985.

Crews, Donald. _Freight Train_. New York: Greenwillow, 1978.

Garrison, Dee. _The Apostles of Culture: The Public Librarian and American Society 1876-1920_. New York: Macmillan, 1979.

Hutchins, Pat. _Rosie's Walk_. New York: Macmillan, 1968.

Meyrowitz, Joshua. "Where Have the Children Gone?" _Newsweek_ 100 (August 30, 1982):13.

Vincent, Gabrielle. _Ernest and Celestine_. New York: Greenwillow, 1982.

Chapter 7

THE PRINTED PAGE AND BEYOND: FORMS OF
CHILDREN'S LITERATURE AND THEIR
TRANSMITTAL TO CHILDREN

Margaret A. Bush

Pictures and narrative on the printed page might be
called the basic and even traditional form in which children's
literature has been created, conveyed and preserved in the
now many years since the invention of print and the ensuing
spread of literacy as a predominant cultural mode. Of course
it has now been more than a third of a century since television, building on the earlier success of motion pictures, began its meteoric rise as the medium of popular choice through
which children receive stories and information. For some
years it was common in some circles to speak of "visual literacy," a concept for which no widely accepted definition seems
to have emerged, but for the most part critics and teachers
have been reluctant to grant the same intellectual and social
stature to the broadcast or projected medium that is accorded
print. Certainly in the mainstream of critical writing on children's literature little examination is afforded nonprint works
except for those based on children's books; it is as though
the print relationship is a prerequisite for legitimacy.

These days "computer literacy" has become a popular
concept. There is a widespread enthusiasm, and one that is
heeded by schools and libraries, for the use of microcomputer
for entertainment, information, and learning. Many writers

are examining the impact of the computer on the intellectual performance of individuals and on the very structure and dynamics of society. Like television, the computer is viewed by some as a competitor of print and one that is both advantageous and detrimental to the social and intellectual order.

These ideas are becoming increasingly important to all of us for they have already begun to alter the very context in which literature for children is produced and used. Our purpose here will be to look at ways these so-called communications technologies and other social and commercial currents are affecting the forms and even the content of literature conveyed to children.

Influence of Television and Computers on Conventional Format

One writer who has thoughtfully addressed the impact of television and computers on children's books and reading is Adele Fasick of the University of Toronto. In a Top of the News article on children's library services in the information age, she makes the following observation:

> Within the past few years there has been an increasing number of information books produced which integrate pictures and text in a new and lively fashion. The information is given in a series of small segments. The reader is not expected to start at the top of one page and work methodically through the text until coming to the bottom of the second page. Instead, the author invites the reader to skip around the page, absorbing the information from text and pictures shown as small clusters. This format does not require the length of attention which a more conventional book requires. It seems to be a format especially appropriate to children familiar with the short segments of television programs.[1]

One might add that such a publication is also a computer-age book since many books in this format are illustrated with computer-generated graphics or computer-enhanced photographs.

The books Fasick describes do receive at least cursory examination in some of the journals which receive children's materials, but we tend to treat them as information sources and not as works of literature. Yet they deserve more thoughtful attention as a form for several reasons. On the one hand, great numbers of books are now produced in this way, and many of them are quite flawed both as children's books and as treatments of their particular subjects. On the other hand, the sameness of format tends to obscure those books which are truly well executed, and we need a better critical understanding if we really care to identify and promote those which are likely to provide pleasure and responsible presentations of information for children.

We have not actually given a name to this type of book although its form has become quite familiar to those who are selecting books for children to use in libraries and classrooms. Its main characteristics are that it is slim, colorful, and miscellaneous in its treatment of the subject. Usually there is a double-spread page on a broad aspect of the topic followed by short, often unconnected, paragraphs offering bits of information. Most often there is no particular sequence in the arrangement of the two-page sections. A substantial portion of each spread is filled with pictorial material. Although children, and probably many adults, tend to think that thin, highly illustrated books will also be easy to read, the majority of these books prove to be at a ninth to twelfth grade reading level when examined by standard readability measures. They do not seem to have been written for children so much as assembled quickly from other sources in order to make a neat, bright, thirty-two-page package. Rather than "integrating pictures and text in a lively fashion," to use Fasick's words, many of these books are fragmented and contain very sketchy explanations of complex material. It is somewhat sad to say at an international meeting that the largest number of these poorly rendered books are distributed simultaneously in several countries and often do not originate in the United States though they are published secondarily here; these are one of the shabbier aspects of a current trend in international co-production of books.

One might dismiss these thin, busy volumes as trivial and unworthy of our attention were it not for the fact that we are seeing literally several dozen of them each publishing season and that they share several characteristics with many

other nonfiction and even fiction books which are being produced. An important factor, also stated by Fasick, is that
"this format does not require the length of attention which a
more conventional book requires." We are indeed faced with
massive evidence of declining reading capabilities and attention span among our childhood population. The miscellany
approach to nonfiction has become very popular; occasionally
such books are thoughtful and entertaining, but often they
are superficial and even monotonous. Cohesive, substantial,
thought-provoking treatments of really interesting subject matter are produced less and less frequently for children. Com-
parably, much of our fiction is developed in a shorter, simpler
form with fewer pages and larger print. Troublesome questions arise out of all of this, and we need to search out and
examine the implications of current research on literacy, learning styles, and intellectual development of today's children.
It may well be that the real audience among children for the
finely crafted fiction and nonfiction is in fact growing substantially smaller.

On a happier note, children's books have also been affected in some very felicitous ways by the visual media. During these years of saturation by television there has been a
parallel rise in the use of photography to illustrate children's
books. Often this is simply a utilitarian matter, with photographs selected from various picture services to accompany a
text. But just as often we see books in which the photographs have been constructed for the particular volume. New
photographic techniques are utilized well, as are the artistic
aspects of photography. The photo-essay has become quite
popular with many photographers and writers specializing in
this format. Some of the best children's books available
through international co-production and co-publication are
handsomely photographed and thoughtfully developed, coming
to the United States primarily from Germany and Japan. Examples which come quickly to mind are the wonderful works
of Hans-Heinrich Isenbart documenting the birth of various
animals,[2] the beautiful natural history books published first
in Japan and then rendered into American editions by the
Lerner Publishing Company,[3] and the informative and appealing handbooks on various pets produced in Germany and published in the United States by Barron's.[4]

Once in a great while we see a children's book developed
in the best style of the television or film documentary. My

own favorite in this category is the richly faceted <u>Joel: Grow</u> <u>ing Up A Farm Man</u>, written by Patricia Demuth and photo- graphed by Jack Demuth (Dodd Mead, 1982). Taking one full year of work, not uncommon for a fine film, the Demuths actually rented an adjacent farm in order to photograph and learn about the agrarian lives and work of thirteen-year-old Joel Holland and his family during the various seasons of the year.

One critical problem persists in our consideration of pho tography as a medium of illustration in children's books: we do not tend to give photography the same level of considera- tion afforded other art forms. In part this is probably be- cause we take photography for granted and consider it as being fairly utilitarian, but we also tend not to understand very well the capabilities of photography. Consequently, we occasionally find books with fairly mediocre photography re- ceiving glowing reviews because the subject matter itself is very appealing.

In addition to the greatly expanded use of photography for both its appeal and its realism, television and film have also influenced the content and shaping of children's books in other ways. Several fine fiction works, both serious and funny, have utilized television as a theme. In the past couple of years we have had several new books which have presented the technical aspects of television to children; on the whole, these have not been very successful in their ex- planations. This year we have a different approach in <u>The</u> <u>TV-Smart Book for Kids</u> (Dutton, 1986). Written by Peggy Charen of Action for Children's Television, and Carol Hulsizer this is intended to extend children's response to their viewing through discussion and the use of puzzles, games and activ- ities; the book also includes a parent's guide. Dell Yearling Books are apparently responding to the small trend called Kid- Vid, in which television productions feature the work of chil- dren as producers, narrators, hosts, etc. A new Dell series called On the Air and Off the Wall will follow the exploits of a group of eight- to seventeen-year-olds who find themselves in charge of a local TV station. Titles include <u>The-Not-</u> <u>Quite-Ready-for-Prime-Time Bandits</u>, <u>Rock Video Strikes Again</u> and <u>Can This Telethon Be Saved?</u>, all written by Barbara Adams. It is not usual to see a book actually take the form of a film, but once in a while this, too, occurs. One of my own favorite examples is the small set by Martha Alexander

called 3 Magic Flip Books (Dial, 1984). Delightfully entertaining in and of themselves, these small stories demonstrate
the basic principle of film animation for children and must
surely have inspired many a young artist to create other
stories in similar fashion.

Board Books

It is not only computer and television technology which
has influenced the current shaping of books, of course. The
widely noted interest in infants and young children and the
increasing sales of children's materials in bookstores have resulted in an amazing proliferation of board books--usually quite
small volumes printed on pages of glossy, durable cardboard.
Until recently these books have not been considered as much
more than a mass-market item. Recently, however, reviewing
journals have begun to pay attention as several well recognized
picture book illustrators have begun to produce work in this
format: Helen Oxenbury, Susanna Gretz, Kate Duke, and Ann
Rockwell, among others. Photography, too, has come to board
books, most notably perhaps in the beautifully simple Red,
Blue, Yellow Shoe by Tana Hoban (Greenwillow, 1986). Another noted photographer, Jill Krementz, recently produced
Jack Goes to the Beach, Lily Goes to the Playground, and
other titles (Random House, 1986). These books are quite
a bit larger than usual and are part of a series called Great
Big Board Books; 7" x 10" in size and a bit heavy in the
hand, these are intended by the publisher to be a bridge for
toddlers who are ready to make the transition to regular paper
page books.

Board books are also moving from very simple stories
and the naming of objects into more complex concepts. Anne
Sibley O'Brien's I Don't Want to Go, It's Hard to Wait, It
Hurts, and Don't Say No (Holt, 1986) are part of a series
which the publisher claims are "designed to foster communication between parent and child." And of course very frank
gimmickry marks the design and packaging of some board
books: Simon and Schuster offers a boxed package, Baby's
First Doll and Book, featuring a Helen Oxenbury board book
and "a squishy-soft stuffed baby";[5] Putnam's My Very Own
Telephone Book is spiral-bound and cut in the shape of a
telephone; yet another series by Dick McCue and Lisa McCue,
Hatching Board Books (Simon and Schuster), features

animal-shaped books, each packed in a plastic egg. Some of these board books are trendy products and may be available for only a short season, but if the season is successful it is likely that spin-offs will soon appear. On the other hand, some of these books represent thoughtful and creative work, and some of the gimmicks are genuinely fun. They deserve the longer life span which serious critical attention might encourage.

Pop-Ups

Another popular form which we tend to consider as a gimmick and a commercial product is the pop-up book. Largely shunned by libraries as ephemeral and non-book items (and for the very practical reason that they are easily damaged), these are generally regarded as products for personal ownership. It should be noted that some bookstores shun them, too, for their precarious shelf-life; and although rumor abounds that many of these are being produced, it would appear that there are currently just a few new ones each publishing season. These books are sometimes described as works of paper engineering because of the complexity of their construction, and they are another notable example of international co-production. While some of the new titles are reviewed in teaching journals and quality magazines such as The New Yorker and Scientific American, they are seldom considered in the standard children's literature and reviewing journals. It's interesting to find that the pop-ups do seem to receive more regular attention in such well regarded reviewing journals from abroad as Growing Point and Junior Bookshelf as well as in The Times' educational and literary supplements. Like board books, pop-ups are often poorly conceived for a quick market; we see this in spin-offs of beloved books such as the Goodnight Moon Room (Harper, 1984) and the Frog and Toad Pop-Up Book (Harper, 1986), which fall far short of the depth and grace of the original books, and also in many informational books which are showy but superficial or even confusing in the information they convey. In our almost categorical disregard of the pop-ups, however, we tend to lose sight of some very lovely artwork and truly ingenious presentations such as may be found in Ron Van DeMeer's Sailing Ships (Viking, 1984), Huck Scarry's Looking into the Middle Ages (Harper, 1984), Alice and Martin Provensen's Leonardo DaVinci (Viking, 1984), and some of the works of

Keith Mosely, Jan Pienkowski, and others. One hopes such
work will continue to be produced with ever more skillful use
of the format, for these are books which truly delight and
stimulate curiosity and imagination; our failure to give them
serious consideration as works of children's literature encourages the proliferation of those which will sell quickly but not
bear up under critical scrutiny. We may find that the truly
fine works will drop from view, to be found only in occasional
private collections alongside the pop-up (or toy and game)
books of past eras.

Audio-Video Formats

We have heard a good deal lately about the rising sales
of children's books in bookstores,[6] suggesting an increase in
personal ownership of books among children, and we have
been hearing for a long time about the popularity of nonprint
formats with children. These two phenomena are now merging with the rapid proliferation of home-owned audio and
video equipment. According to a recent report in Publishers
Weekly,[7] within the next few months we shall be seeing an
extensive promotion campaign for children's audio and video
cassettes to be marketed largely through bookstores. Among
these are new products for children from more than fifty audio
and video publishers; it will be interesting to note the patterns which emerge. One long-time producer of 16-millimeter
films for the education market will rigorously market to the
general public video versions of these films which are "...
developed for educational use and must pass tough school
district board standards. The films must be free from bias
and have socially redeeming value. They must be fun, entertaining, harmless, and gentle."[8]

The products listed by many of these companies fall
into familiar categories: audio and video materials will use
well-known contemporary and "classic" book titles; there are
do-it-yourself materials on fitness and crafts, religious materials, some outright didactic items, overly cute productions
for very young listeners/viewers, vanity publications, television and toy tie-ins, and the expected gimmicks. A talking
teddy bear will be activated by one of six audio cassettes
featuring well-known stories. Book-related products include
audio versions of Sweet Valley High Romances and a Golden
Play Book 'n' Tape series featuring activity books with reusable

vinyl stickers along with dramatized versions of Golden Book stories. One company will offer Board Book/Cassette combinations for older pre-schoolers. A company called CC Studios in Weston, Connecticut, will sell videocassettes of children's books which would seem to be the very same items Weston Woods has sold to libraries and schools as filmstrips, films, and more recently as videocassettes. The H. W. Wilson Company, that venerable purveyor of reference works for libraries, will release The American Storytelling Series; at a price of $99 for a thirty-minute video, this is likely to remain in the province of libraries rather than bookstores. While the audio and video titles will occasionally feature original work produced specifically for this release, in a majority of cases the companies are repackaging works which have already proven their appeal in other uses. As new renderings of the familiar in currently popular formats, they will undoubtedly be very popular in the marketplace.

Clearly the video format, acquired by purchase and home recording of televised productions, offers attractive possibilities for the home viewer. Personal libraries of favorite works surely already exist, and the body of literature represented includes the best of writing, dramatic interpretation, and camera techniques along with the worst in commercialized schlock. Who will critique this format and promote those works of high quality? It seems likely that schools will select works related both to print literature and to curricular subjects, while libraries may choose from a somewhat broader spectrum but will emphasize productions based on books.

During this conference we have seen examples of quite delightful film interpretations of picture books. Since most film is scripted, and much of it relies on artistry and story, the great body of children's literature available in this country provides a rich mine for film-makers. Those of us in the children's literature field tend to base our judgments of book-based films on their faithfulness to the details and qualities of the original books and on the aesthetic qualities of the artistic and visual components. Judgments of more technical aspects of camera work, composition, lighting, and editing are generally left to critics more interested in film-making than in literature. While this serves our purpose of promoting the virtues of print literature, it rather limits our understanding and use of film as a uniquely rich format providing a great range of artistic and intellectual experiences having no print basis. Some children will be enticed into reading through film, and others will enjoy seeing favorite books in new, exciting presentations on the screen; but many children are and will remain predominantly viewers and not readers. We need to develop better critical acumen which will enable us to develop a thinking response to film viewing among children and which will also promote a wider variety of viewing opportunities for them. Left to itself, the marketplace will not accomplish this important function.

Gaps in Today's Literature

While some of the new or newly popular forms of children's books and the audio and video formats offer creative possibilities for the producers of materials and added opportunities for user enjoyment, there are also forces working to narrow and limit the literary ideas and experiences available to today's children. As indicated earlier, the new formats do not reach their fullest potential in serving the intellectual and recreational interests and needs of children. There is a great tendency towards re-working and repackaging popular or proven material, a trend which encourages repeated use of the familiar to the exclusion of works that are fresh and innovative or simply less well known. The commercial factors which have caused publishers to shorten their backlists and the political conservatism which has impinged on school curricula in parts of the country have further diminished the range of quality materials now available to children.

One complaint about the long-standing shortage of material is now being voiced from another quarter. With bookstore sales expanding, booksellers have joined librarians concerned about the scant supply of "middle reader books."9 Only a small body of literature exists for the seven-, eight-, and nine-year-old child who has begun to read independently but is not intellectually or socially ready for full-size novels. Children are being pushed much more quickly through infancy and early childhood and into a long adolescence at a much younger age, so that the span of childhood is becoming much altered. The middle group, less glamorous, if you will, than younger children or adolescents, seems forever to have less attention devoted to its particular needs. While there are always some good materials produced, the shelves of such materials in both libraries and bookstores are never enough;

presumably school and television take up the slack when
reading aloud begins to drop off and the supply of books
that appeal to independent reading narrows. More is the
pity--this is a critical age for the strengthening of reading
skills and habits. The awarding of the 1986 Newbery Medal
to Patricia MacLachlan's Sarah, Plain and Tall (Harper, 1985),
a slim, simple tale artfully told and beloved by readers of all
ages, recognizes the literary worth of simple fiction in a very
special way. It is, of course, a special book. It would be
too much to hope that this little work and its many honors
will inspire writers and publishers to a great production
of the needed books, but perhaps it will provide at least
small encouragement.

A continuing frustration for the buyers of children's
books is the rapid rate at which even recently published
titles now go out of print. Whole chunks of subject matter
once treated respectably in children's books are no longer
available in this form. Librarians everywhere who are concerned about the breadth and quality of materials to serve
children can cite tales of disappointment. Almost nothing for
children is now available on dolphins or on George Washington
Carver or on any of a myriad of subjects appealing to children
or of significance to their heritage or learning. In too many
cases librarians must hang on to dated or worn materials or
refer children to encyclopedias or adult books. Sometimes
very pedestrian or utilitarian titles are still available on subjects where fine work was once published. There is no simple
solution to this vexing dilemma, for its origins are complex.
The causes as I mentioned earlier are both commercial and
social/political; conservative inroads on school curricula in
some states have narrowed the range of subjects taught to
children, impinging in turn on the marketplace.

Finally, as was also pointed out by one of the panelists
earlier in this conference, the children's books and non-print
forms being produced today in the United States fall far short
of reflecting the multi-ethnic nature of our population of children.[10] The tremendous shift in the ethnic configuration of
our society in recent years has nowhere been honestly calcu-
lated or reported, but is well known in our school systems.
The distribution of Asian, Black and Hispanic children is wide
spread but uneven; in some communities the Caucasian population is still an overwhelming majority, but in many and increasing areas it is the minority. Yet the experience of

non-Caucasian children is seen but little in children's books beyond almost standard, token representation in pictures and the fine work of a very few authors and illustrators who are Black, Asian, Hispanic, or Native American. Attention focused on this problem during the so-called civil rights era seems to have lost its thrust. Few new artists and writers are being published, and some of the fine titles of recent years have also fallen out of print. The cultural heritage and contemporary experience of non-white children are thoughtfully presented in a few books and discussed in well-intentioned but utilitarian works of nonfiction. To some extent both television and feature films do a bit better than children's books, but huge gaps exist in children's literature. The shortage of material is twofold; not only are American children's books not truly representative of our population, but there is a serious need for books in the many languages spoken and read by thousands of children and their families only recently arrived in this country. Some libraries are providing such materials, but they still face many problems with identifying, evaluating, and purchasing children's books from other countries. Again, there are no simple solutions, but we greatly need improved communication and availability of materials.

Conclusion

The literature for children is rich beyond reckoning, but it appears that its richness may not reach children as widely or as effectively as we might wish. Those of us who are the creators, critics and purveyors of this literature have more complex challenges than at any time since the mechanical printing of the written word started us down the centuries of children's books. New forms have indeed emerged which utilize, complement, and sometimes compete with children's books. Like books, these forms have their own systems of language, artistry, and technical components which convey ideas, information, and experience. They are deserving of their own critical consideration which does not confine them to the value systems designed for books. As they now share the market once dominated by print materials, they must be evaluated and promoted with the same thoroughness and care afforded children's books.

In arguing for full legitimacy of newer forms, I am by

no means suggesting that we consider books and reading as less important. It is imperative that we continue to promote the very special capacity of books in the emotional, intellectual, and creative development of children. Reading and writing have enormous values which must not be lost--and we see signs of loss. More than ever before, we must devote some of our attention to those economic and social factors affecting the production of materials for children and be truly informed and effective advocates in an almost confounding context.

NOTES

1. Fasick, Adele. "Moving into the Future without Losing the Past: Children's Services in the Information Age, Top of the News, 40 (Summer, 1984): 407-8.

2. Isenbart, Hans-Heinrich. A Duckling Is Born, Photographs by Othmar Bauli (G. P. Putnam's Sons, 1981); Birth of a Foal, Photographs by Thomas David (Carolrhoda, 1986).

3. Lerner Natural Science Books. Most titles adapted by Sylvia Johnson. These include Apple Trees, Frogs and Toads, Snakes, and many more. A similarly handsome series, the Carolrhoda Nature Watch Books, originates in Germany and includes titles on Siberian tigers, ladybugs, storks, and other animals by several authors and photographers.

4. Barron's Pet Care series. Guinea Pigs: A Complete Pet Owner's Manual, by Horst Bielfeld, illus. by Fritz W. Kohler, 1983; Poodles: Standard, Miniature and Toy Poodles, by Hans J. Ullmann and Evamaria Ullmann, 1984; and several other titles.

5. "Children's Books: Up Front," Publishers Weekly, 229 (June 20, 1986): 43.

6. Op. cit., p. 41, and noted variously by Publishers Weekly throughout 1985 and 1986.

7. "New Products for Children," Publishers Weekly, 230 (July 18, 1986): 60-69.

8. "Educational Marketer Learns the Retail Ropes," Publishers Weekly, 230 (July 18, 1986): 56.

9. "Children's Books: Up Front," op. cit.

10. See Dorothy Anderson, "Children's Literature: State of the Art in the United States," in this volume.

ADDITIONAL SOURCES

Compaine, Benjamin M. "The New Literacy," Daedalus, 112 (Winter 1983): 129-142.

Davis, Boyd H. "Tangle in the Story Line," Children's Literature in Education, 16 (Winter 1985): 227-232.

Quayle, Eric. Early Children's Books, A Collector's Guide. London: David & Charles; Totowa, New Jersey: Barnes & Noble, 1983.

Wilson, Pauline. "Youth Services in the Information Society," School Library Journal, 31 (August 1985): 22-24.

PART IV:

FROM THE WORLD OF CRITICISM:
TWO AUTHORS SPEAK

A truism tells us that the quality of a body of literature depends upon the worth of its critics. Two authors share their
insights into important areas of writing: the creation of characters in fiction and the achievement of excellence in poetry.

Chapter 8

CHARACTERIZATION--SOME UNFORGETTABLES

Eleanor Cameron

I remember so clearly from childhood the intensity of my relationships with the beings, human and animal, in those stories I loved best. I suffered and rejoiced with them as if they were alive, as they were to me, so that I felt them to be my friends. And these friendships didn't stop when I'd come to the last page. There were times when I couldn't bear to come to the end (I don't know how many times I read the stories about King Arthur and Hans Christian Andersen's fairy tales) and could do nothing but begin all over or go on with the story as I felt it must go on.

Two influences that mean a great deal to me in character portrayal--as I've learned through years of fiction writing--are the power of place and the power of the unconscious.

About the power of place I once asked Natalie Babbitt, Lloyd Alexander, and Virginia Hamilton, gathered together at a children-and-author occasion in New York, how much place meant to them in the creation of character, and their answers revealed the differences among writers. Both Lloyd Alexander and Virginia Hamilton were definite in their conviction that place had been a powerful inducer, while Natalie Babbitt said that for her it meant little or nothing. She thinks of an idea and then makes up her characters to carry out the idea. She works from the outside in, while Hamilton and Alexander work from the inside out.

79

As for the power of the unconscious, the following statements by Elizabeth Bowen and Ursula Le Guin and the creation of their characters seem to bear out my own discoveries. Bowen, the English novelist, has written, "Between them and me exists no gulf. I could say, they have made themselves known to me--instantly recognizable, memorable from then on. From the moment they hove into view they were inevitable.... They enlightened me, I believe, as to many things. I became, and remain, my characters' close and intent watcher: their director, never. Their creator I cannot feel that I was, or am."[1]

Writes Ursula Le Guin, "I don't write out descriptions beforehand, and would indeed feel ridiculous, even ashamed, to do so. If the character isn't so clear to me that I know all _that_ about him, what am I doing writing about him? What right have I to describe what William did when Helen bit his knee if I don't even know what he looks like, and his past and his psyche, inside and out, as well as I know myself? Because after all, he is myself. Part of myself. If William is a character worthy of being written about, then he exists. He exists, in my head to be sure, but in his own right, in his own vitality. All I have to do is look at him. I don't plan him, compose him of bits and pieces, inventory him. There he is, and Helen is biting his knee, and he says with a little cough, 'I don't think this is really relevant, Helen.' What else, being William, could he say?"[2]

As for my own convictions, I don't see how the fact can be other than that in the depths of the creative unconscious the whole, given character must exist, for the writer has never to wonder what that person would do under certain circumstances. And it has often seemed to me that if you do have to cast around in order to find how a certain character would act, then that character must not naturally and deeply be your own, and that a serious flaw is likely to be woven into the novel which could become increasingly serious felt subtly at first but with increasing proof of artificiality as the novel progresses. For the writer would constantly run the risk of having that character, purely for the sake of an imposed story, do something that would run contrary to his inmost nature.

Unless, of course--and this is most likely if he is a "made" character--he is presented so shallowly that he would have no inmost nature. But even minor characters in memorable novels have inmost natures. The writer perceives them, and even if they come into the novel only briefly, he will have a distinct feeling about their essences, as Walter de la Mare does about the old sailor, the Oomgar, in The Three Mulla Mulgars (The Three Royal Monkeys in this country), and Ursula Le Guin does about Ged's dear friend Vetch in A Wizard of Earthsea, and Katherine Paterson does about Gilly's Black teacher, Miss Harris, in The Great Gilly Hopkins. These may be secondary characters, but we feel them, and we feel strongly that the author knows a very great deal about them--that they were not "cooked up" to take their secondary places. They are a meaningful, perceived part of these novelistic worlds, necessary, inextricably woven into the fabric, and therefore must be known.

Now I should like to tell you, re characters and their roots in the depths of the writer's unconscious, a little about my mother, because this paper, very gradually as I planned it, seemed to want to build itself around mothers. My mother and I were very close, even though we sometimes got at loggerheads in our younger days and couldn't see the other's point of view. She was a power in my life, and at times I rebelled against that power until the time came when I no longer needed to because I understood her, and perhaps myself as well, more clearly. And she became, in my latest books, the mother of the child each novel is about. In each of the later books she is there in essence, though only a part of her, it turned out, is there in each of the three women. There was no need to make an effort to do this--it came about because of place. Place for me, as I've said, makes story by making possible, indeed by making inevitable, certain characters. The mystery to me is why place--and time--should have called up three different essences of the same woman.

In A Room Made of Windows she was one who was compelled to say to her daughter that for her children were not enough because she did not feel whole without a man to share her life. In The Court of the Stone Children she was the kind of woman for whom responsibility comes first, responsibility to circumstance, to making something decent of life, but only within dependable circumstances; so that Nina thinks of her as habitually saying, "We must--we must--we must always" do this, that, or the other. The sense of duty is paramount.

In To the Green Mountains she was one whose dominant qualities were independence and the ability to manage. In this
novel, her management of a hotel led her to desire change in
the headwaiter Grant's life to the extent that she did change
it without discussion with anyone, because she could see so
clearly what it ought to be, how it ought to go.

As for Tissie, Grant's wife, she afforded two instances
of the power of the unconscious to affect the novelist in his
writing, showing me examples of the inevitability of some apparently preordained pattern, if one can only recognize it,
remain open enough to recognize it. Of course I could have
changed it. I could have done anything I wanted with my
own work, but some deeper self knew that it would be un-
wise, unaesthetic, a failure to carry out imaginative truth.

First, I had thought from the beginning (and To the
Green Mountains was in my mind for thirty years before I
finally wrote it) that Tissie would come up to Elizabeth Rule's
room in the hotel with the purpose of threatening her because
she had so changed Grant's and Tissie's private life. I'd
been looking forward to doing a dramatic scene, but upon
arriving at this chapter I was surprised to find that Tissie
had no intention of going up to Elizabeth's room, Tissie having
finally revealed herself to me, in spite of what I had taken for
granted, as not at all the kind of woman who would threaten
another human being with physical harm. The Tissie given
me, my Tissie (who must have been there in my unconscious
the entire time as a completed person so that she could gradu-
ly disclose herself in one aspect after another under the pres-
sure of various circumstances), was a woman of high passion,
yes, full of delight in living, prone to laughter, to dancing,
imitating, acting, teasing, but with, nevertheless, a most
private, withdrawn place deep within that complex self of
hers, a place of dignified reserve. Her friendship with Elizabeth Rule and Kath, unquestioning and trusting all these
years, simply vanished, and she never again had anything to
do with either Elizabeth or with the child Kath, who had
loved her and Grant, and loved, above anything else, being
with them. That was the truth about Tissie, and she made
it known to me.

Second, I did not want Tissie to die. Before I knew
I didn't want her to, I had envisioned the train scene, where

she was run over, with great vividness; I heard the words
of Kath and of Aunt Maud and Uncle Tede, who did not want
Kath to come near Tissie, though Tissie wanted to speak to
her. I could have handled it, I believe, without either senti-
mentality or crudity. But then I discovered that I didn't
want Tissie killed. Not necessary, I tried to tell myself;
but I could not change it, though I ran around mentally inside my head trying to find a way out of my dread necessity.
But Tissie had to die. And I can't tell why except that partly
it was the final piece in the pattern, which I see now, on
looking back, as one of "downhill all the way," step by fatal
step. And I couldn't bring Kath onto the scene of the train
accident because Uncle Tede wouldn't let me. He came toward
Kath with his hands out and turned her and led her back the
way she had come with Aunt Maud following after.

We come now to an exchange one of the editors of Pied
Pipers: Interviews with Influential Creators of Children's
Literature had with Alan Garner.

Q. Your childhood--you lived near Alderly Edge, the
setting for the first two books and a center for the
supernatural. Obviously there were things happening
in your childhood that have perhaps affected you?

A. That's an enormous matter. I could hardly get
through it in two hours. Where does one begin?

Q. I can't believe that you had what might be called
a "normal" childhood.

A. God, no. First of all I was saved from an education by being too ill to go to school. It was very
dramatic--spinal and cerebral meningitis at the same
time, diphtheria, pleurisy, pneumonia. I hardly
went to school before I was eleven. It was largely--
and I think I'm being charitable--that my mother func-
tioned best in a crisis; and now that I understand a
lot more, I see that she precipitated situations by
which I became ill. Quite unconsciously, of course.
A lot of the illnesses were caused initially by severe
periods of emotional tension. My mother was a superb
nurse. It sounds rather sick to say that she made
me sick in order to function, but I saw her do it to
other people. She was a very good nurse and tended
to become rather destructive in other situations.[3]

Now, in <u>Red Shift</u>, a book on three layers of time, the story in the present is carried on by Jan and Tom, I should say late teenagers, in love and trying to find some place to be alone and warm and comfortable in a cold, wet season. They're suspected by Tom's mother and therefore by his father who is led by the nose by his wife, of making love, and this the mother accuses Tom of in the most vulgar, open way. Jan flies out at her and calls her "You cow--!" because they have not been making love, much as they long to, and the mother is tearing apart most cruelly and insensitively what they've had together. Later, Tom calls his mother "the old bitch" because, after having softened towards his parents on the occasion of his birthday, he finds that his mother has been opening letters from Jan and never giving them to him.

In <u>The Owl Service</u> there is a more deeply explored tension between Nancy and her son Gwyn. Nancy is a fine characterization, a good example particularly of how the author brings out a personality through dialogue, mostly between her and Gwyn, and in touches between her and one or two others. Nancy, a housekeeper, was once "the winds of April" according to Huw Halfbacon, the man-of-all-work at a Welsh cottage rented for the summer by London snobs, but she is now lean and knotted and hard and bitter with memories, with a sense of frustrated destiny. As for Gwyn, he is torn between his love of Welsh earth, Welsh singularity, and his fierce determination to better himself away from Welshness in the face of English self-possession, bland English superiority, the kind that so takes itself for granted that it is scarcely conscious of its power to enrage those who suffer under it. And while Gwyn loathes, not his mother's Welshness, but her crudeness and illiteracy, he at the same time detests these thick-skinned Birmingham snobs who've rented the cottage. Furthermore, this loathing of his mother's class, her commonness, and what it means for his own future is all entangled with his fury at her blind, raw, selfish power over him, a fury so intense that his moment of revenge on "the old cow," as he calls her to her face, is one of the jolting scenes of the book.

All of this reminds me of Virginia Woolf's disturbing statement, "Every secret of a writer's soul, every experience of his life, every quality of his mind is written large in his works."[4] This may be an exaggeration, perhaps; but as Lyndall Gordon has pointed out in her life of Woolf, our deepest and most wounding experiences find their way overtly or subtly into our fictions through active happenings, through reflections, through moments of being, illuminations, through characterizations. Woolf believed, Gordon says, that "there are only a few essential hours of life. In the lives of most people they would have to be imagined," creating an essence "from which all that we know them by proceeds." Woolf, attentive to that essence, captured it and found it to be determined by a "shock-receiving capacity."[5]

Through my experience as a writer, I know that my own shock-receiving capacity was most vulnerable in youth and that, as most novelists and poets discover, these shocks leave ineradicable impressions which in some cases are like wounds. They may heal over to some extent, but they are there for life.

For this paper I have chosen some unforgettable mothers, some bad, some good, because always I feel how the characterization of the young protagonist is, you might say, bounced off or resonated from the characterization of the parent. Again and again it is the mother who comes to mind: real mothers, a stepmother, a foster mother, and one not a mother to the protagonist but to an unborn child. All the bad mothers show a profound self-centeredness, a blindness and selfishness incapable of perceiving the desperation of the child, and all the characters evolve with very little authorial explanation (except in the case of The Beginning Place and Tulku, both for older readers) simply through what they say and do.

In Ursula Le Guin's The Beginning Place and in William Mayne's A Game of Dark, both fantasies taking off from reality, the boys escape their self-centered mothers into their own unconscious to find a resolution to their extreme unhappiness. In Cynthia Voigt's A Solitary Blue as well as in Katherine Paterson's The Great Gilly Hopkins--interestingly alike in the situation of mother and child--we are shown the extreme cruelty of these two mothers, the selfishness and blindness that subject both children to slow torture: the continued, persistent deprivation of love and concern when both mothers know perfectly well how their children long for them. But these two pairs of novels, each pair having a basic situation in common, show us how the power of private vision, creating its own unique story according to the experience and essence of the author, has created four entirely different novels--and entirely different characters.

There is a very intriguing portrayal of a mother in Marjorie Kinnan Rawlings' The Yearling, a mother who actually has no first name for the first seventeen pages. We know Jody's father, Penny Baxter, as early as page 9, and we know the name of one of the family's adversaries on page 15, but Jody's mother is only Ma Baxter until page 18, when we finally learn that her name is Ora. On page 89 she's called "the woman," and Jody and Penny choose not to share with her the awesome and beautiful sight of the wild cranes dancing a cotillion. It's she who finishes off Flag, the loved yearling deer, after Jody has been ordered by both his father and mother to shoot it because it's been devastating their crops and there's nothing that can be done, apparently, to stop it. Poor Ora has had one baby after another, all destined for almost immediate death out there in the pioneering forest, until Jody came along.

> She accepted her youngest with something of detachment, as though she had given all she had of love and care and interest to those others. But Penny's bowels yearned over his son. He gave him something more than his paternity. He found that the child stood wide-eyed and breathless before the miracle of bird and creature, of flower and tree, of wind and rain and sun and moon, as he had always stood. And if, on a soft day in April, the boy had prowled away on his boy's business, he could understand the thing that had drawn him. He understood, too, its briefness.... "Leave him kick up his heels," he thought, "and run away. Leave him build his flutter-mills. The day'll come, he'll not even care to."[6]

And these words are sadly prophetic of the book's almost unbearable ending.

Next, an appalling mother, revealed through very little besides what she says. Betsy Byars in The Cartoonist starts right out with her on the first page, where Alfie is drawing his cartoons in his treasured hideaway up in the attic.

> "Alfie?"
> "What?"
> "You studying?"
> "Yes," he lied.
> "Well, why don't you come down and study in front

of the television? It'll take your mind off what you're doing," his mother called.

He didn't answer. He was bent over the sheet of paper on his table. He was intent.

"Did you hear me, Alfie?"

"I heard," he called without glancing up.

"Well, come on down." She turned and spoke to Alma. "Who's the announcer that says that on TV? It's some game show. He says, 'Come on downnnn,' and the people come running down the aisles to guess the prices."

"I don't know, Mom. I don't watch that junk," Alma said." ...

"Alfie!" his mother called loudly. Alfie knew that she was at the foot of the ladder now. She rattled the ladder as if she were trying to shake him down. "I'm coming up there and pull you down by the ear if you don't come this minute ... I don't know what you do up there ... it's not healthy--no windows, no air."

"I like it just the way it is," Alfie said quickly.

'Well, you ought to be more like Bubba.... When he was your age he was outside every day, passing a football, dribbling a basketball--"

"Stealing a baseball," Alma added.

His mother ignored Alma. "You're never going to be on a team."

That's true," he said.

"But, Alfie, everybody wants to be on a team!"[7]

Right there in this brief conversation is the idea, embedded in Alfie's Mom and her adoration of the extremely dubious Bubba, of what is accepted in a good many quarters as the ideal of the red-blooded, healthy, eternally sportsminded boy, either outside playing games or inside watching sports on TV, but definitely not someone stuffed up, off by himself drawing. No one should want to be alone!

Turning now to loving mothers of various kinds, perhaps most of you have read the last Newbery winner, Patricia MacLachlan's <u>Sarah, Plain and Tall</u>, no doubt one of the thinnest, briefest novels ever to have won the Newbery. But it is a slim little novel that moves the reader as many a thicker, more complex and elaborate novel has never done. Why? Because of the simplicity and directness and tenderness of the writing. Because of the felt need, pulling both ways between the children and their father on the one hand, and between the children and the lonely woman on the other, the need to love and to be loved in a certain, particular way. _Feeling_! Listen to Eudora Welty:

> It may be going too far to say that the exactness and concreteness and solidity of the real world achieve in a story correspond to the intensity of feeling in the author's mind and to the very turn of his heart; but there lies the secret of our confidence in him. [8]

MacLachlan said in her Newbery acceptance speech that she is losing her own mother to Alzheimer's Disease and that she wanted to wrap Sarah's story for her mother with spaces like the prairies, "with silences that could say what words cannot." [9] Like a Japanese painting in which there are miraculous, evoking, unpainted spaces. Just so, Sarah, Plain and Tall is full of evocations that take no space on the page but speak like the prairies of all the subtle beauty that is there for the seeing eye. Sarah was plain, but she was full of stories and songs and caring, and we care about Sarah and will not forget her--and I don't think the children will either.

At a Boston symposium at Simmons, I happened to say that on a second reading I found Robin McKinley's Beauty beginning to be a little wearisome because everyone in it, even the Beast, was so confoundedly good and kind, and that, in an engrossing novel, good really needs something powerful to push against. [9] There was a discussion about this, and in the course of it Katherine Paterson remarked that she had particularly wanted to create the character of a thoroughly good woman in Trotter. To my mind, Paterson succeeded triumphantly in doing what she set out to do, for Trotter is thoroughly good but never tiresome because, for one thing, she has Gilly to push against. For instance, Gilly first "sees" that she is not going to be able to wind Trotter around her little finger and that there is no least possibility of manipulating her when Trotter says about William Ernest, "Listen here, Gilly Hopkins, one thing we better get straight right now tonight. I won't have you making fun of that boy.... One more thing. In this house we don't take the Lord's name in vain." Later on, Gilly chooses to read poetry aloud to little old Mr. Randolph, a blind Black man who lives next door, but it is nothing but vanity that compels Gilly to go over to

his house and bring back <u>The Oxford Book of English Verse</u>.
She reads Wordsworth's poem, "Ode." "'Trailing clouds of
glory do we come.' The music of the words," writes Paterson, "rolled up and burst across Gilly like waves upon a
beach." And right there we see that there is a crack in Gilly,
and that if Trotter ever succeeds in widening it--not by forcing, but by being unfailingly herself--something interesting
is going to happen.

Gilly is a tough nut. But again she has a "seeing."
She has made a paper airplane for William Ernest and he has
learned, through Gilly's teaching, to fly it. Trotter is infinitely grateful on behalf of the shy, withdrawn little boy,
who hasn't dared do anything on his own. "'Thank you,'
said Trotter softly. For a moment Gilly looked at her, then
quickly turned away as a person turns from bright sunlight."
Gilly takes Mr. Randolph's elbow to guide him home, "taking
care not to look back over her shoulder because the look on
Trotter's face was the one Gilly had, in some deep part of
herself, longed to see all her life, but not from someone like
Trotter." How hard it is, how infuriating, to receive thanks
from someone whose kindness and understanding we don't want
and must refuse to take if we're to continue within the hard
shell of our own idea of ourselves, inside our own stiff-
necked pride.

But Gilly's final "seeing" is the hardest of all for her
to accept. Having stolen money from Trotter's purse to pay
the bus fare out to California where she knows her mother
lives, Gilly is caught, her grandmother Nonnie is finally found
and sent for, and the grandmother in turn sends for Gilly's
mother. And when Gilly sees her mother at the airport, the
mother she's been waiting all these years for, the illumination
comes hard and clear. This person can't be Courtney--her
long hair dull and stringy, a flower child gone to seed. As
it turns out, Courtney has come only for a few days. She
has no intention of staying, Gilly understands. "She hadn't
come because she wanted to. She'd come because Nonnie had
paid her to.... Gilly had thrown her whole life away for a
stinking lie," the idea that her mother loved her. She wants
now to do two things--vomit, then run away. But she can't
vomit, and so she goes to a booth and telephones Trotter.

And Trotter speaks these extremely valuable words:
"'... aint no one ever told you yet? I reckon I thought you

had that all figured out.... That all that stuff about happy endings is lies. The only ending in this world is death. Now that might or might not be happy, but either way, you ain't ready to die yet, are you? And there is lots of good things, baby. Like you coming to be with us here this fall. That was a mighty good thing for me and William Ernest. But you just fool yourself if you expect good things all the time....' " " 'If life is so bad,' " Gilly says, " 'how come you're so happy?' 'Did I say bad?' " retorts Trotter. " 'I said it was tough. Nothing to make you happy like doing good on a tough job.' "

At this point Gilly can tell Trotter she loves her. " 'I know, baby, I love you, too.' " Gilly blows her nose and washes her face in the women's room and goes back to Nonnie and Courtney. " 'Sorry to make you wait,' " she says. " 'I'm ready to go home now.' " But by home she means her grandmother's house, not Trotter's, where she longs to be. "No clouds of glory, perhaps," thinks Gilly, "but Trotter would be proud." Without Trotter, we weep to think what would have happened to Gilly Hopkins.

Peter Dickinson is an English writer. Of his mysteries for adults, the adjective "elegant" is always used to describe the quality of his writing. For children he's written such fantasy novels as The Weathermonger and The Blue Hawk. And then came Tulku, an astonishing novel for either adults or young adults--a good many libraries haven't been able to decide which. It is the story of a young boy, Theodore, whose missionary father, together with all the people in the mission, has been killed by bandits and whose mission has been burned; and of how he goes off with a woman named Mrs. Jones and her Chinese lover, Lung, to a monastery in Tibet because, as it turns out, Mrs. Jones is to bear the Tulku, the next High Lama. All that happens to Theodore, physically, aesthetically, spiritually, happens because of this astonishing Mrs. Jones. Again, as in the case of Gilly's mother and the other mothers spoken of here, the spirit of the children is bounced off, resonated from, the character of the mother-figure.

It is all very mysterious to reflect that someone as vivid as Mrs. Jones, as startlingly unusual, but above all someone as seemingly unlikely to undergo so vast a change of spiritual outlook during the course of her journey should have come to Dickinson on the spur of the moment. Her reason for being

,in Tibet is an author's whim, and she is a botanist because Dickinson himself happens to be a devoted gardener.

I wrote to Dickinson asking him to tell me a little about his creation of place for Tulku and about Mrs. Jones. I told him how much place means to me in relation to character and asked him if it meant as much to him. I wondered if he'd lived in Tibet, to absorb all he seems to know about it for the book.

He replied:

> I hope it's not a disappointment, but the only journey I took in connection with the book was a regular car journey with two growing boys on the back seat. I used to invent stories to keep them quiet (my The Dancing Bear began like this, and so did The Blue Hawk and earlier The Iron Lion--so, I understand, did Watership Down). One day the boys asked for a new story, "with a good big battle in it," and I remembered a phrase or two from Kim ... when the Lama talks about a fight among the monks using their pen-cases as weapons, and I thought I'd try that. Then I remembered about the Boxer Rebellion, so there was my missionary's son, and the Boxers must [hound] him to Tibet ... and he had to have someone to travel with and so, being a keen gardener, and knowing there were plant-hunters bumming around in that part of the world, I made him fall in with one, and so they got into Tibet and had magical adventures and the boys got their battle in the end and it all worked out reasonably well. So well, in fact, that after two or three retellings I said I wasn't going to do it again because one day I might want to write a book about it.
>
> Two or three years later [and you can see how long it's taking Dickinson's book to grow and ripen with time] I decided I'd do it and settled down to it. I normally write a draft then do the research and then re-write. I read The Way of the White Clouds by an Italian Buddhist monk and one about the Boxer period in China--which turned out to be a mistake, because it was all based on the memoirs of a complete fraud, and then some marvelous translations of poems by Li Po and Tu Fu; the snatch of poetry on page

41 is my imitation. I used an ordinary large atlas to try and plot the journey, but all that was certainly after I'd started to write.

I'd wiped out the Mission and Theodore was standing by the broken bridge and it was raining, and he heard the slap of hooves behind him, and turned, and at that point, or only a paragraph or so before, I said to myself, "Hang on. This guy--the guy who is coming on the horse and with whom Theodore is to go off on his journeys--is going to be boring. I think I'll make him a woman." On the spur of the moment she was speaking cockney, and she was an ex-music-hall artist. I had no idea what she was doing there or why. But once you've set yourself a problem like that, reasons supply themselves if you're on form, and seem valid from the beginning, however improbably.

The same with Tibet. That was imaginatively much harder work than Mrs. Jones. She simply came....
The funny thing is, I don't think of Mrs. Jones as a very original creation. She seems to be, because I must have been on form and so she is alive, but if I hadn't been she would have seemed a puppet made of bits of Annie Oakley and that woman in Cakes and Ale and other golden-hearted tarts and earth-mothers. Fairly original things happen to her, which couldn't have, of course, if I'd stuck with my original bloke.[1]

So there is Mrs. Jones, the outrageously preposterous bearer of holiness: a supremely ironic Eastern Mary with Lung as Joseph, a Mary blasphemous, physical, jolly, overtly sexual, a killer of bandits when forced to it. And it is her music-hall background which gives her her cockney speech, even a certain unattractiveness, like the unattractiveness of the dead-white makeup plastered over her wrinkled face. But to Lung she is "the osprey on the crag ... the song men sing when they march under banners. Her heart beats with the blood of dragons." And there is as well her marvellous smile.

But what of Theo, who is changed because of Mrs. Jones and because of this journey he has been forced to take with her? He tries to pray after the mission has been wiped out, but his words seem cut off, unable to reach God, because he has run away and so has been cast out of the congregation forever. Yet, under Mrs. Jones's fond teasing, he feels distanced from the guilt planted in him by his father's last order--to go, to escape--and he is simply happy now to play his part in the journey and to allow Mrs. Jones to tease him if she will. Farther along in the high, clear mountain air, he tries again to speak to God, but nothing has changed. "Things that happened here," writes Dickinson, "seemed to him to have no weight, no effect on the rest of the world. Any act was simply itself, neither good nor evil. It existed, and that was all, like one of the lilies." Inside him the once-lighted chapel is no longer lit, and his prayers and his Bible reading have become mere habit.

When Lung and Mrs. Jones become lovers, Theo sees and feels their intense happiness so that he is ashamed of his thin, cold disapproval, and he is made to feel it is he who is in the wrong, as if he were, in Dickinson's words, "uprooting some cheerful little flower because it happened to be a weed." But it is in the monastery itself that the greatest and, to Theo, the most incomprehensible change comes over him. It begins when he realizes the devastating intensity of Lung's love for Mrs. Jones, and he is overcome with a sympathy for Lung "as sudden and powerful," says Dickinson, "as the scent of honeysuckle come upon at dusk." He feels, as he prays, that he is being listened to--not his words, but his thought. He has found a footprint, not his own, in the "deserted chapel of his soul." From that time on, again and again, he will find "the same nameless presence waiting to pray beside him."

Dickinson speaks of the problem he set himself and of the reasons that emerge "if you're on form," as he twice put it, so that all seems "valid from the beginning, however improbable." And this reminds me of the extraordinary, seemingly impossible problem Lucy Boston set herself in A Stranger at Green Knowe when she let loose a gorilla from the London Zoo and brought it to Green Knowe. Heretofore all the Green Knowe adventures have happened with Tolly as hero, but now in Stranger it is the little displaced Chinese Ping who becomes friends with Hanno and feeds him and even sleeps in his presence. And Tolly's great-grandmother, Granny Oldknowe, in her wisdom, understands the incredible friendship between the child and the gorilla.

Of seeming improbabilities made to resolve themselves in

the feeling, believing imagination of the writer, himself convinced of what he is writing about, the poet James Dickey has
said something very interesting. "If you want to write about
an owl who can teach a little blind boy in the woods to see,
then you try to imagine how it would be. You know it's not
ever going to happen that way. You know it's impossible.
But it's like Tertullian's proof of God: I believe it <u>because</u>
it's impossible. Then you enter into the experience you've
imagined and try to realize it. And that entering into and
committing-to is what makes writing poetry so damned exciting."11

I'm sure it's what must have made <u>Tulku</u> and <u>A Stranger</u>
<u>at Green Knowe</u> so damned exciting to write for Dickinson and
for Lucy Boston. And I think that both of them brought off
their impossibilities superbly.

Now what strikes me so very forcefully about the books
that I have put together for this paper is that they all express what Virginia Woolf called "the sadness at the back of
life."12 You remember those words of Trotter's when Gilly
phoned her from the bus station--when Gilly had to tell her
she loved her and had to say goodbye. Consider these words
near the end of <u>The Yearling</u>. Penny speaks to Jody after
the yearling has been wounded by Jody himself and then
killed by his mother.

> I'm goin' to talk to you, man to man. You fig-
> gered I went back on you. Now there's a thing ever'
> man has got to know. Mebbe you know it a'ready.
> 'Twan't only me. 'Twan't only your yearlin' deer
> havin' to be destroyed. Boy, life goes back on you.
> You've seed how things goes on in the world of men.
> You've knowed men to be low-down and mean. You've
> seed ol' Death at his tricks. You've messed around
> with ol' Starvation. Ever' man wants life to be a fine
> thing, and a easy. 'Tis fine, boy, powerful fine, bu
> 'tain't easy. Life knocks a man down and he gits up
> and it knocks him down agin. I've been uneasy all
> my life.... I've wanted life to be easy for you.
> Easier'n 'twas for me. A man's heart aches, seein'
> his young uns face the world. Knowin' they got to
> get their guts tore out, the way his was tore. I
> wanted to spare you, long as I could. I wanted you
> to frolic with your yearlin'. I knowed the lonesomene

he eased for you. But ever' man's lonesome. What's
he to do then? Why, take it for his share and go
on.

In the end, Jody goes to his own room.

He found himself listening for something. It was the
sound of the yearling for which he listened, running
around the house or stirring on his moss pallet in the
corner of the bedroom. He would never hear him
again. He wondered if his mother had thrown dirt
over Flag's carcass, or if the buzzards had cleaned it.
Flag--He did not believe he should ever love anything,
man or woman or his own child, as he had loved the
yearling. He would be lonely all his life. But a man
took it for his share and went on.

In the beginning of his sleep, he cried out, "Flag!"
It was not his own voice that called. It was a boy's
voice. Somewhere beyond the sink-hole, past the
magnolia under the live oaks, a boy and a yearling
ran side by side, and were gone forever.13

Now remember the ending of <u>A Stranger at Green Knowe</u>,
when the keeper from the zoo and other officials finally close
in on Green Knowe and corner Hanno, whom Ping has loved
as if he were a kind of father and whom he regarded with the
most profound awe and respect and wonder when he'd first
seen the magnificent animal caged at the zoo.

"Hanno," Ping said in his gentlest voice, for
Ping had, as it were, fallen in love. The world contained something so wonderful to him that everything
was altered. It was not only that Hanno existed, a
creature with the strength of a bull, the pounce of a
lion, and the dignity and grief of a man--too much to
take in, all the animal creation in one--but somewhere
there was a country of such size, power, and mystery that gorillas were a sample of what it produced
in secret, where everything else would be on the same
scale....

And now Hanno saw again his well-remembered
enemy, the man who had taken him captive. His heart
swelled with a fury that was like joy. He stood up,
an avenger from a race of heroes. He was his own
drummer, beating his passionate chest, his own herald

with that roar so horrifying it can never be described, presenting himself for single combat against all comers, and this one in particular. But before he had even launched his onslaught, the unfair bullet had entered his heart, and all that was Hanno had ceased to exist. He lay face downward on the ground.

The keeper, who had got there as if by instinct but too late, now helped the major to turn him over. He looked with grim sorrow at the thirteen-year-old forest face from which all savagery had gone, for a gorilla never looks so tragically human as in the moment of death. Ping looked, too, but not for long. He went indoors to hunt for Mrs. Oldknowe.... And now she saw with overwhelming relief and affection Ping walking with a deliberate jauntiness toward her, his face set like a pale pebble under its smear of blood, his eyes hard like stars in a frost.

"He's dead," he said clearly and too composedly. "It's all right. That is how much he didn't want to go back. I saw him choose."[14]

And consider the ending of Rosemary Sutcliff's tragic Song for a Dark Queen, the splendidly told story, as only Sutcliff can tell these tales, of Boudicca (or Boadicea, as many of us have known her), Queen of the tribe of the Iceni above Londinium in the southeast of Britain in 62 A.D. For years she has tried desperately to keep the honor and independence of her tribe against the demands of the Romans, but in the end she is terribly defeated. Her two daughters are raped and murdered, her people are slaughtered and their villages burned, and she is about to be taken in chains to Rome "to add splendor to a Roman triumph." It is Cadwan of the Harp who has told the story, and now he says, just before she commits suicide by taking poison:

And she turned, gathering her father's sword once more into her arms, and walked away, like a Queen still, up her ruined Hall. In the doorway of the Royal Chamber, she swayed a little, then steadied herself and walked on, and the rough curtain fell to behind her.

Then I took the last of my strength as it were in both hands, and dragged my way out here into the apple garth, where I have made so many songs to sing by firelight, and shall make no more. And let myself

lie down at last, in the long grass against the little
that is still left of the old half-fallen tree. The mist
was wreathing up from the lowland pastures, and the
little white moon-moths fluttering star-pale among the
branches in the dusk.

That was a long time ago, when I was still Harper
to a Queen. Or maybe not so long. I do not know.
A while since, I heard the women keening.

Not any more.

Nothing any more.[15]

Elaine Moss, a respected English critic of children's literature, once wrote a thought-provoking article, "The Adulteration of Children's Books." She was concerned that too
many character studies (the kind of treatment, she felt, that
adulterates children's fiction with the techniques of writers
of adult novels) and too few good stories for children were
being published. She deplores authors who introduce the ob-
scurities and psychoanalytical approaches of adult novels into
children's books at the expense of story. She would like to
see more straight, undemanding stories of adventure and goes
on to say that "If adulteration has taught us anything--and
surely it has--it has taught us that children respond to good
writing. Perhaps the moment has now come for better stories,
well written?"[16]

Well, one can't help asking: does she believe that
editors have ever ceased looking for "better stories, well
written" or that serious writers have ever ceased hoping, and
trying, to write them? To be noted here is that every one of
the books I've spoken of tells an absorbing story. And they
are all made absorbing because of their characters. The fullness of the characterization makes the stories.

The poet John Ciardi reminds us of two ways in which
a book can stand out: horizontally, for everyone alive at this
moment, and vertically, for everyone who will ever read it
through time. When we think of the complexity of adult novels, generally speaking, compared to the apparent simplicity
of children's books, it is astonishing to reflect on the vertical
endurance of a large body of children's literature. I think
that a great part of that enduring power has to do with the
vividness, the convincingness, the imaginative truth of their
protagonists. We think of the apparently simple preoccupa-
tions of the characters created by E. B. White, for instance,

or Beatrix Potter, or Laura Ingalls Wilder, or Patricia Mac-
Lachlan in Sarah, Plain and Tall. The books of these writers
we feel, will go on for decades as opposed to the life span
of a good many complex and difficult novels that grapple with
far larger issues--political, sociological, theological--for adults
Why? What is the answer? Hasn't it a great deal to do with
the singularity of their characters, the "felt life" in them that
children hold dear? Certainly the answer to the vertical
power of Potter's books lies in the imaginative truth of her
animal world, despite the fantastical actions of her animals.

It would seem that all of the great children's writers
know the following maxim instinctively, intuitively, as all of
the great writers for adults know it: Learn to make yourself
akin to people. But let this sympathy be not with the mind--
for it is easy with the mind--but with the heart, with love
towards them. Reynolds Price, interviewing Eudora Welty,
said of her that as her use of radiance began to mount, he
came to feel that all of her work combined to advance a concept of the great writer as a kind of power plant, a large
center of energy, radiating for us, and that the fuel is love,
a deep and tender fascination with human life.

NOTES

1. Elizabeth Bowen, Pictures and Conversations, with a Fore-
        word by Spencer Curtis Brown (New York: Knopf,
        1975), p. 60.
2. Ursula K. Le Guin, The Language of the Night: Essays
        on Fantasy and Science Fiction, ed. and with Intro-
        ductions by Susan Wood (New York: Putnam's, 1979)
        p. 49.
3. Justin Wintle and Emma Fisher, The Pied Pipers: Inter-
        views with the Influential Creators of Children's Lit-
        erature (New York: Paddington Press, Ltd., n.d.),
        p. 223.
4. Lyndall Gordon, Virginia Woolf: A Writer's Life (New
        York: Norton, 1984), p. 6.
5. Ibid.
6. Marjorie Kinnan Rawlings, The Yearling, with Illustra-
        tions by N. C. Wyeth (New York: Scribner's, 1939),
        p. 18.
7. Betsy Byars, The Cartoonist (New York: Viking, 1978),
        pp. 3-7.

8. Eudora Welty, The Eye of the Story: Selected Essays
    and Reviews (New York: Random House, 1978), pp.
    127-128.
9. Patricia MacLachlan, "Newbery Acceptance Speech," Horn
    Book 52, No. 4 (August, 1986): 412.
10. Peter Dickinson to Eleanor Cameron, 24 April, 1985.
11. James Dickey, Self-Interviews, recorded and ed. by
    Barbara and James Reiss (New York: Delta Books,
    1970), p. 33.
12. Gordon, Virginia Woolf, p. 85; a quotation from Woolf's
    essay, "On Not Knowing Greek," Collected Essays,
    3 vols. (New York: Harcourt, c.1925-1966), I:13.
13. Rawlings, The Yearling, pp. 403-404, 405.
14. Lucy M. Boston, A Stranger at Green Knowe. Drawings
    by Peter Boston (New York: Harcourt, 1961), pp.
    43-44, 153.
15. Rosemary Sutcliff, Song for a Dark Queen (New York:
    Crowell, 1978), p. 174.
16. A talk given in November 1973 and printed in Signal;
    reprinted in: Elaine Moss, Part of the Pattern; a
    Personal Journey Through the World of Children's
    Books, 1960-1985. (New York: Greenwillow, 1986).

BOOKS MENTIONED

Byars, Betsy. The Cartoonist. New York: Viking, 1978.

Boston, Lucy M. A Stranger at Green Knowe. New York:
Harcourt, 1961.

Cameron, Eleanor. The Court of the Stone Children. New
York: Dutton, 1973.

Cameron, Eleanor. A Room Made of Windows. Boston: Atlantic, Little, Brown, 1971.

Cameron, Eleanor. To the Green Mountains. New York:
Dutton, 1975.

De la Mare, Walter. The Three Mulla Mulgars. New York:
Knopf, 1919.

Dickinson, Peter. The Blue Hawk. Boston: Little, Brown,
1976.

Dickinson, Peter. The Dancing Bear. Boston: Little, Brow 1973.

Dickinson, Peter. The Iron Lion. New York: P. Bedrick, 1984.

Dickinson, Peter. Tulku. New York: Dutton, 1979.

Dickinson, Peter. The Weathermonger. Boston: Little, Brown, 1969.

Garner, Alan. The Owl Service. New York: Ballantine, 1981. (pbk.)

Garner, Alan. Red Shift. New York: Ballantine, 1981. (pbk.)

Govinda, Lama A. The Way of the White Clouds. Boston: Shambala Press, 1970.

Le Guin, Ursula. The Beginning Place. New York: Harper, 1980.

Le Guin, Ursula. A Wizard of Earthsea. Berkeley, CA: Parnassus Press, 1968.

MacLachlan, Patricia. Sarah, Plain and Tall. New York: Harper, 1985.

Mayne, William. A Game of Dark. New York: Dutton, 1971.

McKinley, Robin. Beauty: A Retelling of the Story of Beaut and the Beast. New York: Harper Jr. Books, 1978.

Paterson, Katherine. The Great Gilly Hopkins. New York: Crowell, 1978.

Rawlings, Marjorie K. The Yearling. New York: Scribner's 1939.

Sutcliff, Rosemary. Song for a Dark Queen. New York: Crowell, 1978.

Voigt, Cynthia. A Solitary Blue. New York: Macmillan, 1983.

Chapter 9

"HOW CHARMINGLY SWEET YOU SING!"

Myra Cohn Livingston

The Owl and the Pussy-Cat went to sea
    In a beautiful pea-green boat:
They took some honey, and plenty of money
    Wrapped up in a five-pound note.
The Owl looked up to the stars above,
    and sang to a small guitar,
    "O lovely Pussy, O Pussy, my love,
    What a beautiful Pussy you are,
          You are,
          You are!
    What a beautiful Pussy you are!"

Pussy said to the Owl, "You elegant fowl,
    How charmingly sweet you sing!
Oh! let us be married; too long we have tarried:
    But what shall we do for a ring?"
They sailed away, for a year and a day,
    To the land where the bong-tree grows;
And there in a wood a Piggy-wig stood,
    With a ring at the end of his nose,
          His nose,
          His nose,
    With a ring at the end of his nose.

"Dear Pig, are you willing to sell for one shilling
    Your ring?" Said the Piggy, "I will."

So they took it away, and were married next day
    By the Turkey who lives on the hill.
They dined on mince and slices of quince,
    Which they ate with a runcible spoon;
And hand in hand, on the edge of the sand
    They danced by the light of the moon,
        The moon,
        The moon,
They danced by the light of the moon.

It has been well over a century since the Owl and the
Pussy-Cat set sail in their pea green boat. I like to think
of the myopic, bespectacled, asthmatic, rheumatic, epileptic,
impecunious Edward Lear, who always likened himself to an
owl, waving them off. Certainly he must have chuckled at
the boldness of the cat proposing marriage, as Lear himself
was never able to do. Surely he patted his rounded stomach
in satisfaction, knowing that for once there was plenty of
money, delicious food and an easily affordable wedding ring!

It is not necessary that children, or even we, recognize
that "The Owl and the Pussy-Cat" is a fantasy of all that
Lear wished: to flee from the "moneytrying intoget smokey-
dark London-life" and the "great folk" to whom he was indebted for buying his paintings but whose society bored him.
It is only enough to know that for one hundred and sixteen
years we have listened to his verse, sensing what he is trying
to tell us of accomplishing the impossible, of the value of
imagination and of hope.

Each of us needs a pea green boat, a song of love and
perhaps even a dance by the light of the moon. Each of us
needs a haven in the mind where imagination plays, where
one may dare, in the midst of the most difficult obstacles, to
dream. Each of us needs an Edward Lear, who speaks to the
child in us of hope.

Said the Table to the Chair,
"You can hardly be aware
How I suffer from the heat
And from chilblains on my feet.
If we took a little walk,
We might have a little talk;
Pray let us take the air,"
Said the Table to the Chair.

Said the Chair unto the Table,
"Now, you <u>know</u> we are not able:
How foolishly you talk,
When you know we <u>cannot</u> walk!"
Said the Table with a sigh,
"It can do no harm to try.
I've as many legs as you:
Why can't we walk on two?"

So they both went slowly down,
And walked about the town
With a cheerful bumpy sound
As they toddled round and round;
And everybody cried,
As they hastened to their side,
"See! the Table and the Chair
Have come out to take the air!"

But in going down an alley,
To a castle in a valley,
They completely lost their way,
And wandered all the day;
Till, to see them safely back,
They paid a Ducky-quack,
And a Beetle, and a Mouse,
Who took them to their house.

Then they whispered to each other,
"O delightful little brother,
What a lovely walk we've taken!
Let us dine on beans and bacon."
So the Ducky and the leetle
Browny-Mousy and the Beetle
Dined, and danced upon their heads
Till they toddled to their beds.

There can be no doubt that all of us gathered at this
conference are tables--those who believe that it can do no harm
to try to overcome time and distance and differences and explore the castle in the valley, the alleys and perhaps even
get a little lost! Edward Lear, to my mind, is distinguished
above all other verse writers, among other things, for his
recognition that hope and dreams are not to be sought singly;
the Owl must have his Cat, the Table its Chair, the Daddy-
Long Legs his Fly, the Duck his Kangaroo, and the Jumblies

one another. It is by being together that creatures have
the desire, wit and courage to fight against the "theys," the
naysayers. And so we gather together to share and to offer
to one another the best of literature for the growth and hu-
manization of the children who play on the shores of the Pacific Rim.

Rhyme and verse are often given to us through oral
transmittal that passes from adult to child, and child to child,
changing a bit here and there but kept alive by each generation. Paul Hazard has marvelled at the English nursery rhyme
and the respect given to children in England. No one would
bother to develop such rhymes for children in France, where
"very rarely do we give flight to our dreams. As soon as
pure imagination gets loose we put a bridle on it. We bring
it back to more moderate slopes, our natural region." The
English, he writes, "are not unconscious of the fact that by
placing rhythm at the beginning of life they are conforming
to the general order of the universe."

Nursery rhymes, which Walter de la Mare tells us "call
for as little in the way of introduction as ... Santa Claus"
and are "surer of perpetuity than the pyramids of Egypt,"
are part of our poetic heritage. And so is the Reverend Isaac
Watts, who believed that study and hard work were essential
for children, offering verse that focused on "redeeming love
and renewing Grace," verse that would "convey piety in reflecting upon nature" and "melt the hardest souls to the love
of virtue." Determining that children remember best what is
taught in rhyme, he published his Divine and Moral Songs
in 1715. To this day one of his verses lives on in many a
contemporary anthology.

> How doth the little busy bee
>   Improve each shining hour
> And gather honey all the day
>   From every opening flower.
>
> How skillfully she builds her cell!
>   How neatly spreads the wax!
> And labors hard to store it well
>   With the sweet food she makes.
>
> In works of labor or of skill
>   I would be busy too;

For Satan finds some mischief still
   For idle hands to do.

In books or work or healthful play,
   Let my first years be passed,
That I might give for every day
   Some good account at last.

Horrified at Watts, his pious morality and bigotry, William Blake responded with his <u>Songs of Innocence</u> and <u>Songs of Experience</u>. It is the priests who bind the sluggard's garden with briars and thorns, Blake said; it is the false nurse who does not allow the children to play a bit longer, the unfeeling adult who rails against the pleasures of food and the foolishness of dreams. Lewis Carroll's attack was couched in parody:

How doth the little crocodile
   Improve his shining tail
And pour the waters of the Nile
   On every golden scale!

How cheerfully he seems to grin,
   How neatly spreads his claws,
And welcomes little fishes in
   With gently smiling jaws!

To Carroll, Dr. Watts was the crocodile who sought to improve children through his "golden scales," his hymns, all the time feigning a false cheerfulness that destroyed the right of children to real play, dreams and pleasures. Carroll fought mischief by making it against Southey, Watts and all others who would deny children their few years of innocent joy.

However we may view the attitudes of these early writers towards children and poetry, their work has survived to this day in varying degrees because of the responsibility they felt either to strengthen the child's moral fiber through serious observation of nature and strict adherence to religious virtues, as exemplified by Watts, or to honor their dreams, their imaginations, their right to escape from reality as in Carroll and Lear. The world of reality and play, with a minimum of piety yet some xenophobia, lies in the garden of Robert Louis Stevenson; the world of nonsense is inhabited by the Walrus and the

Carpenter, Father William, and the Jumblies. Walter de la Mare recognized the necessity for both worlds, laced with fantasy rather than nonsense, and the tradition lives through the work of many contemporary poets who present their worlds in varying proportions of reality and/or humor but with adherence to an unwritten code of standards as to theme and poetics.

Poetry is not immune to change, however. During the past ten years we have seen some astonishing changes in a code which, if I may be allowed the metaphor, is beginning to ripple the sea of the owl and cat, kick up some dust on the road of the Highwayman, and cast a pall over the landscape of which Tennyson sang.

> The splendor falls on castle walls
>   And snowy summits old in story:
> The long light shakes across the lakes,
>   And the wild cataract leaps in glory.
> Blow, bugle, blow; set the wild echoes flying.
> Blow, bugle; answer, echoes, dying, dying, dying.
>
> O hark, O hear! how thin and clear,
>   And thinner, clearer, farther going!
> O sweet and far from cliff and scar
>   The horns of Elfland faintly blowing!
> Blow, let us hear the purple glens replying:
> Blow, bugle; answer, echoes, dying, dying, dying.
>
> O love, they die in yon rich sky,
>   They faint on hill or field or river:
> Our echoes roll from soul to soul,
>   And grow for ever and for ever.
> Blow, bugle, blow; set the wild echoes flying,
> And answer, echoes, answer, dying, dying, dying.

For the most part the splendor is still with us, should we care to choose it. We must certainly be heartened by the excellence of many who write poetry for children today, an excellence which did not exist in such abundance when my mother first recited to me "The Owl and the Pussy-Cat." The staples of my own childhood reading are still about: Stevenson, Blake, Christina Rossetti, Lewis Carroll, Edward Lear, Elizabeth Madox Roberts, and the light verse of A. A. Milne. But consigned to the back shelves are versifiers whose names have, for the most part, been forgotten. The rhyming haiku of Miller's Little Pictures of Japan has been, praise be, replaced by a purer, truer form. There are more than 100 Best Poems for Boys and Girls. Longfellow, Eugene Field, and James Whitcomb Riley are resurrected only by the sentimentalists, and Laura Richards' xenophobia is largely forgotten. New voices, ever appearing, speak with a surer knowledge of children's emotions, of a reality that moves beyond lamplighters and English chauvinism, and a nonsense that leaves the Sugar Plum and the Amfalula trees in the shade to die.

Yet there are signs that we stand in danger of backsliding into images and words that would negate this spectrum of a broader, more humanizing world--a world that recognizes the contributions of all races and countries; a world that considers it prudent to walk along the Pacific Rim, to come to grips with the responsibility of offering to the young a literature that speaks in universals. We have made some strides, but we have only just begun. And to do this we must, I believe, be aware of what it is that good poetry, excellent poetry, gives to children--and what we should work to discard if poetry and its music, if literature and the best in language are to live.

This is not to suggest that poetry will, as long as we have tongue, die, but rather that we are seeing what Fred Inglis, in The Promise of Happiness, calls a "disintegrated poetics ... a loss of gentility in the tones of the voice, an increase of candor, and a consequent and large-scale redefinition of decorum in the conventions which control what may be said to children...." Inglis focuses on fiction, but this degeneration is as true for poetry. Is it ridiculous to speak of disintegration and degeneration in poetry when so many children are literally starving for food? I think not, for what can be more dangerous to our world than starved imaginations, minds devoid of hope, of laughter, of dreams?

> Tom, he was a piper's son,
> He learnt to play when he was young,
> And all the tune that he could play
> Was "Over the hills and far away";
> Over the hills and a long way off,
> The wind shall blow my top-knot off.
> [Opie, Oxford Dictionary of Nursery Rhymes]

Over the hills and a long way off--what line of the most elo-
quent poetry can match the yearning, the promise of this
simple nursery rhyme, a line that both figuratively and lit-
terally speaks to us of the possibilities for the children we
serve and of the dreams they pipe for themselves?

As adults we realize that what lies ahead, over the hill
or across a sea, no matter what the cultural heritage, is born
of values for which we are responsible. "Every story we tell
a child," the poet Ted Hughes has written in "Myth and
Education," "is a whole set of blueprints for dealing with
himself and for dealing with his own imagination." To Hughes
the great works of imaginative literature are "hospitals where
we heal, where our imaginations are healed...." But when
the stories are less than the great, they become "battlefields
where we get injured."

If stories are hospitals and battlefields, so is poetry,
and perhaps even more so. For poetry is absorbed through
its music and rhythm, through coenesthesia into our blood.
Its rhythms, its phrases, its images return to us throughout
life. If we do not offer the best in poetry, that most suc-
cinct form of literature, if we give only doggerel, didactic
lessons in verse, silly neologisms, poverty-stricken clichés,
ridiculous images, we cheat our children of those values which
sustain and strengthen.

There is a responsibility we assume when we bring poetry and children together. Yet for many poetry is in itself
a difficult and esoteric form. If we cannot define it, many
say, how can we know the difference between what should
be shared and what should not?

One way to approach better understanding between the
worst verse and the best poetry might be to think about the
charmingly sweet song which Lear's owl sings, a song which
surprisingly makes no use of the hoot or screech or onomato-
poetic WHOOO we normally associate with the owl. This is itself a departure from the bird of whom we remember hearing
when

> A wise old owl lived in an oak;
> The more he saw the less he spoke;
> The less he spoke the more he heard.
> Why can't we all be like that wise old bird?

Lear does not give us a lesson in keeping silent in order to gain wisdom. On the contrary, Lear's bird is quite a romantic, devil-may-care sort of fellow who stays away from the proverbial cliché-ridden oak and is sent off to sea with what in reality is his enemy, the cat. Instantly, therefore, we and the children are given a fresh image. Our imaginations have been released and go to work.

There is nothing wrong, let me add quickly, in approaching the owl through its usual song. Indeed it may be the very way to reinforce the young child's ego.

Who?
Who?
Who is it?
Who?
Isn't it you
who sleeps in the day
and wakes up at night
to go prying around?
Who?
Who?
Who is it?
Who?
Isn't it you
who has feathers so quiet in flight
that wings go flapping
as silent as clapping
without any sound?
Who?
Who?
Who is it?
Who?
      Isn't it you?
[Opie, Oxford Dictionary of Nursery Rhymes]

Young children will most certainly want to answer Eve Merriam's question that it is not they but the owl who says WHO and flaps with quiet feathers. This riddle poem with its use of repetition, onomatopoeia, inner rhyme and simile is crafted with great care to stir the imagination and appeal to children's sense of wonder. For slightly older children, David McCord offers a lyric poem which encourages even further a child's response to humor and word-play:

> I think that many owls say Who-o:
> At least the owls that I know do-o:
> But somewhere when some owls do not-t,
> Perhaps they cry Which-h, Why-y, or What-t.
>   Or when they itch-h
>   They just say Which-h,
>   Or close one eye-e
>   And try What-t Why-y.

"Owls Talking" is but an extension of children's imaginative ability to listen and avoids the cliché of oak, tree and wisdom, offering instead the amusing idea that owls, like humans, may even itch.

Here is another, by Madeline Chaffee, based on the sound of the owl:

> Oh, did you hear the wind last night
>   A-blowing right at you?
> It sounded just as though it said,
>   "Ooo-oo--oooo!"
>
> The wind now has a playmate,
>   Just as most children do.
> He sits up in a tree and hoots,
>   "To-whoo, to-whit, to-whoo."
>
> So when you hear the owl and wind
>   Just at the close of day,
> They're calling to each other
>   To come out now and play.

It does not take a highly developed sense of poetics to recognize a poor versifier here who has committed any number of grievous errors in her understanding of what poetry is all about. Her cloying question, "Oh, did you hear the wind last night/A-blowing right at you?" is, of course, metrically perfect, for versifiers will add an "Oh" and "a-blowing" to insure they do not stray from the prescribed rhythm. They know little of the value of pauses or breaks in sing-song meter. What we should not forgive is the ridiculous anthropomorphism, personification and miserable stab at metaphor that has rattled around in her imagination, producing the idea that the wind's sound and the owl's cry are so closely related as to miraculously make them playmates!

It is important to note the happiness of this little piece, how wonderfully cosy it is that a strong wind and a hooting owl portray joy and fun and call to each other to play. Play what? the child may well ask. Does the wind buffet the poor owl about or swoop up mice for his playmate to eat? We should note how the versifier tries to entertain the child with a question to which any sensible child, who didn't hear the wind at all last night, might well answer: NO! And does the wind go "a-blowing right at you"? Probably not, unless the child was outdoors after dark in the middle of a field or road. I need not even dwell on the smack of didacticism that subtly wants to know if the child also has a nice playmate!

It is one thing to ask of poetry that it stretch the imagination, that it embody wonder, that it contain music such as is achieved in the poems by Merriam and McCord, but quite another to stretch so hard that the image becomes incredible. But the versifier is forever anxious to please. One of the most pleasing devices is the use of Mr. or Mrs., which appears in the title of this verse by Edna Hamilton, "Mr. Owl":

> I saw an owl up in a tree,
> I looked at him, he looked at me.
> I couldn't tell you of his size,
> For all I saw were two big eyes;
> As soon as I could make a dash,
> Straight home I ran, quick as a flash!

To share this bit of dull verse is also to point out how versifiers shun the mention of any emotion but joy. In this case fear is neatly sidestepped. We are told only that the child, who wasn't even asked about size (which of course had to be there to rhyme with eyes), offers the perplexing information that she left "as soon as she could" and went home. Please note as well the glorious cliché, "quick as a flash."

The owl's looks and call are, indeed, a source of fear for many. A poem from the Indian tribes of our Southwest (in Houston, Songs of the Dream People) tells us

> There came a gray owl at sunset,
> there came a gray owl at sunset,
> hooting softly around me.
> He brought terror to my heart.

This is an honest emotion, the kind that versifiers sh__
in an effort to gloss over untoward thoughts, to ease pain.
For theirs is a romantic look, a faulty concept of the "golde__
days" of childhood. Occasionally one will attempt to inject a__
bit of fantasy which, in this case, in a poem by Sylvia Read
called "Owl," comes off as

> On Midsummer Night the witches shriek,
> The frightened fairies swoon,
> The nightjar mutters in his sleep
> And ghosts around the chimney creep.
> The loud winds cry, the fir trees crash,
> And the owl stares at the moon.

We note here another hallmark of the versifier: to tel__
us what happens in words that carry none of the rhythm or
force of what the poem is about, but rather to catalog a list
of things in the hope that somehow saying them will build u__
to a picture of Midsummer Eve. One wonders, of course,
why this verse is called "Owl" at all. We might ask why the
owl is not hooting or looking for food or flying off, unless
we suddenly realize that because fairies swoon the poor owl
must do something that rhymes with swoon, and looking at
the moon is as good a thing as any. It is difficult for me,
furthermore, and perhaps for you, to think of fairies swoon__
ing at the shriek of witches when the verse is called "Owl."
But let it be.

Poetry should not, I believe, push a child into fear,
but neither does it deny that one might be frightened.

> Tu whit
> to whoo
> he stares
> right through
> whatever
> he looks at
> maybe
> YOU
> and so
> whatever
> else
> you do
> don't
>   ever

```
            ever
                be a
                    mouse
                or
            if
        you
    are
        STAY
            IN
                YOUR
                    HOUSE
    old owl
    can you be really
    wise
    and do those great big          or by jiminy
    sunflower eyes                  on a chimney
    see THINGS                      or whooshing by
    that WE                         on velvet wings?
    can never see                   Let's hie to bed
    Perched on the tiptop of your tree   and leave him be.
```

Here, the poet Conrad Aiken says, is reality. Owls
do seem to stare right through things and it is best you not
be the mouse that owls enjoy eating. But the poet, unlike
the versifier, speaks of "sunflower" eyes, tucking in a few
alliterations, repetition, a metaphor and a touch of humor.
If not a perfect poem, it is at least one that portrays the owl
as he might appear to children who have every reason to hie
themselves to bed. Similarly, May Swenson's poem, "The
Woods at Night," avoids the stereotyped bird and offers us

```
        The binocular owl,
        fastened to a limb
        like a lantern
        all night long ...
```

We can probably never be totally objective about the nightly
song of Shakespeare's "staring owl, Tu-whit;/Tu-who, a mer-
ry note," nor of Tennyson's white owl who "in the belfry sits
... alone and warming his five wits," for they are part of our
heritage. But if what we seek from poetry is imagination
and wonder, we will certainly choose for older children poems
which do not repeat for the hundredth time the facts we know
about owls' calls, but focus instead on a balance between the
reality of the owl's existence as a bird of prey and the mystery
of his nighttime excursions. The poet John Haines says

If the owl calls again
at dusk
from the island in the river,
and it's not too cold

I'll wait for the moon
to rise,
then take wing and glide
to meet him.

We will not speak,
but hooded against the frost
soar above
the alder flats, searching
with tawny eyes.

And then we'll sit
in the shadowy spruce and
pick the bones
of careless mice,

while the long moon drifts
toward Asia
and the river mutters
in its icy bed.

And when morning climbs
the limbs
we'll part without a sound,

fulfilled, floating
homeward as
the cold world awakens.

Just as Haines uses silence, so does Randall Jarrell use
rhythm to make us feel the sensual presence of the owl in
"The Bird of Night."

A shadow is floating through the moonlight.
Its wings don't make a sound.
Its claws are long, its beak is bright.
Its eyes try all the corners of the night.

It calls and calls: all the air swells and heaves
And washes up and down like water.

The ear that listens to the owl believes
In death. The bat beneath the eaves,

The mouse beside the stone are still as death--
The owl's air washes them like water.
The owl goes back and forth inside the night,
And the night holds its breath.

Jarrell's use of form and sound, his repetition, consonance, assonance, alliteration, his simile and personification and masterful control of rhythm say much of the difference between verse and poetry. This is no time for exegesis, but these few examples do point up how differently the versifier and the poet handle their language and tools; how the freshness or keenness of the poet's eye, the sensitivity of the poet's ear, and the careful order and selection of detail raise the level of what we, as readers, can think and feel.

In genuine poetry there are no sugar-coated questions and false emotions, no oak trees or feigned wisdom, but rather an aura, most pointedly in Haines and Jarrell, of mysterious movement more compelling than any statement about fear. And so, like the night, we too must hold our breath.

It is entirely possible, of course, that the owl who calls outside your night and lives in your imagination is none of these. But there is such a wealth of fine poetry and good verse from which to choose that selection of any but the best does children a great disservice. What most of us seek in literature is some answer to our human condition. "What matters," George Steiner tells us in Tolstoy or Dostoevsky, "is truth and splendor of human experience in the light of conflict." That we are able to seek some measure of conciliation in our lives, some resolution to personal conflict, is one of the reasons for good writing, literature, poetry, and art.

We cannot hope to find this meaning in science. Science, according to I. A. Richards, "can tell us our place, but it cannot tell us what we are or what the world is about." For this knowledge we turn to the arts, which speak to our emotions and imaginations. They are all we have to keep us human. We cannot, on the other hand, ignore science. The twentieth century like all eras has its prophets of doom, and there is every chance we may all be blown up. But it will not be because of what science has unleashed. It will be, in the end, because we have failed to respond with imagination and to pass on to our children such tools as will enable them to learn to re-think and re-order in imaginative ways.

Poetry, I believe, is a way to imagination. Learning of other cultures, other languages, other customs and centuries and eras is a way to lead children to grow and expand. In 1968 my first anthology, A Tune Beyond Us, was compiled in the belief that choosing poetry from varying countries and different languages would alert the young to new possibilities, to stretch their hearts and minds. In subsequent anthologies I have chosen from the best of poets of all times and places. I feel the urgency, the need to offer even more now, for during the past ten years I have become increasingly alarmed over the loss of imagination in the young. No longer are many children given the time to make their own pictures, to imagine and dream. More and more they rely on others to make their pictures for them. Television may be partly to blame, it is true, but we must also take into account educational systems that do little to encourage children towards use of the imagination. If not used, the imagination dies. The way I know best to encourage imagination is through sharing poetry, through metaphor, through asking a child to think of the night holding its breath, to picture a Bong tree, to give life to a Table, to listen for echoes dying.

Imagination can be nourished and healed, as Ted Hughes suggests, in the hospitals of fine poetry. It can also be injured on the battlefields of the mediocre. And there has been as Fred Inglis notes, a poetic disintegration which appears in various guises. It is not difficult to spot those who follow Watts' precepts with didactic messages. Much of the poetry of a Guatemalan anthology that recently came my way exhorts the child to good behavior, substituting an ant for the busy bee, steeping children in fear of dreadful retribution for their lies and little sins.

Within the past few years in this country a number of self-proclaimed reformists have rewritten nursery rhymes so that all nonsense is destroyed, all joy routed. A parochialism has guaranteed, for example, that as in poor verse no evil may exist; the crooked man is straightened by the Bible, and God restores sight to the man in the bramble bush. Reality and unpleasantries are replaced by grins and happiness. The

real world is abolished. One must keep a sense of humor
about a recent Mother Goose rewrite in which Little Boy Blue
has Little Girl Green, Jack Horner has Nell Horner, and yes,
Georgie Porgie has Margie Wargie. Even the old woman in
the shoe has become "The Old Couple Who Lived in a Shoe"
whom the author chastises for having too many children and
proper lack of "a plan."

But it is hard to manage a smile at the irresponsibility
with which some so-called nonsense dwells on creatures who
devour each other; recalcitrant children who wreak havoc
with teachers, parents and friends; children at the mercy
of vampires and ghouls with never an adult in sight to help
them; children who make toilet soup and a girl who steals
bicycles and leaves them inside her house, "the one stuffed
with garbage and half a dead mouse." There has indeed
been an increase of candor and a loss of decorum. It is a
sort of verse of which none of us need be proud--and merci-
fully, if enough of us choose well, it may die.

It is also possible that you may feel, as I do, an over-
emphasis of late on light and humorous, even nonsense verse
at the expense of attention to the more serious sort of poetry.
Nonsense verse occupies an important place in the child's
life, for as Kornei Chukovsky tells us, it enables children to
distinguish reality from fantasy and in so doing provides them
with a sense of self-worth. We must be delighted, all of us,
by the contributions made by Shel Silverstein, X. J. Kennedy
and N. M. Bodecker; but it grieves me to see the metaphoric
work of Valerie Worth and Lillian Morrison, for example,
slighted or compared unfavorably to light verse and the instant laugh. Years of sharing poems and verse with children
have taught me that levity is the quintessential beginning for
an introduction to poetry. But many adults have, I think,
gone overboard, equating easy verses with short bursts or
sequences that guarantee a child will be entertained and respond instantaneously by laughing. Children do not, I need
not tell you, laugh all of the time.

I am also a bit put off by the current craze for colorful packaging in books of poetry that insists every verse or
poem be illustrated and by those who base their reviews or
purchases on the dust jacket or the pictures. Poetry, if it
is poetry, is intended to stretch children's imaginations, to
encourage them to make their own pictures. I am beginning

to wonder if there is a child alive who might picture the one who stops by the woods on a snowy evening as anything but a jolly, present-bearing, stout Santa Claus, a European peasant in a rumbly cart, or a teenager on a white horse. Heaven forfend that a child be allowed to view the poem with some white space beside it! But then perhaps I am speaking too adamantly for the imagination. I find myself leaning more and more toward the Japanese haiku, like this one by Jōsō [translated by Harry Behn] for which children must invent the images.

> That duck, bobbing up
> from the green deeps off a pond
> has seen something strange...

Perhaps it is better in Papua New Guinea, where there is only an oral tradition and children must supply their own mental pictures.

As to form in poetry, I admit little enthusiasm for prose aligned on a page to resemble poetry. If the art of the poet is to order, to select and to present some image in memorable form, that art is beginning to fade. I do not think any great harm is done, but with a loss of meaningful sound in our language we push the young further from poetry and deeper into their pop music. Children's need for rhythm, for coenesthesia, is great. Seldom can they sit still when the poetry calls with a music which T. S. Eliot tells us "is heard so deeply that it is not heard at all/But you are the music while the music lasts." Writing that pays no attention to rhythm, to patterns of sound, might be more honestly called prose. I would re-echo Robert Frost that many today are playing tennis without a net. On the other hand, many adults are led astray by the lilt of an anapestic beat, hearing only a joyful rhythm that covers up shoddy verse. Balance, said Mrs. Muffington, balance in all things!

As to poetry beyond this country, I am in the process of learning. And learning poses far more questions than answers. During the past year, in preparation for this paper, I have been engaged in a search for materials which is both heady and maddening--a voyage, as it were, in which the sea has been rough. International booksellers offer a minimum of help when it comes to poetry, for poetry itself is difficult to translate. Years ago when I was compiling a large anthology, Poems for Christmas, I met the problem head-on.

Juan Ramón Jiménez has written a poem entitled "Village,"
which I first read in a dull translation which ignored the essential metaphor. I tackled the job of translation myself,
only to discover there was no way I could retain the original
rhythm and rhyme and come out with anything worthwhile.
Eventually, after rejecting any number of translations, I
chose that of Robert Bly. Here is his version.

> The lamb was bleating softly.
> The young jackass grew happier
> with his excited bray.
> The dog barked,
> almost talking to the stars.
> I woke up! I went out. I saw the tracks
> of the sky on the ground
> which had flowered
> like a sky
> turned upside down.
> A warm and mild haze
> hung around the trees;
> the moon was going down
> in a west of gold and silk
> like some full and divine womb ...
> My chest was thumping
> as if my heart were drunk ...
> I opened the barn door to see if
> He was there.
>
> He was!

I have been indebted to translations since I began my
first poetry anthology; my admiration and respect for them
continually grows. I spoke earlier of one theme that runs
through Lear of the need for others who will help to make possible the plunge or the escape or the discovery. Those who
have been most helpful to me in this newest of projects I
thank warmly--Shelley Quezada in Boston, Carolyn Johnson
in Fullerton, Okiko Miyake in Japan, John Gough in Papua
New Guinea, and Jesús Cabel in Peru. Most of all I wish to
thank Jenny Factor, who came to me as a creative writing
student in first grade; as a high school junior, she has been
working on an internship with me this past year. Her enthusiasm, painstaking work and careful research have made
it possible for both of us to explore together the poetry of
some of the Spanish-speaking Pacific Rim countries. At this
point both Jenny and I are challenged to try to put together

an anthology for English-speaking children of some of our favorite poems. Perhaps by the time of the Fourth Pacific Rim Conference we will have something to offer.

Meanwhile, I frame my questions and Jenny asks hers. Why is it that dwarves figure so prominently in Latin American poetry? What is the special bond between mother and child found in Gabriela Mistral and so many others that barely exists in poetry for the young in this country? Why is it that Guatemalan poetry re-echoes so strongly the work of Dr. Isaac Watts with its exhortations to industry? What is the symbolism of insects? What is the chief voice used by poets--the narrative, lyrical or dramatic? What forms do they use and why? Is the music of Spanish more suitable to some themes than others?

And I pull down from my shelves anthologies from Canada that offer a heady list of poets whose work has not crossed the border. Here are ballades which remind one that the influence of France is still strong; and here is a ballad, a most traditional form which would seem to come from the seventeenth century, written by a contemporary poet, and a sonnet on Noah. Stories and ballads abound, stories of fantasy; yet animals and nature poems form the bulk of the collection. Does it happen only in this anthology, I ask? Is it representative of the poets of Canada whose work children read? If I were to pick one anthology, one only, from all the anthologies published in the United States, would it hold a fair cross-sampling of the poets writing here today?

The Australian anthologies intrigue me. One is filled with staples of the English nursery and works by many contemporary Americans. In another, where Max Fatchen echoes the Ruthless Rhymes of Harry Graham and A. B. Patterson's ballads seem to come straight from Kipling, I find that others such as Doug McLeod and Norman Lindsay have their own brand of irreverence, possibly cloned from Michael Rosen in England. I plan research to discover the origins, hoping that this tendency has not started in the United States but fearful it has.

But is an anthology a fair way to judge what children read--the popularity of a poet? What anthologists choose may not be representative of popular taste among children. Perhaps had I read another Guatemalan anthology I should have found less of Dr. Watts. If I could spend time talking to those who live in these countries, I would have a firm basis on which to test some ideas.

I bother friends who are going and have been to China. There is no way, I am told, that the Chinese have time for the frills of poetry in education today. Yet Carolyn Johnson produces a slim paperback of nature poems, a bilingual edition with work by artists whose names I have never heard. They must be painters, not poets; they are not listed in my many translated editions of Chinese poetry. I call the UCLA Oriental Librarian for information.

With Japanes haiku I am more comfortable. I have long loved the work of Issa, Bashō, Shiki, Jōsō and Onitsura. As a poetry consultant and in anthologies, I use haiku constantly. Wind in My Hand, the life of Issa by Hanako Fukuda, is a staple in my creative writing classes, and I admire Kazue Mizumura's haiku for the young, published in this country. Okiko Miyake has been kind enough to send me other Japanese poetry in translation and has written to me about a children's poet whose work she has permission to translate. This is promising and exciting for future exchange. I will need to correspond with those who can guide me in my reading.

John Gough, with whom I had a slight public correspondence several years ago in Children's Literature in Education--for we disagree about the value of the poetry anthology--has become an intermittent correspondent. He writes to me of the oral tradition in Papua New Guinea, of some new poets in Australia, of what he remembers about poetry in school. "Poetry was certainly a very second-rank interest compared to story reading.... As far as I was concerned a 'good' poem had a strong adventure as its basis.... I know I liked Alfred Noyes' 'The Highwayman.'"

The files grow; the notes stack up. I rave and rant over an article on literature for children in Chile with never a mention of Gabriela Mistral and her splendid efforts to encourage others to write poetry for children. I write to international book dealers for whatever poetry books they can send. Many do not answer. Will stories do, some of them ask, with pictures?

No, they will not do, for I am smitten with a need to

pursue this research. I have a hypothesis and theories about the value of oral transmission and the inroads of television, about the subject matter in the poetry of Latin American countries and about the strong values of the Asian countries and their adherence to nature themes. And if ever I should have any doubts about the value of this work, I can go to a report Jenny Factor prepared on her Argentinian translations.

"My favorite poem," she writes,

> is written by a not-so-famous poet by the name of Aguero. It is about crickets, and the first eight lines perfectly balance the tinkling of the crickets with the twinkling of the stars--paralleling the sound image of one to the sight image of the other. The last two lines break meter and have a music of their own. I remember looking at them while the words still made no sense:

> > como si un dedo infantil
> > tocara una sola tecla

> Well, "dedo infantil" is an infant's finger, "tocara" means to play, and "una sola tecla" is a single key (like a piano key). It translates, "As if an infant finger were playing a single note." And I could see the stars and the crickets and the children poking at their piano keys as if it all were right in the room with me. And I kept on thinking that no one else I knew had ever seen this image which I had unlocked. Perhaps it could not be translated, but I thought how much I would like to try so that they could see it too.

There is a poem in an anthology for children published in Chile by Rafael Pombo which tells of a selfish owl who asks a dove why everyone hates him. It is your fault, says the dove. "Love, oh owl, and they will love you." The concept of a selfish owl is one I have never encountered in English poetry and is probably as good an example as any of the need all of us must feel, each in our respective fields, to learn more about the symbols, values and beliefs of other cultures.

More than one hundred years ago the Owl and the Pussy Cat set sail. On the first night of the conference there was dancing by the light of the moon. During the week we shall probably hear a small guitar and sweet singing. During the conference banquet, if our imaginations are so inclined, we may dine upon slices of quince and use our runcible spoons. We are well met, and I am certain that were he able to attend, one particular Victorian "landskipper" would greet you "absquoxiously ... full of blomphious and umpsidicious congratulations" for coming to the Third Pacific Rim Conference on Children's Literature.

As it is, I shall simply pass on his greetings and tell you how charmingly sweet you listen.

REFERENCES

Aiken, Conrad. Cats and Bats and Things with Wings. Atheneum, 1965.

Barrows, Marjorie. One Hundred Best Poems for Boys and Girls. Whitman Publishing, 1930.

Behn, Harry. Cricket Songs. Harcourt Brace and World, 1964.

Blake, William. Songs of Innocence. Dover, pbk., 1971. Songs of Experience. Dover, pbk., 1984.

Bly, Robert, tr. "The lamb was bleating softly," in Lorca and Jiménez: Selected Poems. Beacon Press, 1973.

Carroll, Lewis. Alice's Adventures in Wonderland. John C. Winston Co., 1923.

Chaffee, Madeline A. "The Owl and the Wind," in Poetry Place Anthology, Instructor Books, 1983.

Chukovsky, Kornei. From Two to Five, rev. ed., tr. and ed. by Miriam Morton, Foreword by Frances Clarke Sayers. University of California Press, 1968.

de la Mare, Walter, introduction to Nursery Rhymes for Certain Times. Faber and Faber, 1956.

Decker, Marjorie Ainsborough. The Christian Mother Goose Book. Decker Press, 1978.

Eliot, T. S. Collected Poems of T. S. Eliot. Harcourt, Brace and Company, 1934.

Father Gander. Nursery Rhymes. Advocacy Press, 1985.

Fukada, Hanako. Wind in My Hand. Golden Gate Jr. Books, 1970.

Gough, John. Holograph letter to author.

Haines, John. "If the Owl Calls Again," in Winter News. Wesleyan University Press, 1966.

Hamilton, Edna. "Mr. Owl," in Poetry Place Anthology, Instructor Books, 1983.

Hazard, Paul. Books, Children and Men. The Horn Book, 1960.

Houston, James, ed. Songs of The Dream People. Atheneum, 1972.

Hughes, Ted. "Myth and Education," in Children's Literature in Education, March 1970.

Inglis, Fred. The Promise of Happiness. Cambridge University Press, 1981.

Jarrell, Randall. The Bat-Poet. Macmillan, 1966.

Jiménez, Juan Ramón. Primeros Libros de Poesia. Aguilar, 1967.

Jōsō. "That Duck," in Cricket Songs: Japanese Haiku, trans by Harry Behn. Harcourt, Brace, Jovanovich, 1964.

Lear, Edward. The Complete Nonsense of Edward Lear. Dover Publications, 1951.

Lear, Edward. Letters of Edward Lear. T. Risher Unwin, 1907.

Livingston, Myra Cohn, ed. Poems of Christmas. Atheneum, 1981.

Livingston, Myra Cohn, ed. A Tune Beyond Us. Harcourt
  Brace and World, 1968.

McCord, David. One at a Time. Little, Brown and Co.,
  1977.

Merriam, Eve. The Birthday Cow. Alfred A. Knopf, 1978.

Miller, Olive Beaupré, ed. Little Pictures of Japan, v. 2
  of My Travelship. Chicago: Book House for Children,
  1925.

Opie, Iona and Peter. The Oxford Dictionary of Nursery
  Rhymes. Clarendon Press, 1951.

Read, Sylvia. "Owl," in The Random House Book of Poetry,
  Jack Prelutsky, sel. Random House, 1983.

Richards, I. A. Science and Poetry. Regan, Paul, Trench,
  Trubner & Co. Ltd., 1935.

Romero, Maria, ed. Antologia de Poesia Infantil, 1980.

Shakespeare, William. Love's Labour's Lost.

Steiner, George. Tolstoy or Dostoevsky. Alfred A. Knopf,
  1959.

Swenson, May. Poems to Solve. Charles Scribner's, 1966.

Tennyson, Alfred Lord. Poetical Works. Thomas Y. Crowell,
  1885.

Turner, Ann. Tickle a Pickle. Macmillan, 1986.

Watts, Isaac. Divine and Moral Songs for Children. L. C.
  Page, n.d.

Watts, Isaac. Horae Lyricae. Jepthah Sheed and Co., 1813.

PART V:

CHILDREN MEET BOOKS

These five reports come from adults concerned with matching
literature and young persons. First of all, children of minority cultures need books about themselves. Joan Brockett
describes the movement in New Zealand to provide stories
with Maori protagonists, and Shelley Quezada outlines the
difficulties of selecting books in Spanish for libraries in the
United States serving Hispanic children. Author and illustrator Ashley Bryan, having shown the power of attracting
children to poetry through his reading of Black poetry and
folklore, shares his techniques with others who would follow
in his footsteps. Shanta Herzog suggests how children's
books adapted for film can lead reluctant child readers back
to thinking and reading. Elizabeth Miller demonstrates her
commitment to bringing children and books together through
a total library environment.

Chapter 10

TOWARDS A MULTICULTURAL LITERATURE:
ENGLISH AND MAORI IN NEW ZEALAND CHILDREN'S BOOKS

Joan Brockett

This is not the place to embark on a lengthy history
of New Zealand from its beginnings as a British Colony to its
present independent status within the British Commonwealth.
Suffice it to say that almost 150 years ago the Treaty of
Waitangi was signed which made certain promises to the Maori
people, the tangata whenua, the people of the land. This
treaty has never been ratified, and many of the promises
made at that time have not been fulfilled--in particular those
relating to land rights. In addition, as a result of various
official and educational policies and to an extent as a result
of some of the views on language held at that time, many
Maori children of my generation later grew up with little
knowledge of their own language and some, sadly, their
own customs.

It is necessary to say this because of recent developments in New Zealand in the context of which our children's
literature is undergoing certain changes. New Zealand has
over the years been steadily developing a significant literature for children. Book experience is basic to the teaching
of reading in our schools, and we are proud of the place
some of our writers have won internationally; Dorothy Neal
White, Margaret Mahy, Dorothy Butler are just three of note.
Now I believe we have an exciting opportunity to develop a

129

multicultural literature which is specifically for our children but will have an impact, I hope, beyond New Zealand.

I have referred in the title to a multicultural literature. Maoris and Pakehas are not, however, our only citizens--in fact until very recently the city from which I come had the largest Polynesian population in the world and also a large group of Asians. But because of our commitment to the tangata whenua and a belief that the road to multiculturalism must, for our country, be through biculturalism and bilingualism, we must concentrate for a time on the bicultural aspects of our literature.

Three recent developments in New Zealand have had considerable significance. The first is the acceptance of "taha Maori," the Maori dimension, as a vital element in our school curriculum. Second is the development of Kohanga Reo, literally "nests," for pre-school Maori children to learn the Maori language and Maori values under the guidance of their elders in a warm, non-institutional setting. Many of us see this as the most exciting and significant movement in early childhood education in New Zealand since the pre-school movements first began. Finally, in April of this year a bill which will make Maori an official language went through its first reading in Parliament. This gives Maori and English equal status in New Zealand.

Betty Gilderdale in A Sea Change talks of the anxiety of those over forty to have children's books reflecting New Zealand life and New Zealand settings, an anxiety which she believes has led to publishers' losing sight of the higher demands of good literature. This may well be true, and perhaps one can regard it as a warning, but I have vivid memories of a story world peopled with upper- and middle-class characters who lived in country houses, went to elite boarding schools, and clearly spoke in voices which were not those of my New Zealand contemporaries. How soon one learned that the New Zealand accent was a poor relation of the truly English voice! I empathised immediately with a five-year-old called Manu in Patricia Grace's novel Potiki. His school career came to an abrupt conclusion on his very first day. First there were the cracks in the floorboards through which a small person might slip, then there were the other children who "fizzed like bees"; but worst of all, "they had no stories for him."

As the children from the Kohanga Reo move into schools--
and this is already happening--there will be an increasing demand for high-quality books in Maori. Attempts have been
made to provide translations of well-known children's books,
and while Eric Hill's Where's Spot? and Eastman's Are You
My Mother? no doubt translate reasonably well, one wonders
whether the zany verbal humor of Dr. Seuss's Cat in the Hat
can be retained in Maori.

Booksellers in my suburb report that these translations
into Maori are generally bought by Pakehas, and this may
indeed be seen as a willingness on the part of these parents
to encourage some degree of bilingualism. Some Maori teachers, on the other hand, believe that dual texts, especially
of well-known stories, will only reinforce Maori children's
feeling that Maori may be considered a second-class language.
I hope that publishers will avoid the temptation to jump on
to this particular bandwagon and translate everything with a
New Zealand background that comes to hand.

If I were a Maori parent--and I am clearly not that,
nor do I intend to speak on their behalf--I would, at this
stage, want those books translated which reflect as much as
possible Maori values and beliefs. Perhaps the most obvious
of these is the view of self, which is nonindividualistic and is
expressed in relationships to a place, to kin structure, and
to descent. For the Maori the individual is less important
than the group, and the individual has accepted moral obliga-
tions to the group. One could well expect these and other
factors to be expressed in any stories translated into Maori;
and it goes without saying that translators must be carefully
chosen who demonstrate a sensitivity to both languages. The
whole area of translation is a subject of its own and one that
has been insufficiently explored.

Up to now many of the books published in Maori have
had original texts in English. There are two Maori writers
of great significance in the development of picture books for
young New Zealand children. Patricia Grace, whose novel
Potiki I have already mentioned, is already an established
writer for adults. Her collection of short stories, Waiariki,
has a special place in our adult literature as the first short
story collection by a Maori woman. Her first children's book,
The Kuia and the Spider (in the Maori version Te Kuia me te
Pungawerewere, translated by Hirini Melbourne), is superbly

illustrated by Robyn Kahukiwa. In the English version it is
skillfully written and has special appeal in its warmth and
humor for both Maori and Pakeha children; while Kahukiwa's
illustrations fit the story perfectly.

Grace's later work, Watercress Tuna and the Children of
Champion Street, speaks directly to children of Maori, Pakeha
Tokelauan, Cook Island Maori, and Samoan background--a
truly multicultural book, once again translated into Maori by
Hirini Melbourne. The tuna with the magic throat lives be-
neath the watercress at Cannon's Creek; since Cannon's
Creek is a real place, it may well be swimming there now.
One day Tuna made a twist in his tail and bounced out of
Cannon's Creek, over the tavern, over the shopping center,
over the primary school, and on to Champion Street. To a
New Zealander it is clear that Champion Street is in an area
of State houses, not in middle-class terms the most promising
setting for the magic which follows. But from Tuna's magic
throat come the essential props for the dances of the various
children he visits; and they dance, all day, all night and don
go to bed until morning. This is a joyous book, and I am reminded of the words of our race relations conciliator who spok
recently not of anti-racism, but of celebrating the difference.
This is a true celebration. A Maori writer for the periodical
Tu Tangata who attended the launching of this book spoke
of the wonder of children accepting each other before they
pick up adult prejudice which sometimes masks as realism.
This is perhaps the reason many of us involved in children's
literature believe that children in their early years must have
the best possible literature.

A second writer of note is Miriam Smith, whose book
Kimi and the Watermelon is illustrated by David Armitage.
This book has been hailed by Maori reviewers as an important
book expressing Maori values. Miriam Smith says she was
consciously expressing something not yet found in New Zealand children's writing and that she was writing for adults
as well as for children. Important elements in the book, she
felt, were the different family situation, with the grandmother, uncle, and child living together; the effect of time
measured by the season; and--something which gave me pause
for thought--the relationship between old and young reflected
in Kimi's working beside her grandmother rather than playing
with toys. On the surface this is a simple, straightforward
little story, but within there are depths of meaning.

It is this extra dimension, together with the Maori use of symbolism and imagery, which adds a special quality to Maori writing for children--something I see only rarely in English writers. Maurice Sendak and Jenny Wagner are obvious exceptions. Maori children grow up with a tradition of storytelling, and as they listen they absorb the beautiful language and the imagery. No explanations are given--it is as if they take from the story what they need at that time and gradually absorb the meaning. When Roimata, the mother of Manu of whom I spoke earlier, decided he wouldn't return to school, she sought for what was right for a child who had a fear of disappearing and who could not find his stories. Then she realized, "Everything is here. We learn what we need and want to learn and all of it is here." They needed just to live their lives, seek out their stories, and share them with one another.

There have, of course, been Pakeha writers who have written stories with a Maori background. Ron Bacon, who wrote The Boy and the Taniwha, The House of the People, and many other books, is now withdrawing from this sort of writing and has publicly stated that he believes the time has come for Maori writers to take over. There is a growing insistence among some Maori people that their stories should be retold by their own people. This applies particularly to legends and traditional tales, but Lois Burleigh, who wrote Amiria's Hat, the story of a famous Maori woman on whose hat a pigeon rested, found, despite all her efforts to follow correct protocol, that at least one member of Amiria's family felt the story should not have been written by a Pakeha. In the past Maori legends have been readily available to New Zealand children, but I hope now that all our children will have these written for them by Maori writers in something which approximates more the style in which they were originally told. There is, too, an untapped wealth of stories in our street names and place names.

I recently came across the old story of The Gingerbread Man retold in Maori for Kohanga Reo children. The traditional gingerbread man had been likened to Maui, a demigod known sometimes as Maui the quick-witted and Maui the trickster, who also has the capacity to change himself into other creatures. It had never occurred to me that the gingerbread man was very like Maui, especially in his teasing of the people he met. Of course he could not be eaten up at the end, so the final picture shows the gingerbread man triumphant and the dead fox floating feet up in the river.

This brings me to a very practical problem in relation to Maori texts--the reality of cost of publication. To provide beautiful books it is probably essential for them to be in an English text as well as in Maori. I suggested earlier that in New Zealand the teaching of reading is based on good book and language experience. Our readers are written by writers of considerable stature--Margaret Mahy is one--and illustrators are carefully chosen. Publishers producing supplementary material are equally responsible in their attitudes, so we know that our children are getting early readers of high quality. This has meant an increasing number of small books in Maori, beautifully illustrated and produced by the Education Department and readily available at small cost. Some funding has been available from various government sources for publishers interested in publishing books in Maori. We could not afford them otherwise.

Publishers and editors have always been nervous about trying out on the international market books which use New Zealand vocabulary. We have now attained the dignity of our own version of the Oxford Dictionary, and Lynley Dodd's Hairy McLairy from Donaldson's Dairy is selling overseas under its New Zealand title even though it's only in New Zealand that a little corner store, open all week and all day, is called a dairy. Recently the novelist Witi Ihimaera suggested we should no longer offer glossaries or explanations within the text of Maori or New Zealand words which we used in our daily conversations. Freed from the necessity to make explanations or to re-phrase, writers like Joanna Orwin, author of Guardians of the Land and Ihaka and the Prophecy, are writing children's novels which would read aloud perfectly anywhere in the world.

As I put together this material I realised how optimistic I must seem about the future development of an identifiable New Zealand children's literature for all our children. Of course we cannot be complacent--it is going to require a lot of time--but there is a great deal of good will as well as anger, and way down almost off the edge of the world we may be able to go quietly ahead. But I am reminded of a poem by Allen Curnow. He looked at the Moa (a huge bird, now extinct) in Canterbury Museum in the city where I lived as a child. When the Moa was first reconstructed, the curatorial expertise which we have now did not exist, and he is bent and propped up on iron crutches. Curnow muses:

> Interesting failure to adapt on islands,
> Taller but not more fallen than I, who come,
> Bone to his bone, peculiarly New Zealand's.

His final lines accurately express my own thoughts as we move towards a multicultural future:

> Not I, some child, born in a marvellous year
> Will learn the trick of standing upright here.

Let us hope that we will indeed learn this particular trick for the sake of all our children.

BOOKS MENTIONED

Bacon, Ronald Leonard. The Boy and the Taniwha. Auckland and London: Collins, 1966.

_____. The House of the People. Auckland: Collins, 1977.

Burchfield, J. The New Zealand Pocket Oxford Dictionary. Oxford: Oxford University Press, 1986.

Burleigh, Lois. Amiria's Hat. n.pl., n.pub., n.d.

Curnow, Allen. "The Skeleton of the Great Moa in the Canterbury Museum, Christchurch," in The Penguin Book of New Zealand Verse, Ian Wedde and Harvey McQueen, eds. London: Penguin, 1985.

Dodd, Lynley. Hairy McLairy from Donaldson's Dairy. Auckland: Mattinso Rendel, 1983.

Eastman, P. D. Are You My Mother? New York: Beginner Books, 1960.

Gilderdale, Betty. A Sea Change. Auckland: Longman Paul, 1982.

Grace, Patricia. The Kuia and the Spider, Illus. by Robyn
Kahukiwa. Auckland: Longman Paul, 1981.

_____. Te Kuia me te Pungawerewere, Illus. by Robyn
Kahukiwa. Auckland: Longman Paul, 1981.

_____. Watercress Tuna and the Children of Champion
Street. Auckland: Longman Paul, 1985.

_____. Te Tuna Watakirihi me nga Tamariki ote Tiriti o
toa. Auckland: Longman Paul, 1985.

_____. Potiki. London: Penguin, 1986.

_____. Wairiki. Auckland: Longman Paul/Three Con-
tinents, 1976.

Hill, Eric. Where's Spot? New York: Putnam Publishing
Group, 1980.

Orwin, Joanna. Guardian of the Land. Oxford: Oxford
University Press, 1985.

_____. Ihaka and the Prophecy. Oxford: Oxford Uni-
versity Press, 1984.

Seuss, Dr. The Cat in the Hat. New York: Beginner
Books, 1957.

Smith, Miriam. Kimi and the Watermelon, Illus. by David
Armitage. Auckland: Brick Row, 1983.

_____. Ko Kimi me Tanamereni, Illus. by David Armitage.
Auckland: Brick Row, 1983.

Chapter 11

BRIDGING THE PACIFIC RIM: SELECTING AND REVIEWING LATIN AMERICAN CHILDREN'S BOOKS

S. Shelley Quezada

My paper is given primarily from the point of view of a librarian responsible for the development of library services to a growing Spanish-speaking population. It will focus on the importance and difficulties of securing and reviewing Spanish language books published in Latin America. I shall outline the reviewing process and say why we must begin to develop a better coordinated network with Latin American publishers.

Hispanics in the United States

The Hispanic population now represents the largest growing ethnic minority in the United States. It is estimated that by the year 2000 this group will increase to 77 percent of the total population, with limited proficiency in English. This figure, of course, does not include undocumented workers of Hispanic origin who are presently estimated at more than several million. The Hispanic population is young and highly urbanized, and it maintains strong attachment to a language and a culture which cut across all racial boundaries. It is estimated that more than 14 percent of the Hispanic population speaks only Spanish, and another 25 percent of people of Hispanic origin who are born in the United States have difficulty with English.

Assimilation into mainstream U.S. culture can be a painful process for any ethnic group. For both newly arrived and more established Spanish-speaking immigrants, the lack of ability to speak, read, and write English often leaves them living in cultural enclaves. They are often distanced from mainstream society and disenfranchized to the point of feeling that they have no share in what is happening in the world around them. For many Hispanics, language is the strongest communicator of their culture, and they are reluctant to relinquish it. Children of Hispanic heritage living in the United States may speak and read Spanish, but it is not uncommon for second generation children to speak only the language of their parents and to have no reading ability in Spanish. These children will often reject the Spanish language, viewed as a sign of inferiority, and refuse to speak or pretend that they do not understand the language of their parents. This presents a problem in providing service to this population because it means that not only do we need quality materials in Spanish, but we must also search out both bilingual and English-language materials which accurately reflect the Hispanic experience and culture. These books ar equally important, therefore, for Hispanic children who are newcomers and those who cannot or choose not to read Spanish. These materials are important as a part of a service to children who live in large pluralistic neighborhoods; they foster cross-cultural sharing in the English language, which is the common denominator for children of different cultures who live side by side in our communities.

Service to the Spanish-speaking community is predicated upon a better understanding of the complexities of their culture. Latin America embraces more than twenty-one nations. Broad generalizations about Hispanics are often made in which people from diverse cultures and backgrounds are lumped together and given any number of supposedly shared characteristics; at the same time, as an aggregate group they are also compared with other populations of limited English proficiency which are vying for a place in American society. Recent studies by cultural anthropologist Shirley Brice Heath which are discussed in her outstanding book, Ways with Words,[1] give insight into the way that different cultural groups learn to use oral and written language. A two-year program offered at Boston's Roxbury Community College, "Teaching from Strengths," has trained many teachers to work with children of diverse cultural backgrounds, many of whom are speakers of English as a second language. The teaching methodology of this program has important implications for librarians, editors and publishers, for if we are adequately to serve the Hispanic population in this country, we as service providers must develop an understanding of their cultural background and speak to their individual cultural strengths. Specific guidelines for the development of library services have been drawn up by Yolanda Cuesta of the California State Library and Patricia Tarin of the Los Angeles County Library. These guidelines have been reviewed by Reforma, the Association of Spanish-speaking librarians, and approved by the American Library Association. Other titles offer an understanding of the Hispanic point of view.[2]

The Role of the Reviewer

What then, is the role of the reviewer of books in Spanish in this process? Because materials are one of the key elements in any library service or program, helping to produce, select, and disseminate books appropriate to the needs and interests of all groups which fall within the library's responsibility is crucial. In the past few years, major efforts have been launched by reviewing media such as Booklist, School Library Journal, Bulletin for the Council on Interracial Books for Children, and The Horn Book to include Spanish-language books as part of their regularly featured reviews. In addition, Lectorum,[3] a journal which has been established a few short years, is totally devoted to reviews of Spanish-language material for both adults and children. It includes numerous articles on a variety of topics ranging from children's literature to Latin American film.

The reviewing process has not been without its complexities. The following are some of the problems I have encountered:

- Difficulty in identifying Latin American distributors

- Delays in ordering material from Latin America

- Scarcity of copies of children's material published; titles go out of print quickly

- Poor quality of paper, binding, illustrations

- Limited selection because of many didactic or overly

moralistic texts

- Domination by publications from Spain, which limits Latin American initiatives to produce books for children

- Internal social or economic problems which affect the ability to produce children's books

With few exceptions, when the subject is foreign language books, it is often the responsibility of the reviewer to search out his or her own material. When I first began to select Spanish books for The Horn Book a few years ago, it was necessary to write to quite a number of Spanish-language book distributors before finding one who would supply me with material for review. There are few publishers in Spain and even fewer in Latin America who will provide examination copies for reviewing media or large public library systems. While some publishing houses in Mexico, Argentina and Venezuela have produced elaborate book catalogs describing their publications, many Latin American publishers communicate their holdings only by circulating simple lists of titles with no indication of age level or content. It is extremely difficult, then, to keep up with the output in children publishing from so many individual countries unless the reviewer develops contacts with Latin American publishers and professionals who seek to promote a greater understanding of children's literature abroad.

It is also extremely important to develop contacts with professionals who actively promote the dissemination of Latin American library materials within the United States. For the past few years, I have been extremely fortunate to receive support from Linda Goodman at Bilingual Publications[4] and more recently from Teresa Malawer of Lectorum, both situated in New York City, who have supplied me with some of the best and most recently published books in Spanish. The reviewer has a tremendous advantage in working with a U.S.-based distributor because of the assurance that any title which is reviewed will most likely be in stock and available for purchase. It is frustrating for librarians to read reviews of material which they would like to acquire but for which they are unable to find a source for purchase.

A second problem in identifying and securing materials from Latin America is the scarcity of copies printed. In

eru, for example, children's literature by Peruvian authors
ay well be only privately published and must be secured
rom the author. In many Latin American countries a mere
ve or ten thousand books will be printed--hardly enough to
erve the internal needs of a country, much less provide addi-
onal copies for export.

Poor format is another problem. Reading material
eemed appropriate for children is commonly developed in con-
nction with local educational agencies, and cost-cutting
easures often necessitate printing these books on flimsy
aper with perhaps limited, two-color illustrations and poor
inding. These books are often published to serve as grade-
eaders, providing an inexpensive, accessible reader for large
umbers of children; quality is not an issue. This is especial-
y true in Guatemala, where with few exceptions children's
aterial is distributed primarily through the schools. In
hird World countries it is often difficult to produce material
hose quality of paper and binding would sustain multiple
irculations. Moreover, poor print and less attractive illus-
rations do not appeal to Spanish-speaking children in the
nited States, who are accustomed to more variety and choice.

atin American Children's Books

The growth of children's literature in individual Pacific
im countries closely parallels that in the rest of Latin Amer-
a. An outstanding author of original children's stories may
e well known principally within his or her own country but
ot widely disseminated outside. Examples are Marcelina Paz
f Chile and Carmen Lyra of Costa Rica. For years Spain
as dominated the Latin American market, producing large
umbers of translations of well-known European folktales and
assics such as Mujercitas (Little Women) or La Isla del
esoro (Treasure Island). While no one can deny the need
 have European and American folktales and classics trans-
ted into Spanish, until recently there was less incentive to
earch out the wealth of original folklore from Latin America
nd make it available for children.

The impact of internal struggles and economic problems
n the development of children's books cannot be ignored.
he political situation in Guatemala has been so tumultuous
uring the past six years that it has forced the suspension of
he documentation of oral history and folklore which had been

carried on for several years by the University of San Carlo
As with Cuba more than twenty years ago, the current stat
of children's literature published today in Nicaragua most o
viously reflects the political attitude of its present governm

A veritable renaissance among publishing houses in
Latin America is taking place, however, which is having a
profound effect upon the development of children's literatur
by original authors and is promoting a rediscovery of a national folklore. Some of the evidences are these:

- Foundation of chapters of IBBY in Latin American
  countries

- Cooperative editing of children's materials

- Greater dissemination of criticism of children's literature through international journals

- Participation at international book fairs

- Awareness of a growing market for children's book
  outside individual countries.

The International Board on Books for Young People,
IBBY, has the goal of promoting a better understanding of
children's books and reading and has established national s
tions in 43 countries with individual members in another 14.
A resurgence of interest in children's literature in Latin
America is evident in the establishment of IBBY chapters in
Argentina, Brazil, Chile, Colombia, Cuba, Ecuador, Mexico,
Panama, Peru, and Venezuela. In addition, Paraguay and
Uruguay participate through individual memberships. The
Costa Rica chapter, which has recently been excluded from
IBBY because of the cost of membership, continues to func
as a formal organization, the Instituto Infantil y Juvenil. I
retains the goals of encouraging Costa Rican authors to wri
children's books and of promoting a love of reading among
children. The importance of national participation in IBBY
is demonstrated by the development of a network of Latin
American countries which now voice their opinions through
newsletters and meetings and in the pages of the IBBY mag
zine Bookbird. Although published in English, every issue
of the magazine now contains an insert in Spanish which su
marizes current trends and enables readers in Spanish-spea
countries to communicate with one another.

Individual initiatives in Latin America are working to preserve an important part of national literary heritage. For example, eleven years ago in Guatemala, a center for oral folklore was instituted at the University of San Carlos where staff systematically transcribed the wealth of Guatemalan folktales from the itinerant storytellers who abound in this country. In spite of the political upheaval of the past six years, there is hope for Guatemala and other Central American countries because of growing cooperative efforts among the Central American university presses. Shared editorial expertise and a dedication to service to children hold the promise that more high quality children's editions will be made available for circulation both in Latin America and in other countries.

Strong leadership from Latin American publishers is now improving the quality and availability of children's books. For example, the consortium of Central American universities, EDUCA, has brought together an outstanding group of children's stories in its Coleccion Cumiche, which was developed to affirm the literary heritage shared among Central American countries. These countries, part of the Pacific Rim, take the lead in an important new direction for publishing in Latin America. Because of this successful publishing venture, stories from Guatemala, El Salvador, Panama, Nicaragua, and Costa Rica will receive wider dissemination in both Central America and South America. Moreover, these materials will now be available for purchase in libraries in the United States which serve a growing Central American clientele.

Co-edited editions of Latin American children's books are also being published under the guidance of Banco del Libro in Caracas. The best original folktales and stories from a number of countries are selected, edited, and produced with original illustrations by artists from those countries. A recently printed co-edition gathers the popular tales of the picaresque or rogue hero, a tradition from Spanish literature which is prevalent in many versions throughout Latin America. These diverting stories are collected and published as Cuentos Picarescos para Niños de America Latina (1983). Similar volumes in this series present compilations of ghost stories or other thematic material chosen from diverse Latin American countries and of interest to children. Co-editing allows countries with a rich oral tradition but little local support to benefit from sharing editorial expertise and producing good quality material at an effectively low cost.

Mexico's Secretaria de Educacion y Cultura (Departme
of Education) is also a major publisher of children's material
many of which are inexpensively produced in paper covers.
Sold at street kiosks and available by mail, these high-qual
low-cost editions are actively promoted by the Mexican gove
ment. Some of the most beautiful productions of folktales
are now available from a growing group of dedicated Mexica
publishers. New impetus has generated the Coleccion Piñat
(Mexico, D.F.: Editorial Patria), whose editions feature
vivid, colorful illustrations to delight the beginning Spanish
reader. In addition, CIDCLI, under the editorship of Patri
Van Rijn, has published an incredible variety of traditional
Mexican folklore in the past few years featuring original wo
by Mexican authors and artists.

Carmen Garcia-Moreno, a speaker at the Pacific Rim
Conference and contributor to this volume, is a strong advc
cate for both Mexican children's books and Mexican libraries
As founder of the Mexican chapter of IBBY and a constant
participant at the Children's Book Fair in Bologna, Ms. Mor
selects recently-published Mexican children's books for dissemination outside of Mexico. She is an author in her own
right, having published The Story of Benjamin, the tale of
a book-loving mouse who is also featured on her daily radio
broadcast from Mexico City which promotes reading to youn
listeners. Through Ms. Moreno's efforts the Premio Antonic
robles, a national prize for children's literature, was institu
in 1981 with the support of the Mexican chapter of IBBY.
Since its inception, this prize has encouraged hundreds of
potential authors and illustrators to submit manuscripts of
children's books.

Given our limited budgets in the United States, librar
must select only the best in writing and illustration; therefc
we must use the same critical standards in choosing Spanish
language books for our collections as we do for English-
language books. As the publishing industry in Latin Ameri
begins to realize the potential which the United States mark
represents for well-written Spanish-language materials and a
it continues to support efforts such as participation in inter
national book fairs, more awareness of children's books from
Latin America will result, as well as a substantially larger
market from which to select.

Need to Develop a Network of Support for
Latin American Publishing

How do librarians and professionals concerned with access to good quality material overcome some of the problems
of selection and acquisition? First, we must actively promote
a growing network of people who are both reviewing and publishing books. The children's editor at Booklist, for example,
told me that she receives numerous letters from subscribers
requesting materials from particular areas of the world. Writing to editors and publishers one's concerns about the quality
and availability of books in Spanish and in English will demonstrate the demand for this kind of material. We must also
send a strong message to Latin America that a market exists
for excellent titles which contribute importantly to the understanding of the various countries. Examples are Kurusa's
La Calle es Libre (Caracas, Venezuela: Banco del Libro,
1981), which depicts life in the "lost cities" surrounding
Caracas, and--an excellent example of contrasts in modern
Mexico--Editorial Patria's El Campo y la Ciudad, by Luis
Aboites (1983), which shows Mexican people living in large
cities. These titles realistically depict life in Latin America,
which has long been portrayed with primarily rural stereotypes. Seeking out material which deals with Latin America
in its urban setting is extremely important in dispelling the
myth that most Spanish-speaking people come from the country, ride burros, and sleep under cactus. The presence of
Carmen Garcia-Moreno and other representatives from Latin
America at the Pacific Rim Conference is a good place to begin to form a strong network of ties with Latin America. At-
tendance at international conferences provides an arena for
sharing ideas about trends which affect all people who have
strong concerns about the state of children's literature.

More American librarians, educators, and book publishers should seek to participate in book fairs such as the
Feria Internacional del Libro Infantil y Juvenil, sponsored by
Mexico's Secretary of Education, or the Spanish Language
Book Fair held at New York University in 1985. American
publishing companies attending the gigantic Feria Liber,
Spain's major annual book fair, should search for new children's material from Latin America, which is also represented
at this event. It is important that book publishers attending
the Bologna Book Fair should also seek possible books for
translation into English.

Devaluation of currency in Latin America makes the cos of travel abroad quite prohibitive; therefore one must seek ways to enable each Latin American chapter of IBBY to send at least one representative to Bologna with a selection of books from his or her country. In the United States, more librarians should subscribe to U.S. publications which contair excellent material on Latin America, and to Parapara, the jour nal which features Latin American children's literature and which is published by Banco del Libro in Venezuela.

Just as UNESCO has worked to gather and publish six volumes of Asian folklore, Folktales from Asia for Children Everywhere (New York: Weatherhill, 1975-1978), so IBBY or another international organization should seek to produce a similar volume of stories translated from Latin American autho and illustrated by Latin American artists. A comparative stud of Latin American and U.S. folklore would show strong parallels between the crafty Tio Conejo and Brer Rabbit, for example, or between the picaresque Juan Bobo and the hero of the American Jack tales.

Prizewinning titles published in Latin America deserve wider attention. In addition to Mexico's Premio Antoniorroble we must be aware of other important prizes awarded for outstanding Latin American children's books. Examples are the Premio Carmen Lyra of Costa Rica, the Premio Nacional de Literatura of Chile, which has been awarded to a children's author, and the Casa de las Americas of Cuba.

Bilingual Material and Translations for Children

As our Hispanic population grows in this country, we have a responsibility to provide more about their culture, not only for the Hispanic children but for the other children who live and go to school in the same communities.

In the past ten years, an excellent example of bilingual materials has been published reflecting the diversity of Hispanic people and cultures present in the United States today. Children's Book Press of San Francisco[5] publishes bilingual books about many Pacific Rim countries, including books in Spanish and English from Mexico, Panama, Guatemala, Costa Rica, Peru, Chile, and Colombia; two new titles about the Moskito Indians of the Nicaraguan coast are scheduled for publication in 1987. Publisher Harriet Rohmer's choice of vigorous stories, combined with meticulous detail in translation and use of artists and writers from the countries of the stories' origins, makes them unique. Moreover, these materials promote cross-cultural understanding because they are written in two languages.

In addition to acquiring materials in Spanish, librarians and professionals involved with children's books must support an increasing number of translations of children's books into English. In recent years, American publishers have substantially reduced the number of books which are translated into English. The chairperson of the Batchelder Award Committee laments the decline in the publication of books in translation available to children in the United States; she attributes this to a number of factors, not the least of which is the takeover of smaller publishing companies by large, multinational corporations. At one time the Batchelder Committee had more than fifty translated books from which to select their prestigious annual award; now there are significantly fewer. In her keynote address for this conference, Mildred Batchelder stated that about sixty English-language books have been translated into the Japanese language, however I am quite sure that an equal number of books have not been translated into English.

Two years ago I was unsuccessful in finding a U.S. publishing company to produce an English-language version of an outstanding Mexican picture book from Aztec mythology. Ironically, this beautifully illustrated myth, a version of how the stars and the moon came to be, was recently sought out by publishers in Sweden for translation, and now Swedish children can enjoy this handsome book. With the paucity of quality literature for and about Hispanic children published in the United States, one can only lament that U.S. publishers make so little effort to look toward Latin America as both a partner and a source. What can be the argument for the absence of an English translation of the work of Brazilian author Lygia Bojunga Nunes, 1982 winner of the Hans Christian Andersen Award and the first such medalist from the Third World? An author who is considered distinguished in the field of international children's literature deserves wider dissemination, especially in English, which is read almost universally.

Conclusion

Public library services to children must respond to the individual needs of each community. The purpose of acquisition and related areas of service is to provide materials which will allow each child from a non-English-speaking culture to understand, know, and preserve his or her past while moving into the future. The acculturation, assimilation, and socialization processes, if they are to be successful, require that each individual has a sense of pride in his or her own culture. All people who are involved in providing service to such children must support the efforts to write, illustrate, publish, disseminate, and acquire the best and truest of these materials.

NOTES

1. Shirley Brice Heath, Ways with Words: Language, Life and Work in Communities and Classrooms. Cambridge: Cambridge Univ. Press, 1983.
2. Daniel Flores Duran's Latino Materials: a Multimedia Guide for Children and Young Adults (New York: Neal Schuman, 1979) presents an insightful discussion of many of the myths and stereotypes which are perpetuated about Hispanic culture; Robert Haro's Developing Library and Information Services for Americans of Hispanic Origin (Metuchen, NJ: Scarecrow Press, c. 1981) gives an excellent profile of the cultural diversity of the Hispanic population with specific recommendations for library service to children.
3. Lectorum Publications, 137 W. 14th St., New York, NY 10011.
4. Bilingual Publications Co., 1166 Broadway, New York, NY 10023.
5. Children's Book Press, 1561 Ninth Ave., San Francisco, CA 04122.

Chapter 12

A TENDER BRIDGE: READINGS FROM
BLACK AMERICAN POETS, AFRICAN FOLK TALES,
AND BLACK AMERICAN SPIRITUALS

Ashley Bryan

My program for the Third Pacific Rim Conference on
Children's Literature began with a reading of varied poems
by Black American poets: Langston Hughes, Gwendolyn
Brooks, Paul Laurence Dunbar, Nikki Giovanni, and Eloise
Greenfield. Next came the reading of an African tale which
I had retold. I also shared songs from my two books of
Black American spirituals. Those who were in the audience
know that my presentation was not in the form of a paper.
What I can do here is to offer some notes on my work.

We have a vast literature of English and American poetry that is rarely performed. Yet poetry, like song, is
meant to be heard. Poems inspire a range of vocal possibilities which can bring warmth to the printed word and surprise the listener with a deeply felt response.

I begin my programs with readings from Black American
poets because their work is directly related to the explora-
tions of voice I seek in retelling African tales. Long before
the printed word, poetry enveloped story and made story
memorable. Today, when I come across African tales which
I choose to retell, they are in brief and colorless form; they
hardly do more than document the story motif. First I

research the sources. Then I apply this material, my background, and the techniques of poetry to my retelling of the tale. I hope by these means to evoke the oral tradition from which these stories came, for the vocal play that printed poems inspire has offered me a key to the writing down of the oral tradition. Thus, when I read Black poetry and then my version of an African tale, the audience has a direct experience of the connection.

I closed this program with songs from my two books of spirituals, Walk Together Children and I'm Going to Sing! These songs, a gift from Black people from the time of slavery are considered America's greatest contribution to world music. The spirituals are loved and sung throughout the globe.

When presenting a program I hold the book, even though I know the poem or story by heart--since obviously I have studied poetry and memorized many poems. I use this method of presenting poetry, tales, and spirituals because I wish to remind the audience that the vitality of voice lives in the book I hope that by presenting the heart of my work to the audience, I have helped bring that work closer to the hearts of others.

Editor's Note: The African folktale which Mr. Bryan read was The Cat's Purr (New York: Macmillan, 1985). Walk Together Children and I'm Going to Sing! (Macmillan, 1981 and 1982, respectively) are Mr. Bryan's volumes of Black American Spirituals.

Chapter 13

BOOKS AND MOVIES--THERE IS MORE TO FILM AND TELEVISION VIEWING THAN POPCORN AND COKE

Shanta Herzog

You may wonder why we are talking about television at a children's literature conference. The fact is that no matter where we live, television is creeping up on us, and the media are fast becoming an important influence in our children's lives. Even in India, seven years ago, television was not in everybody's home, but it was something you went to watch in a neighborhood community hall or the like. Television and the media are there, and here, and they are important. I wish to describe how we can use this influence to help explore literature with children. Sometimes it is very hard, since today's children are so much interested in watching things that they are not particularly interested in reading. Well, maybe we can use that viewing experience to take them to books, to the arts--not just to reading, but to any form of art: dancing, music, the graphic arts.

Perhaps because I have worked with so many librarians in this region, I feel that librarians, even more than teachers and parents, can accomplish this goal. The teacher is constrained to follow a curriculum; the librarian can spend time talking to children about a film. The teacher thinks, "I have to talk about social studies today, I have to pay attention to Lesson Plan #9 and cover it in 45 minutes." The librarian can say, "Although today I must spend three hours working

151

at the reference desk and make plans for tomorrow, still in the brief periods I have with the children themselves I am not constrained by the subject. By time, yes, by responsibilities, yes. But when I am with the kids themselves I can talk about almost anything under the sun." And it is for the librarian-- or for the teacher or parent--to decide how one can use a viewing experience to lead anywhere one wishes. This is what I wish to demonstrate.

First, a few facts. In the United States children spend more time in front of the television than it takes to get a college degree. By the time they graduate from high school most students will have spent 50,000 hours watching TV and only 11,000 in school. So television has to be a great influence. Another thing is happening, perhaps not in other countries, but here. Children are becoming big business. One reads about the baby boom, one sees many toy stores, one hears about marketing; everybody's talking about children. In this paper I will not evaluate television programs or movies, but I do want to state that suddenly, because of the children's market, all kinds of people are saying, "Let's make a children's program!" One of the safest things they can do is to adapt a well-known children's book for film. It has been done successfully, using advanced techniques. It is our obligation to realize the skill and artistry involved in these techniques. Milan Herzog's remarks on this subject are appended to this paper. For example, simply photographing the book has given way to animated drawings, which in turn have been succeeded by animated puppets, as in John Matthews' Curious George. Matthews has taken the technique a step further in Frog and Toad Are Friends, and he is using an even more sophisticated method in his next film, based on Beverly Cleary's The Mouse and the Motorcycle, in which live action and animation are joined and in which the mouse's head and eye movements are achieved by remote control while the rest of the body movements are done by hand. In order to appreciate Matthews' techniques, one should see "Frog and Toad" Behind the Scenes and also show it to children. Incidentally, a number of people at this conference are responsible for the making of Behind the Scenes, because when we showed Frog and Toad once at a breakfast meeting with Arnold Lobel, many librarians asked, "Why can't we have a film that shows how Frog and Toad was made?" And so it was done.

I believe the popularity of showing films in the library
has been established, whether the films are versions of familiar books or something quite different. We are aware that
we can attract children to the library to see films even though
they would not come to look at books. What we must do,
then, is to exploit the movies we show in order to propagate
something we all believe in, and that is reading. After a
film program you could simply say, "Thank you very much.
We hope you had a good afternoon. Come back next week,"
and that would be the end. Or you can use film not only
for its ability to entertain, but as a springboard for inspiring
children to think and read. (Debby Yashar's helpful pro-
cedures for such a showing are appended to this paper.)

Other ways of exploiting a film include the following:

- Using an appropriate film to instill a creative effort.
  One librarian, for example, after showing a musical
  film asked children to bring something from home
  the next week which they thought could make music.
  So they brought spoons and colanders and dishes,
  and they marched all around the library. I don't
  know whether the other library patrons enjoyed the
  experience, but the children had thought about the
  film and they had created something.

- Providing paper and crayons so that the children
  can draw their immediate reactions to a film or asking the children to draw their reactions at home
  after thinking about the film. These images can be
  placed on the bulletin board to make the children feel
  part of the library's program.

- Stopping a 10- or 15-minute film at just the right
  moment, when everyone is thoroughly involved, and
  asking, "Now what is going to happen next? How
  is the film going to end?" This is hard to do, since
  everyone is interested in seeing what is on the
  screen. But once you've stopped the projector,
  you've started them thinking. And nothing happens
  to the projector; nothing happens to the film.

- Running the film backward, if the projector has a
  reverse button. This is a way to have fun and to
  instigate thinking and talking.

- Seeing that the book from which the film has been made is on hand. After the film is over, open the book, such as <u>Curious George</u> or <u>Hug Me</u>, for purposes of comparison. Do the viewers see that the illustrations are the same or different in the two media? Is the story different? Did the Man in the Yellow Hat, for example, catch Curious George the same way in both media? If the method was different, why do the children think the filmmaker made a change?

- Asking the children to act out the film themselves after the showing. After <u>Hug Me</u>, for example, what would they try to do to acquire a friend if they were lonely porcupines needing a hug? Would they hug a telephone pole? Would they hug the telephone in their houses? The table? What <u>would</u> they do?

- Making use of maps. Asking, "Where was the setting of the film?" "Where did this folktale come from?" "Where are the major jungles in the world?" "Where do porcupines live?"

- Stretching into the world of books. <u>Curious George</u>, for example, was set in the jungle. Ask the children whether they can think of other books with a jungle setting. Is there another book in which the color yellow is featured? The possibilities here are limited only by your imagination and sense of fun.

I've been talking about the use of film and television in the library or school. If you don't have these available where you work, discover a television program popular with children at home. You can build a program around that, using the same techniques. The same methods can be used with commercial movies the children see.

Depending upon the group of children you are with and your own capabilities, the opportuntiies for exploiting film and television are endless. One needn't stick to the story one has seen, one needn't be serious. Asking crazy questions actually stimulates the imagination. And sometimes things go wrong, but you can be creative--tell the children a story, talk about related books, be flexible. One day, for example,

I showed <u>Harold and the Purple Crayon</u>, and afterwards every-body wanted to draw. I had no paper or crayons, and I was angry with myself, but we managed to talk a lot about the film. Not every activity is a success, but that's life, and that's how we learn. In the meantime, you have helped chil-dren get more out of the film, and you have had an oppor-tunity to help them think and use their imaginations.

Perhaps you feel you need some help. Our organiza-tion, The Children's Film and Television Center, produces a magazine which provides synopses of films, suggestions and ideas for follow-up, and other relevant matters. An impor-tant book on the subject is Patricia Greenfield's <u>Mind and Media</u>, about the impact of the media on children and how to use these to advantage.

I advise you to make yourself a friend of the media. Challenge and stretch yourself, and you will challenge and stretch children and take them into another area of experi-ence, into the world of imagination.

PRINT AND FILM TITLES MENTIONED

Children's Media International

Magazine: Publ. by The Children's Film and Television Center, Univ. of Southern California School of Cinema-Television, University Park, Los Angeles, CA 90089-2211.

Curious George

Book: Written and illus. by H. A. Rey. Boston: Hough-ton, 1941.
Film: Los Angeles: Churchill Films, 1984.

Frog and Toad Are Friends

Book: Written and illus. by Arnold Lobel. New York: Harper, Jr., 1970.
Film: Los Angeles: Churchill Films, 1985.

Frog and Toad Behind the Scenes

Film: Los Angeles: Churchill Films, 1985.

Harold and the Purple Crayon

> Book: Written and illus. by Crockett Johnson. New York: Harper, Jr., 1958.
> Film: Weston, CT: Weston Woods, n.d.

Hug Me

> Book: Written and illus. by Patti Stren. New York: Harper, Jr., 1977. (Publ. simultaneously in Canada by Fitzhenry & Whiteside, Ltd., Toronto)
> Film: Pacific Palisades, CA: Bosustow Entertainment Productions, 1981.

Mind and Media: The Effects of Television, Video Games, and Computers (The Developing Child Series)

> Book: By Patricia Greenfield. Boston: Harvard University Press, 1984.

The Mouse and the Motorcycle

> Book: By Beverly Cleary, illus. by Louis Darling. New York: Morrow, 1965.
> Film: Los Angeles: Churchill Films, 1987.

MILAN HERZOG: ADDENDUM

There are no more creative persons in the film industry than the makers and shapers of the film itself. These are the people who decide that the film can be made; they precede the creators, the artists. As I was walking yesterday through the mazes of beautifully illustrated books on display at this conference,* every one of them provoked that inner feeling--which is experienced by what in the feature business is called the executive producer or producer, or in more modest terms simply administrator or head of production-- that this book probably deserves more than just being there. But could each book be made into a film? Could it be made into an animated film, should it be made into a live film, and if made, would it cost a million dollars, or forty million, like Star Wars? It isn't always the length of a film that determine

---

*Representative children's books from ten participating countries at the conference were on display throughout the week.

its cost or the complication of making it. Sometimes one might be considering only a two-minute segment. In fact, I don't think Curious George or Frog and Toad would have been made had the communicative administrator not tested the technique first on two other films until that technique finally reached the relatively high degree of perfection one sees in Curious George and which, in Frog and Toad, has been taken a step further and is now being taken even further.

To make such a commitment is like the start of an epic poem. It took one year to make Curious George--one year-- not just for one person, but for a whole team, sometimes seven, sometimes five, sometimes one solitary man just making one little thumb. So it is an art form which brings life to the book. And I think it is an important contribution which we filmmakers, television makers, media makers provide. The medium is such that we can particularly influence those whose visual quality, whose visual agility is greater than their ability to read. For them we have created a certain reality which although it has sprung from a book, becomes either less terrifying or more acceptable, more familiar; and it somehow penetrates very deeply into their memory. I've had experiences in which, fifteen years later, somebody will stop me and say, "You know, I saw you in Kansas City when you were showing that film, and I still remember...," and he will recite details from that showing. Films do sit deeply in some persons' memories. Often what I read stays longer, but sometimes my memory is a compound of reading and seeing. At any rate, we must know the valuable role that film plays in some lives.

DEBBY YASHAR: ADDENDUM

In planning a film program, the first and most important thing to do is to view the movie yourself before showing it to children. Otherwise, you might be in the embarrassing position of wishing you hadn't! While viewing the film for quality, also think of questions you might ask the children after it's over. At the actual presentation, take time to introduce the film to the children. And be prepared for emergencies if something goes wrong with the projector or the like. Be flexible.

After the showing, ask pertinent questions--ask about little things at first. For example, what kind of ice cream cone was Elliot the porcupine eating in <u>Hug Me</u>? Then ask more thoughtful questions in order to get children involved in what happened and why.

The most important reason for following a film showing with questions is to stimulate thinking. All too often children simply sit in front of a screen, wide-eyed and glassy-eyed, not really knowing what they are seeing. At least if one introduces the film, asks the children to really watch what they are seeing and think about it, then asks them to talk about their thoughts, they will go out of the library knowing that they've seen something. Perhaps later they'll think about it even more. They might even go out of the room with a book or two which the librarian has introduced unobtrusively in connection with the program.

To repeat, however, the most important result of this method is the thinking child.

Chapter 14

A LIVING LIBRARY IN ACTION

Elizabeth C. Miller

Introduction

To describe a living children's library in action is about
as complicated as describing a living person in action, but I
shall try to do that briefly. The children's service I am describing is that in the Invercargill Public Library, Invercargill, New Zealand; and I hope through inadequate words to
convey some of the soul of our activities.

The bones of a living library are, of course, the books;
but I do not plan to discuss them or their selection, even
though they are the focal point of all that we do. The life-
blood is, perhaps, communication, which makes positive children's literature accessible on many levels. This communication is activated and made possible through the physical environment, the programs, the activities, the day-to-day goings
on, and, of course, the books--and through the interaction
of children with staff and of staff with one another.

I believe that a free, professionally-run and -staffed
public library, with a generous department designated as the
children's own library, is one of the most important gifts a
society can give to its young ones. Going to the library,
being free to select and reject, being able to seek a children's
librarian for help when help is wanted--these are a vital part

of any child's education; and this part should begin long before formal education begins.

And as with formal education, giving the child a librar is not merely a matter of putting that library and its resources in a physical space. The library must be promoted and brought to life, and the child must be given the incenti and skills and confidence to use it. I believe in a total library environment for young people still in their formative years, with defined boundaries, so that they know where they are safe and free, they know what they can expect in terms of service and relationships and resources, and they know their right to seek help and be assisted. This does not mean that they are confined to the children's room with no access to adult stock, but rather that they can make thei forays into the adult room from the safety of their own place We have an overlap period when they belong to both departments, and this makes the transition very easy.

In a carefully planned, well-stocked library, people from babyhood on may find resources for their mental, physi cal, spiritual, and social development of a kind and variety not possible from any other source. Here is gathered the cu ture, the knowledge, the experience, the story of all times and of all races--the birthright of every child. With a staff aware of its responsibility to open that treasure store to those who enter and to see that each one will find herself or himself represented with integrity, the sky is the limit fo the riches which can be discovered and utilized by every chi not just the natural bookworm.

We have called our children's library the Young People Library. Initially this was done to overcome the natural reluctance of some older children to use its resources. But it also highlights the fact, often ignored or forgotten, that chi dren are people--a special kind of people but real people with rights. These small people need the security that come with having the same librarians there each time they visit, people who remember them and like to pin on the walls the pictures they make and the poems, stories, and letters they write. Our desks and walls are often smothered in odd offe ings; my office, with its open door, is crowded with paper-foldings and puppets, drawings, and strange little gifts. W display their models and collections, take an interest in what the new baby did yesterday, listen with genuine sympathy t the grieving when the budgie dies, discuss the best way to put on eyeshadow, and are ready to discuss seriously all the concerns of childhood. We are people who see them on the street and greet them, stopping to have conversations in shops and parks.

I do not think children grow and learn as effectively in a fragmented environment as they do in a total, in-depth situation. Superficial learning imparted through teaching which is isolated, to a large degree, from the relevant environment is difficult to assimilate, easily forgotten, and often not incorporated into one's life. The learners are left incomplete and unsatisfied. It seems to me that everything that makes us real and individual is achieved in the in-depth way. Our abilities to reason, imagine, and create are established thus, and so are our attitudes and values. Certainly children learn their mother tongue best, as studies show, through the opportunity to communicate from birth in a person-to-person situation, as a normal part of living. Just as language skills and understanding develop more fully under these circumstances, so also is reading skill acquired more efficiently and easily if the child is talked with, read to, and listened to as a matter of course. I would go so far as to say that, despite the many methods of teaching reading which have been practiced, the true readers have learned because this "environment of reading" has been offered them in their homes, schools, and libraries. The best way to learn to read is to do it.

The best teachers I know use in-depth methods--and so do the best librarians as they provide an environment in which children can live fully and which they can absorb through all their senses. How does a librarian put into practice this concept of total library which will offer the child in-depth learning and develop communication skills?

The Physical Environment as One Part of the Communication Between the Child and the World of Literature

Children need their own special place, with walls and a welcoming doorway. This can be provided even in towns with miniscule populations. The small New Zealand town of Lawrence has created a tiny, magical room for children, whose painted pictures have been sealed on the floor, and the whole

room is not much bigger than my bedroom. Even the use of
semi-permanent screens can be better than nothing. Small
children, and even bigger ones, need to see clearly the space
in which they will be able to grow on their own terms, unen-
cumbered by even tacit disapproval or by intrusions from
adults. Children can often be overwhelmed; in their own library space they are free from adult conformist attitudes which
in many cases curtail their natural curiosity and openness.

It is good, too, for children to be able to bring adults
into their own special place and share it on their own terms.
I always experience a lift of the spirit when I hear a child
"showing off" the books, the birds, the games, the displays
(and sometimes even their librarian) to a dad, an aunt, or a
visiting grandparent--and the child does this with great pride
and an air of delighted ownership.

In their own room children may test themselves safely
and learn to be independent. They learn to search and discover, to relate to others and to respect them, to perform
their own transactions, to make choices. Even coming into
the library is a choice when there is a door and there are
walls; you have to take action. You open the door, you go
in, and then you decide how far you will go; you may even
decide to back out.

I remember the nervous little boy who came to our pre-
school program with his mother for nearly a year before, in
his own time, he decided he was safe and could allow her to
leave him with the other children while she joined in the parent session. What rejoicing there was, what excitement!

We do not have an actual door at Invercargill, but we
have stairs, and we make them work in the same way, for
we place pictures and enticements all the way up to draw the
children; and when they turn the landing corner, the room is
there before them.

Doorways are also symbolic of the books, which are the
dominant aspect of the library the child has chosen to enter.
Books are doorways into an experience, not windows for mere
observation. We try to show the children in myriad ways
that these doorways, these books, are at their service.

I believe that the décor of this library we are discussing

is very important, too. It needs to be bright and relaxing, and everything needs to say "welcome" to the child who enters. The atmosphere should not be overpowering or intimidating. There needs to be plenty to see and to experience, and it all needs to be child-proof. We have pictures at a child's eye level as well as higher up, and the pictures change frequently; things hang off the high ceilings. There are displays, art works, models, carvings, dollhouses, posters, children's own creations and offerings such as birds' nests found or daisies picked; birds and fish (and for a year my small chihuahua); chalkboards and a small children's puppet theater for their own use at all times as well as the large one for special performances; plants, toys, headphones; signs in Maori as well as in English; and a great deal more.

Some of these objects are permanent in order to give a sense of familiarity and continuity; some change in order to stimulate interest. All add to the feeling that this is a lived-in place with a welcome for anybody and everybody, not just for the bright ones, the bookworms, or the middle-class pakehas. We have plenty of materials for children to use creatively--crayons, scrap paper, coloring-in pictures, cloth, scissors, templates, and so on. We make booklists and program sheets to take home, and copies are sent to all the schools. I cut bookmarks from donated greeting cards for the children to keep.

In our library you fall over children lying on the floor surrounded by armfuls of books; over dads playing chess with the children; a family sharing a puzzle; a mother feeding her baby and reading aloud while the older ones select books and the little ones draw. You hear impromptu puppet shows and you see adults creating and discovering along with the children during the programs. Grown-ups are encouraged to read with, play with, do with the children. Lately we have been delighted to see a Chinese family make the library their second home as they practice their English and socialize with their new neighbors.

Community involvement is vital, for we depend upon the community for many of our resources. I am known as one of the best beggars in town. One elderly lady regularly mails me the feathers shed by her three budgies, because she once noticed we were using some to line eggshells at Easter. A young mentally-handicapped woman saves me all the foil wrappings from the chocolates she eats and sometimes mails them, but at other times sends a peremptory message that I must come and get them. Then she eagerly waits for the letter of thanks which always follows. We beg scraps from firms and useful junk from the public, and we have a warm relationship with many sources of supply. Our room is, as a result, always stimulating, never static, and perhaps a bit untidy to conventional adult eyes. But all these contributions help to make the library not just a separate place, but a presence in the community.

Another important reason for the privacy of walls is that both the children and the staff do better without an inhibiting sense of being watched; children's noise in an open-plan library, and even their laughter, can annoy adults. Children are free in their own special place to satisfy their curiosity and their need to explore without undue constraints by those who do not understand their needs. Parents, I find, feel more secure when they realize they do not have to rein in their children's delight and that their children will not wander too far. Staff members unacquainted with children's programs and their importance do not stray in. (I have often heard adults commenting, as they walk right through a storytelling program, "It's only kids.") Finally, watched children tend to play to the audience rather than to get on with the matter in hand.

Staff Activity as Another Area of Communication

I believe that it is most creative and highly desirable for all the work of the library to be accessible to the children. They have a right to experience in-depth learning about the functions of the library and to learn by example, by seeing, by participating. When all aspects of the library are open to children, they develop a perspective. They begin to feel at ease with the resources and with the staff. This is not possible where work is centralized and performed by staff other than those working with children. Our work benches and desks are in open view, as well as all the work of ordering, selection, processing, weeding, and repairing, and of planning and executing displays, programs, and promotions. All this work, ordinarily done behind the scenes, can be discussed and understood. Even new technologies are explained to children, and they can see new systems and tools being used as servants--not taking the place of people, but being used _for_ people.

Tiny children as well as older ones appear often at my elbow wanting to know what I am doing, and I tell them. There are no secrets. Our method opens up endless two-way opportunities for learning and communicating. Staff members are available at all times, and children are participants. Children, and their adults as well, frequently join in our staff discussions, offering ideas, making gifts, sharing their talents.

I also find it valuable that, because we are children's library staff and are not rotated, we too experience the library in a total way. I know of no children's library which has enough staff to allow for specialization to any large degree. So to be effective when staff is small, versatility is required. Each member must be able to occupy any space, perform any task, and respond to any need. Children's library staff need to know their stock intimately and specifically, and to be involved with it at all stages and in all areas. Children expect every staff member to know everything; and because we are all involved in all aspects of the work we can share what we do spontaneously as needed.

Since staff members are accessible to children all the time, they have an extraordinary opportunity to observe children's behavior, their language, and their needs. The result of alert observation is to become more responsive and useful to the children. At the same time, because of our close relationships with the children, we have the bonus of a membership which presents very few disciplinary problems. Not that we are surrounded by young angels, but we are on the spot to handle incipient difficulties, and the young people realize that, just as they are respected, trusted, and enjoyed, they have a responsibility not to impinge upon others' rights or spoil library participation for themselves and others.

Staff Relationship with the Children as an
Aspect of Communication

We impose no formal, unbendable rules for behavior, book use, or any other aspect of library participation upon the children. There is no formal teaching, there are no demands. We make it clear that we are there to open doors to those who come and that we hope they will open some for us. They may select and reject, and they may make suggestions if what they want is not forthcoming. We encourage them to ask questions, make suggestions, challenge policies--anything. And if they prefer to write comments rather than to make them face-to-face, we provide forms. These we answer, and we frequently take action upon them.

In this way, as well as in informal ways, they discover that we are interested, that they have a voice, but that even we are not totally free--that there are boundaries for us in the form of budgets, staffing levels, availability of books or resources, and so on. And I have found that children are realistic. As long as they know that we are honest with them, that we listen to their point of view even if we do not agree with it, and that we value them as people, they will accept and live with our guidelines and decisions, even though sometimes it is a reluctant acceptance.

Another important aspect of this in-depth method is that the children see and experience the staff in action and in interaction with one another and with the people they serve. A child picks up the message that these are adults who are safe to approach because they are warm, supportive, and accepting towards one another as well as towards children, adults who are truly interested in children and are busy all day doing things to make the library work--"for me, a child."

To sum up this section, I should like to quote Clarence Budington Kelland: "My father didn't tell me how to live. He lived, and let me watch him."

Learning by Example and Involvement to Use the Library to Make Literature Accessible

In order to use the library well, its members must learn to use the tools, and to develop the skills to use them. Many libraries use the class visit and the library lesson pattern as a means of sharing these skills and teaching the use of these tools. I try not to use any formal teaching, since I prefer to excite the children about the library, about books, about story, and about learning. We must keep telling them that books are for them and that they read for themselves and they learn for themselves, not for the teacher or anyone else.

It is best, I think, that the learning of skills be part of every visit the child makes. This becomes especially apparent when one realizes that not every child will be part of a class visiting the library, nor will a set program necessarily come at a time when a particular child is ready to absorb the knowledge. I like to make the teaching of library skills a day-to-day part of our relationship with the individual child, to be offered at the moment of need. We leave the more formal aspect to the school.

In-Depth Learning in an Environment Where Children Are Challenged and Free to Practice and Experiment with a Wide Variety of Skills and Experiences

Learning and growing develop as children find themselves free to share with one another and with adults as they browse, as they do research, as they participate in programs—as they live in the library.

Growth in communication with others happens on many levels and in all situations. It also happens between flesh-and-blood people and book people. I put a Ramona doll in the display case with a letter sent by Beverly Cleary when she mailed the doll. A little girl stood open-mouthed and breathed, "Is it really from Beverly Cleary?" I have grown inches taller in her eyes now that she knows I write to her "very favorite author," and we have talked at length about Ramona and other book people.

When we have a book-centered activity, we leave plenty of room for each child to develop an original idea, and creativity develops. At the same time, the child learns to discard what does not work and learns to share ideas with others. Relationships grow. Not only do children share, but we hope they will become relaxed with people—relaxed about not knowing all the answers, for example, or about knowing more than others even when those others are adults. We see the children developing social skills, taking risks, beginning to value themselves and others.

Self-assurance increases. We help children evaluate

information and its presentation by encouraging them always to trust thmselves and to think. Their experience in our programs as well as our daily assistance helps them develop skills in problem solving, in using words, and in understanding their power. We play with words and come to see them as tools for communication. We practice making images and dreaming, then acting on the dreams. When we tell or read stories we watch children caught up in magic and wonder; but we also thereby help them develop their skills in reasoning, deducing, and anticipating. We help them shape a faith in their own judgments and become comfortable about making mistakes.

These growths, and many more, do not happen easily in a room where little is going on. To create the environment for these developments we practice a door-opening concept. The staff members work hard at keeping our minds and attitudes open and flexible, and we take active steps to keep the minds of the children open so that they will learn to see and experience literature in a total way. We constantly watch for what we may be doing or saying that may close the mind.

A good example of closing the mind may be found in the definition of the two major areas of book arrangement in a library. Almost every time I ask a child for a definition of the words "fiction" and "nonfiction" I am told that fiction is not true and nonfiction is true. Communication and growth slow down when teachers and librarians insist on finite definitions and pigeonholes. I believe that to state these things about books or about any book is to set limits on the truth and on children's thinking and reasoning. We should encourage them to question books, us, other adults, their peers, the media--which include libraries--and to be constantly alert to new ideas, new ways of thinking and seeing and being. We want them to learn that there are many kinds of truths and many facets to each truth, and that truths are found in many places. We want children to recognize that any one book, or any group of books, can only contain a facet of truth that is the writer's view and experience of the truth. Truth may be found everywhere and anywhere, not just in books with numbers on their spines.

We want children to be always becoming, never finished. They should find that each book is a doorway and that they may open the door and explore beyond it for themselves. Children must decide for themselves whether they are discovering truths to add to their store by experimenting and exploring and learning to change and discard as need be. Talking with others facilitates this process, and we will listen and share.

Because of this philosophy we need to plan all our activities to allow each person to be an achiever when entering her or his very own library. Each child must be allowed and helped to develop a personal growth plan. Note that I have not used the words "each reader." We cannot expect every child to be a reader in the sense that he or she will gulp down stories and books. But what we must hope is that all will learn that the library can serve their needs and will not necessarily expect devotion to the printed word in return.

Extension and Promotion as Part of Communication and In-Depth Learning

I have always believed that a wide range of activities is an integral part of implementing the philosophy I have been describing. They are a primary method of opening the door into the world of books, offering keys and providing clues and skills for the discovery of personal treasure. To try to meet all kinds of needs we include the following: regular storytelling and reading, puppetry in a variety of forms, weekly interest sessions, special programs whenever opportunity or inspiration offers, parades; pot-luck literary teas, reading programs, and workshops for both children and adults. We always provide holiday programs, and we have our annual Christmas Parade around the city streets led by a child Mary riding a real donkey called Johnny. Winter term usually sees fortnightly musical concerts by children using the library piano. We offer a full service of library visits to schools and preschools. Youth groups, too, use our services, and we test for readers' badges. A penfriend service is popular, and we have a sister-city link with Lorain, Ohio, U.S.A.

My meetings with some famous authors have given the children the opportunity, rare down under, to feel connected to real writers. I share with them my autographed books and posters, and letters. We know Beverly Cleary, who brought us our library monkey puppet. Mollie Hunter, Spencer Shaw,

Margaret Mahy, and others have visited us, too. We encourage mothers to register their babies as soon as possible, and we send them a letter while they are still at the obstetrical unit telling them why they should use the services of the library and enclosing a registration form. We also run a weekly pre-school program and share the language skills of storytelling, fingerplay, and other activities with mothers and children--and the occasional father.

We also go out into the community to let people know what is being done and why. We want others to be involved, to feel positive about the library and about books. And so we make posters and booklists, broadcast a weekly radio program, plan newspaper items, give talks and seminars, hold a monthly storytellers' meeting, and keep alert to the need for other services and try to offer them. We have gone into the malls and playgrounds to tell our stories as well as into the schools and similar places; we encourage and we entice and we work hard, for a children's library is a free service and there is no compulsion on anyone to use it. We must particularly attract the adults, for the children are dependent on their good will in the matter of library provision and use.

Conclusion

I believe a children's library must be a place where a total experience is available, where in-depth learning occurs all the time, and where the doorways of communication between child and child, between child and adult, between child and book, are always open.

I would want the children's libraries of the world, of my country, and of my city in particular to be places of magi and journeying, of growing and endless becoming.

PART VI:

THE ORAL TRADITION

The continued power of old tales to move the minds and hearts
of children was recognized at the conference by a Storytelling
Festival as well as by a variety of papers on aspects of folklore. Spencer Shaw's introduction to the festival is followed
by Jewell Coburn's admonition that the translator of folklore
be sensitive to the original culture. Jane Ricketts talks
about her attempts to preserve traditional tales in the South
Pacific by audiotaping native storytellers. Ronald Jackson,
aware also of the decline of old Polynesian ways, describes
the value of storytelling in a preliterate society. And Edna
Hurd reveals the pleasures and surprises of scholarship in
the area of folklore.

Chapter 15

CROSS-CULTURAL UNDERSTANDING THROUGH THE
ART OF STORYTELLING*

Spencer G. Shaw

"It's storytime! Welcome storytellers!" These simple
words have echoed in every age and culture of humankind,
from the preliterate periods to the most advanced stages of
civilization. They have provided a bridge over which listeners and tellers have crossed from a world of reality to beckon-
ing realms of imagination and fantasy. Leaving behind the
commonplace of the present, willing companions have responded
timelessly to the demanding call of an ageless art.

The Origins and Influence of Storytelling

Storytelling has its roots deeply imbedded in the beginnings of articulate expression. Regardless of their culture
or their geographic regions, the reciters and singers of these
dawning eras related their stories in which they made the time,
the place and the drama as one. The locale of their tales
could have been the long, white roads of Greece, the hot,
dry sands of the Egyptian deserts, the trackless forests of

---

*Excerpted from the lecture, "The Art of Storytelling," given
by Spencer G. Shaw in Tokyo, Japan, July 23, 1984, before
the Society for Children's Libraries, the Japan Library Association, and the International Board on Books for Young People.

the American wilderness, the beautiful islands of Hawaii, the
rugged terrain of the Scandinavian countryside, or the villag
marketplaces and terraced farmlands on the islands of Japan

Extending beyond the limiting boundaries of one conti-
nent or one civilization, the universal appeal and uses of
storytelling have been indestructible. The tellers of tales
have defied any bonds of captivity that may have been imposed upon them, for the captive people in any culture even
tually have encircled the captors with their oral artistry.
Storytelling has transcended the evils of censure and the efforts of suppression with its strong appeal to the concept of
freedom of thought. It has overcome ridicule and disbelief
among those who spurn its manifold roles to entertain, to in-
form, to inspire, to instruct and to transmit cultural and etl
nic legacies. Storytelling has confronted the challenges whi
have been generated by every new medium of communication,
from the advent of pictorial images to the most advanced tec
nological wonders. In the words of the eminent folklorist,
Stith Thompson:

> The teller of stories has everywhere and always foul
> eager listeners. Whether his tale is the mere report
> of a recent happening, a legend of long ago, or an
> elaborately contrived fiction, men and women have
> hung upon his words and satisfied their yearnings f
> information or amusement, for incitement to heroic
> deeds, for religious edification, or for release from
> the overpowering monotony of their lives. In village
> of central Africa, in outrigger boats on the Pacific,
> in the Australian bush, and within the shadow of
> Hawaiian volcanoes, tales of the present and of the
> mysterious past, of animals and gods and heroes, an
> of men and women like themselves, hold listeners in
> their spell or enrich the conversation of daily life.
> So it is also in Eskimo igloos under the light of seal
> oil lamps, in the tropical jungles of Brazil, and by
> the totem poles of the British Columbian coast. In
> Japan too, and China and India, the priest and the
> scholar, the peasant and the artisan all join in their
> love of a good story and their honor for the man wh
> tells it well....

> This oral art of taletelling is far older than history,
> and it is not bounded by one continent or one

civilization. Stories may differ in subject from place to place, the conditions and purposes of taletelling may change as we move from land to land or from century to century, and yet everywhere it ministers to the same basic social and individual needs.[1]

What Is the Heritage of Storytelling?

Storytelling is rich with heritage, for it has never existed in a vacuum. It has ministered to basic societal needs; it has revealed the existence of a common humanity, an instinctive belief in the worth and dignity of the human spirit. Storytelling has revealed horizons beyond known horizons, enabling tellers and listeners to discern the possibilities and the limits of their potential capacities. It has been a portal through which the hearts and minds of humanity may travel from the present into the past, thus retaining the best of tradition that is in touch with today.

The heritage of storytelling has made possible the preserving of cultural legacies. It has provided an intergenerational link in home environments as members of a family circle embrace the creative expressions that are shared regardless of the intellectual attainment of tellers and listeners. Embarking on an endless journey through the centuries, storytellers in diverse societal groups have presented their gifts to eager listeners. Assuming many roles--as historians, genealogists, recorders, priests, teachers, and entertainers-- these skilled practitioners of the ancient art form of storytelling have crisscrossed many lands. Stately courts and impoverished lodgings have resounded to their harmonious refrain of beloved tales. Truly, the historical continuity of storytelling as an art form cannot be minimized. Older than recorded history, geographically boundless, and indigenous to every cultural group, storytelling by both accomplished and unskilled tellers has been a catalyst for the transmittal, as living organisms, of the heritages and cultural traditions of all people.

The Uses of Storytelling

Through the power of the spoken word as recaptured in a traditional art form, reflective pilgrimages into cultural traditions may be undertaken. Closed doors may be opened to reveal the rich fabric of humankind's lore. Through the art of storytelling a strong, beautiful chain may be forged, linking the distant past with the present.

If this bond is to occur, let us accept the premise: What is past is prologue. Where do we proceed from here? Let us accept the mandate to keep alive the art of storytellin and the gifts of stories. Let us commit ourselves to meet the demands which the folk art of storytelling sets forth. Let us excel in its mastery and reap the incalculable and oft intangible rewards. Let us travel roads still unknown and perceive the interconnections of cultural inheritances in different physical and social environments. Let us share the wealth of stories to serve as guideposts in seeking enjoymen keeping alive institutions and history, and strengthening a sense of self-worth and self-dignity. Let us touch every facet of emotion, for if these facets remain untouched, the intellect will cease to comprehend. In this regard, let us re member the words of the educator, as recounted in the book Totto-chan: the Little Girl at the Window:

> Having eyes, but not seeing beauty; having ears, but not hearing music; having minds, but not perceiving truth; having hearts that are never moved and, therefore, never set on fire. These are things to fear. [2]

Let us bridge every difference of age and interest with our storied offerings, thus providing a communion of spirit betw children and children, children and adults, adults and adult between similar and diverse cultural groups. Before us the is an unopened door--a story to be shared, waiting listeners dreams to be fulfilled.

In the winter of 1969 it was my pleasure to have been invited to serve as a scholar/librarian-in-residence in the Graduate School of Library Studies at the University of Haw During this period I was asked to present assembly program for the pupils in the Lincoln School in Honolulu. In honor of the occasion two pupils, Randall Kikukawa and Gordon We wrote an introductory verse that provided an imaginary key with which the storyteller would unlock the door to stories. Now let us pretend we are lighting a storytelling candle and listening to the refrain of our young friends' poem:

The candle is lit,
Story Hour begins,
A door of magic unfolds.
All ears are attentive,
All lips are hushed,
Waiting for the story to be told.

The story begins,
The storyteller starts,
We wait for the tale still untold.
All eyes look up straight,
All minds concentrate,
On the story that is now being told.[3]

NOTES

1. Thompson, Stith, The Folktale, (New York: The Dryden Press, 1951), pp. 3, 5.
2. Kuroyanagi, Tetsuko, Totto-chan: the Little Girl at the Window, translated by Dorothy Britton. (Tokyo/New York: Kodansha International; New York: dist. by Kodansha International/USA through Harper & Row, 1982) p. 88.
3. Kikukawa, Randall and Wee, Gordon, "Story Hour." (Honolulu, Hawaii, Lincoln School, February 12, 1969) Unpublished. (Personal Files)

Chapter 16

METHODS OF TRANSLATING FOLK LITERATURE FROM ONE CULTURE TO ANOTHER

Jewell Reinhart Coburn
with Duong Van Quyen

The translation of the arts of one culture into the context of another with the objective of achieving deepened mutual understanding among peoples is a theme of the 1986 Third Pacific Rim Conference. It is the perspective of this paper that, indeed, a successful methodology can be develope to produce the desired outcome.

As the author-researcher of a trilogy of books inspired by the Southeast Asian dilemma of the 1960s and 1970s, I hold the view that accurate, purposeful, highly informative, and entertaining translations of ethnic literature can be accomplished when appropriate consideration is given to the following:

- Authenticity

- Universality

- Information and Education Value

- Entertainment Value

- Captivating Writing Style

178

- Moving and Accurate Visual Style

It should be observed that these six characteristics are not numbered. The reason for this deliberate omission is significant. It is the author's view that none of these traits necessarily precedes or supersedes another; all are of equal importance in effectively pursuing the goal.

Many of us, I am confident, have read folk literature outstanding for its authenticity and strictness of literal translation, which nevertheless falls woefully short in communication and entertainment value. It reaches the reader in ways that scarcely would inspire interest, let alone respect or compassion for the human condition of those portrayed. It is my position that in order to succeed in such an intercultural endeavor, the translator-author must be not only a fine writer but part diplomat, part sociologist, part historian, part psychologist-researcher. Thus, only by employing a many-faceted, comprehensive, holistic approach can a writer hope to capture and communicate an authentic gestalt of the material at hand.

Not all would-be writers and translators of ethnic works can manage to live, as the present author did, in the countries that provide their subject matter. The following ingredients, however, are important for a successful outcome:

- Prolonged personal acquaintance with or, better yet, immersion in the culture of choice;

- A mingling if not a blending with the people on a day-to-day basis until each culture becomes comfortable with the other;

- Sensitivity to the values of the people, their dreams, their fears, their deepest concerns;

- Familiarization with the customs, traditions, and the prevailing political and religious views that influence their daily lives;

- Workable professional contacts with both intellectuals and citizens of less learning, for the purpose of carefully balancing the realities and views of one group with those of the other; and

- Awareness--for the purpose of recording and in-
  corporating them into the completed work--of the
  sights, sounds, smells, and moods of that country
  and its people.

This outline provides the filaments with which the literary web is woven. Without a well-honed sensitivity to nuance
of the culture of choice, the attempt to retell its folk literature may well turn out to be no more than "little half-chickian
The reader thus receives only a part of a picture, and that
part is all too often permeated with uninformed author bias.
This author places strong emphasis on rigorous attention to
the portrayal of ethnicity, but never in isolation from the
other qualities listed.

Stories must be traced and interpreted with careful, if
not painstaking, scholarship. One must study countless
sources to determine the degree to which a given folktale belongs to a given people. Cultural spillage, for example, is
commonly encountered. Themes are found repeated in the
cultural heritage of many countries the world over. For example, the charming rascal Xieng Mieng,[1] the popular boy-
hero in Laotian folk literature, is to that culture what Huck
Finn has become to our own. It is significant that Xieng
Mieng's origin is obscured in legend, whereas Mark Twain,
of course, receives credit for Huck's existence. Or, known
for his feats of cunning and strength, Cambodia's Brave
Kong[2] has characteristics in common with our own Paul Bun-
yan. Obviously, a determination must be made as to what
stories, or treatments of stories, are truly representative
of a given people.

Customs common to one people may be difficult to understand, distasteful, even repugnant to another, and yet
may be an integral part of the body of its folk literature.
What should the translator's position be?

One of the most poignant tales found in Vietnamese folk
heritage is sometimes entitled "The Love Crystal,"[3] which I
chose, in consultation with Duong Van Quyen, my Vietnamese
resource, to call, "Crystal Love." The first title refers to
the concrete, or what happens in the story in a physical
sense. The title I chose drives to the heart of the story's
universal yet markedly ethnic theme.

The tale is about a lovely but cloistered daughter of a Mandarin official. Daily, she whiles away her time reading light literature, doing needlework, and dreaming as she sits by the window of her father's great house overlooking a picturesque, winding river. One day she becomes aware of a lovely sound. Watching closely, she determines its source to be a flute that is being played by what appears to be a fisherman floating down-current on the far side of the river. To the daughter's delight, she finds this to be a daily occurrence. She learns to anticipate the fisherman's song. With her imagination heightened, the maiden begins to dream. She imagines that the distant fisherman is strong and handsome and that his lovely, haunting melody is played especially for her. So obsessed with this idea does the maiden become that she falls quite desperately in love with the man on the far side of the river.

When her father, the great Mandarin, learns why his daughter has grown wan and weak and will not leave the window of her room, he is forced by his paternal love to summon the fisherman to his daughter's presence. When the man arrives, however, the girl sees that instead of being virile and handsome, he is gnarled and bent, and a wretchedly poor commoner. In disgust, the girl turns away. The fisherman is led from the great house, not to be heard of again until his small boat is found floating free, carrying the body of the man who brought shame to a lovely Mandarin's daughter.

It is at this point that all the Western versions of this story which I have read draw to a close with the statement that when the fisherman's boat is found, all that can be seen is a crystal, a symbol of unrequited love; hence the title, "The Love Crystal."

The authentic story, however, goes on in an interestingly different direction, one that easily could be construed as unacceptable to readers with a Judeo-Christian background. There exists a tradition in certain Asian cultures that when one dies, loved ones bury the body. After three years, the body is exhumed, the flesh is lovingly cleaned from the bones with fragrant water, and the bones are carefully reburied. Such a practice is anathema to a people inculcated with a concept of reverence for the deceased that is demonstrated by leaving the body judiciously undisturbed. In point of fact, the Old Testament contains injunctions against handling a body.

The corpse is considered to be unclean, as is he who has touched it. And yet, to omit or dilute the authentic ending or to substitute an alternative conclusion not only robs the story of its authenticity, but also diminishes its message and the impact it could have for the reader.

Consider this more authentic rendering from the present author's retelling in "Crystal Love":

Sadness gripped the humble fisherman's shack for he did not return for many days. Finally a search was set. It was found that his lonely boat had drifted far off course and that he had died and drifted with it. Friendly seamen returned the boat with its ill-starred cargo and, according to custom, the fisherman's family tenderly cared for his body and then gave it to the earth from which it came. As for the maiden, unaware of the fisherman's sad destiny, she returned to her reading, embroidery and days of dreaming.

Exactly three years passed. In keeping with tradition, the fisherman's family gently removed his body from the earth in order to care for and preserve his bones and thus to free his spirit.

They tenderly lifted the coffin to the earth's surface and prepared for the ritual of cleaning the bones with fragrant water, after which they would lay them with reverence in the small, crockery urn that would be their final resting place.

When they opened the coffin they gasped at what they saw. There, gleaming and sparkling in the light of day, lay a piece of flawless crystal.

"How can this be?" they cried. And they stood back because of the brilliance of the stone that lay before them.

"We should find nothing but bones," they exclaimed "but here we find a perfect heart. Preserved as crystal. A stone of breathless beauty!"

The fisherman's humble family gazed long at the crystal and they pondered this mystery, for great had been their love for their crippled brother whose greatest gift to life had been but his lonely, lovely songs.

Years passed and one day the Mandarin's daughter happened to call to her maid servant to bring her tea.

Her servant responded with a tray on which sat a porcelain tea set and a single fine cup.

"Such a remarkable piece of hand work," exclaimed the Mandarin's daughter as she looked at the fine crystalware. "Where did this come from?"

The servant explained that it was but one of the many gifts given by humble village folk to show honor and respect for her father, the great Mandarin. And the servant left the room, the tea on the tray beside the crystal cup.

The maiden lifted the pot of tea and poured it into the cup. She set the pot down immediately for suddenly she heard a faint, distantly familiar melody. She looked about the room but saw no one. Then she glanced back at the cup and there to her astonishment, floating on the surface of the tea she saw a tiny boat and in the boat she saw the image of the fisherman.

When she recognized the haunting melody she was overcome with grief, for only then did she comprehend that the heart that can make music is more precious than a homely face. She knew then how deeply she had missed the beauty of the fisherman's music. Thus did she guess the fisherman's destiny and what her indifference had accomplished.

The maiden wept tears of remorse and as she did, a tear fell into the cup. When it touched the crystal, the cup shattered into a spray of a million tiny diamonds. Just as quickly they disappeared.

Love, it is believed, is so strong a force that it imprisons the very soul. When one dies of a broken heart, his soul may be forever trapped.

The maiden's tears were tears of contrition and because of them peace was finally brought to the fisherman's soul.

And as for the maiden? She resumed her reading and embroidery--but as for her dreams, they were never again so carefree.

Note the comments of the omniscient author as well as the following footnote for additional explanation:

From earliest times burial rites were an important part of Vietnamese religion and life. It is believed that there exists some sort of continuity of the dead one's personality. Also, there is the belief in the possibility of some contact between the living and the spirit of the dead.

To many Vietnamese, the community consists of the living, the very personal spirits of dead relatives and intimate friends, and of the less personal spirits of nature--all having the potential of contact with each other. Thus do the place of burial, the manner of burial, and the frequent, succeeding commemorations of the dead take on significance in Vietnamese everyday life.

It is a commonly held belief among Vietnamese that should a person die while in a state of anxiety--perhaps the result of rejected love, attitudes of hatred, jealousy, or of false accusation--the soul or spirit is not free.

At this point the reader can readily understand why the preferable title is "Crystal Love," which speaks more to the purity of motive than of a physical phenomenon only.

Therefore, it is my practice to retain as much of the original story as possible, but to use two principal methods in dealing with such challenges:

- Allow for the introduction of the omniscient author who speaks directly to the reader and furnishes explanations; and

- Footnote difficult concepts with lucid descriptive material.

Arbitrarily omitting a subject integral to a given piece of folk literature can diminish the potential for realizing the desired level of intercultural understanding. No matter what the country or the people, universal themes are to be found. However, ways of achieving common objectives may differ, and such are the sources of a people's uniqueness. I make it my practice to be open to those qualities, those dynamics that are in common with others. These are the touchstones, the soul-binders among peoples. On the other hand, differences, rather than being ignored or suspect, should be dealt with and included for their capacity to arouse curiosity, heighten interest, and add to a story's suspense. Companion, therefore, to the desire for building bridges between cultures through the gathering and retelling of folk tales is the potent motive of capturing and thus preserving those unique qualities of a culture which are threatened by extinction.

The extent to which the folk literature of one country is valued by another is often measured by its power to entertain. Herein lies one more very significant challenge to the reteller of folk tales. Adroitly, the writer must establish character, draw settings, communicate theme, and sculpt the finished piece in a fashion titillating to his readership. Therefore, the reteller of tales must become, to a considerable degree, multicultural. As he grows in sensitivity to the subtleties of the culture under study, he must also be keenly responsive to his readership.

The artistic shape characterizing a piece of literature can also serve to enlighten us concerning the psychological and esthetic nature of a people, and provide a guide to the effective retelling of a story in a manner entertaining to the reader of another culture. For example, many Asian folktales have a picaresque or episodic quality. The characters go through one escapade after another, a device designed essentially to entertain and not necessarily to demonstrate character--an approach somewhat uncommon in Western literature. Because of the Western reader's orientation to variations of the ancient Greek dramatic form wherein the play had a distinct beginning, middle (rising action), climax (turning point of the action), denouement (falling action), and conclusion (drawing the story line to a satisfying end), the purely episodic begs reshaping. This demands a delicate balancing act between the effort to retain authenticity and to spark reader delight.

One last point must be made. Since the sharing of insights and information is integral to the successful translation of folk literature from one culture to another, the quality and synchronicity of visual illustrations are of paramount importance. If we agree that "one picture is worth a thousand words," then great care must be given to the pictorial interpretations of retold tales. Just as it behooves the author to become multicultural, so should this be the aim of the illustrator. The joy derived, therefore, from working closely with illustrator as well as scholar stems from the realization that the end result will be a product of the highest level of artistic coordination.

An example is an illustration for the wonderful Vietnamese tale of women warriors recounted in "Sister Queens,"[4] a legendary version of two wives of noblemen who saw a need and refused to shirk from it. Rather, they inspired their sisters to don military attire and wage battle against intruding forces, win the fray, and crown the achievement by proclaiming themselves queens.

One of the story's many charming illustrations by Nena Gregorian Ullberg called for a pictorial account of one of the sisters confronting the ladies of the court with the challenge that they lay down their needlework and their gentility and pick up arms to defend their province.

At first the illustrator, not familiar with the Asian practice of leaving one's shoes by the door before entering a home, was asked by the scholar Duong Van Quyen to remove all the ladies' shoes in the illustration as they sat demurely in the grand rooms of the sister's fine home. Next arose the issues of costume and hair style. Ms. Ullberg had envisioned the dynamic woman leader as someone with long, flowing tresses. Our scholar suggested the opposite. Research validated the scholar's position. In that day, and even in this, to a considerable extent, the traditional hair style of mature Vietnamese women is to pull the hair back tightly and form a bun, around which is placed a crownless, brim-like hat, which gives the impression of a halo.

Such minutiae may seem trivial and insignificant to some. Yet to the end that understanding and appreciation of others' ways are the goal, such fine points contribute richly to the overall grasp of a culture.

And what may be the hallmark of having achieved such a noble objective as the interlacing of cultures? Perhaps it is the intellectual and emotional involvement one feels when reading or hearing a tale from another land. Conversely, when one reads his own folk literature, retold and written in another language, and feels it is convincing enough to have been written by one of his own countrymen--perhaps this is the real litmus test for such an endeavor.

NOTES

1. Jewell Reinhart Coburn, Encircled Kingdom: Legends

and Folktales of Laos (Los Angeles: Burn, Hart,
1981), pp. 37-40.
2.   Jewell Reinhart Coburn, Khmers, Tigers and Talismans:
From the History and Legends of Mysterious Cambodia
(Los Angeles: Burn, Hart, 1977), pp. 37-42.
3.   Jewell Reinhart Coburn, Beyond the East Wind: Legends
and Folktales of Vietnam (Thousand Oaks, CA: Burn,
Hart, 1976), pp. 45-49.
4.   Ibid., pp. 76-77.

Chapter 17

MI TALEM WAN STORI

Jane Ricketts

Telling stories has always been part of the way of life for people who live on the islands of the South Pacific. Today this storytelling tradition is still very much alive in the eleven countries which make up the region served by the University of the South Pacific. In Fiji, Tonga, Western Samoa, the Solomon Islands, Kiribati, Tuvalu, the Cook Islands, Vanuatu, Niue, Tokelau, and Nauru, families still gather together to listen to traditional stories, perhaps in the evening around a kerosene lantern on the floor of a thatched house, or at midday under a shady tree in the middle of the village, or maybe on the beach beside a canoe. The storytellers are normally the old people, the language is, of course, the mother-tongue, and the audience--the "sea of upturned faces" includes people of all ages, including the very young.

Later on, as students, some of these young people will tell the same stories in English to their classmates at the University of the South Pacific. I first heard a number of these stories from students taking my course, Introduction to Children's Literature. This storytelling component was included in the course for several reasons: first, so that students would realize that literature for children exists as part of their own heritage, to be valued along with the books from outside; second, so that students from different island countries could share one another's cultures and traditions throug

listening to one another's stories; third and most important,
so that students would be aware of the need to preserve the
storytelling tradition, particularly after the introduction of
television due soon in Fiji, the largest country of the region
(population: 600,000).   The government of Fiji and the Australian company granted television rights have assured people
that the programs screened will include a proportion of local
material and that television generally will promote local culture; but in spite of these assurances, many people expect
to see a decline in cultural activities after the introduction of
television.

The stories could be seen as "literature for children."
Yet listening to them in English one feels that some of them
are hardly that.   James Toa's story from Vanuatu, for example, would strike many western ears as being most unsuitable
for children.   It is a story of adultery and murder, as this
summary shows:

> Talai, the protagonist, lived many years ago on
> the island of Aoba, one of the islands of Vanuatu
> and the storyteller's own island.   He and his wife
> were prosperous and happy although they had no
> children.   They raised pigs and chickens and tended
> their garden.   One day Talai loaded his canoe with
> pigs which he intended to exchange for pigs from a
> neighboring island according to the custom of the
> time.   He instructed his wife to look after their farm
> during his absence.   He was away for some time.   On
> his return his suspicions were aroused.   At their
> garden he hid and lay in wait for the man he believed
> to be his wife's lover.   The man came and a desperate
> fight took place.   Talai killed his rival and buried
> him in the garden.   Worse was to follow when Talai
> punished his wife for being unfaithful.   He forced
> her to dig up the body of her lover and to eat the
> decaying flesh.   It was too much for her and she
> died.   Weeping bitterly, Talai buried her body in the
> garden.   Early next morning the villagers saw his
> canoe disappearing over the horizon.   He never re-
> turned.

This is strong meat surely for little children, but James
heard the story at his grandmother's knee.   He remembers:

It was one of the traditional stories I enjoyed
most when listening to my grandmother. Like most
children in our family, I heard this story when I was
a small boy. We would sit beside our grandparents
after supper, paying close attention to the stories
they told us. Often when the story ended, I would
be fast asleep on the mat beside my grandmother.

James also recalls that sometimes they were aware of the
presence of evil spirits in the darkness outside, but that inside the house they felt warm and safe. Perhaps this atmosphere of warmth and security within the family circle
which surrounds the child during the telling purges these
traditional stories of their horror for the young listener. It
seems to me that in this situation the child takes from the
stories only what he can cope with emotionally at the time;
full understanding comes gradually. Certainly James's retelling of this story brought out the full impact of its traged;

Robert Leeson makes the same point about traditional
English stories in a chapter entitled, "Once Upon a Time:
Folk Tales and the Young." He writes:

One might guess that as the young grew into the
work their parents did, which was one part of their
education, and into the games which were another
part of their learning, so they grew into the stories
which were the third part of their life's teaching.
There are matters in all folk tales which a child can
understand; there are often others which require maturity of mind and body to fully appreciate.[1]

How do we pass on our traditions to our children?
Are stories mere entertainment or do they have a more important function in society? Good stories are, of course, entertaining. If they were not, children would not want to listen to them over and over, and they would not remember the
all their lives. I believe, however, that traditional stories a
also a very important means of passing on traditions. To
quote Leeson again:

The oral tradition contained everything which preliterate society thought worthy of notice and worth
passing on. And so it was especially important to
the young generation. Just how important we can
only guess.[2]

Some of the ideas and beliefs passed on in traditional
stories have significance only for that particular cultural
group. For example, a story told by Poasa Aiga has a special meaning for Samoan listeners. It is a humorous story
of "Mafi the Fisherman."

> Mafi was a vain and virile scallywag, more inter-
> ested in enjoying himself than in obeying his elders.
> He was renowned for his success both as a fisherman
> and with the women. One day he caught a lot of
> fish. He was reluctant to give the biggest fish of
> his catch to the paramount chief according to the cus-
> tom. Instead, he planned to give it to the family of
> his girlfriend. Mafi instructed his younger brother
> Sione to tell the chief when he next visited the fam-
> ily that he, Mafi, had gone to another island. Mean-
> while he hid under the bed. He did not realize that
> his feet were sticking out--and Mafi's feet were dis-
> tinctive because a shark had taken all the toes off his
> left foot. The chief told Sione, "Next time Mafi goes
> away, tell him to take his feet with him."
>
> The story of the missing feet alarmed the Chief's
> daughter, Sina. Mafi was unaware of this and con-
> tinued to show his prowess. He caught the largest
> fish in a competition, losing his lavalava in the pro-
> cess; and Sina presented him with a prize, a lei of
> frangipani. She placed a flower behind his left ear
> and asked him to dance. At the end of the dance she
> told him, "Mafi, I really like you as a person but I'm
> sorry, I cannot marry you until you tell me the
> secret of your missing feet."

Mafi's cheeky behavior appeals to a Samoan audience.
In Polynesia, however, the system of chiefdoms is a very important part of the structure of society. The Polynesian audience knows that Mafi's disrespect for the chief will lead to
his downfall.

The beautiful love story, "How the Fine Mats Came to
Tonga," told by Sister Anunisia, conveys several traditional
ideas to local listeners: the importance of fine mats in Tongan
ceremonial and the historical basis of the close but sometimes
troubled relationship that exists between Tonga and Samoa.

> Long ago there was a handsome chief in Tonga

named Senilau. Stories of his fame spread beyond the shores of Tonga and reached Samoa, where a beautiful princess named Hinaleanoa lived. She was very curious and longed to see this handsome man for herself. Curiosity got the better of her, and off she went to Tonga.

She swam and swam until eventually she came to an island. She did not know it, but this was Senilau's own island and the people were celebrating his coming of-age. This was also the time for him to take a wife. Hina was so exhausted after her long swim that she fell asleep on the beach with her clothes spread around her in the sun to dry.

It was there that some of Senilau's young men found her. Awed by her beauty, they said to each other, "Let's make a noise. If she wakes she's one of us. If not she must be a witch." Startled by the noise, Hina awoke and grabbed her clothes to herself. The young men welcomed her to their village and took her to Senilau. When Hina and Senilau saw each other they fell instantly in love and he asked her to be his wife.

For a while they were happy, but then some of Senilau's women who were jealous of Hina poisoned his mind against her and convinced him she really was a witch. He did not have the heart to kill her. Instead, he imprisoned her in the pigsty, where their baby son was born. Hina was brokenhearted and very homesick. Her people heard of her plight and sent a little bird to her with a message. Early one morning, they came in canoes and spread fine mats from the shore to the pigsty. Then they took Hina and her baby back to Samoa.

Senilau followed them, begging Hina for forgiveness and pleading with her to return with him to Tonga. Hina forgave him, but she did not go back. Sadly, Senilau swam home. Halfway between Tonga and Samoa he decided to turn into a big rock. If Hina ever did decide to return, he wanted her to be able to rest there on her journey.

These stories may convey specific cultural values to small groups of people, as I have suggested. Implicit in them too, are universal human values appealing to a much wider audience. James Toa sees the barter system emphasized in the story of Talai as an important part of his cultural heritage, now kept alive only in stories like this one; but there is universal meaning in the sorrow and regret felt by Talai at the end of the story.

The story of Mafi, too, has universal appeal; Mafi is not just a Samoan character--he is a character in the picaresque tradition. Behind the story is the message that order and custom must be observed. Similarly, the story of Senilau and Hinaleanoa tells everyone something about the nature and the power of love.

Duncan Williamson is a storyteller who keeps alive the vital oral literature of his people, the Travellers, an ancient nomadic people of Western Scotland. He writes, in his book, Fireside Tales of the Traveller Children,

> On cold winter nights when early darkness enclosed the old travellers' camps, a father would turn round and take his children beside him. "Listen children, sit down and be quiet--I'll tell you a story." My father knew in his own mind, at these times, that he was going to tell us something that was going to stand us through our entire life. Probably he had no tobacco for a smoke; probably we didn't have a bit of meat to eat, we had no supper. But we sat there listening to our father telling us a story and we were full, not full with food, but full of love of our father's voice. And even though he was hungry himself, he was teaching us to be able to understand by his tales what was in store for us in the future, telling us how to live in this world as natural human beings--not to be greedy, not to be foolish, daft or selfish--by stories.[3]

Pacific stories also tell children how to live in this world as natural human beings. This is something we all need to know. We all need stories to help us, the stories of our own culture first and then those given us by our neighbors. Duncan Williamson goes on to say, "Then television along with radio came into vogue and travellers had no more time for sitting around a campfire talking." It would be a pity if the advent of television meant that the families in the Pacific, too, would have no more time for storytelling and that stories, including the ones recorded here, were not passed on to the next generation.

NOTES

1. Robert Leeson, Reading and Righting (London: Collins, 1985), p. 23.
2. Ibid., p. 22.
3. Duncan Williamson, Fireside Tales of the Traveller Children (New York: Harmony Books, 1985), introduction.

Chapter 18

A BRIEF HISTORY OF CHILDREN'S LITERATURE
IN POLYNESIA

Ronald S. Jackson

This is an age of wonder and a time of fun and learning for a child. From the time a child begins to see the
sights and hear the sounds of the world about him, the miracle of learning begins. From the beginning of time children
have learned about their world through entertaining stories.
These stories, sights, and sounds are the literature of children.

Books and television are used quite heavily in the western world as a means of conveying information and literature
to children. But in some cultures, even today, the written
word is not the major means of communicating literature to
the child. Telling stories, singing songs, and playing games
have been the time-honored methods of entertaining and teaching children throughout the world. Even the strictest societies have used these methods to develop the literature and
convey the history of their cultures to their children, sometimes even after the information has been written down.

A superficial review of history shows that while civilization advanced, man literally printed his way out of the dark
ages. It is man's ability to read, write, understand, and
articulate ideas that makes him literate. With the advent of
the printing press, Gutenberg provided us a means of

recording and conveying literature, philosophy, and information from one generation to the next and from one culture to another. Early on, however, the written word was only for adults. It was felt that the printed page was too valuable to be wasted on children.

When printed material did appear for children, it was very stiff. The first books were didactic in nature and dealt with moral issues. Children may have gained some information and understanding from reading books, but the bulk of their literary knowledge still came from observing and listening to adults. The children listened to stories, sang songs, and played games as a means of becoming a part of their society and culture.

Today, in the western world, there are many books for children which entertain and delight them. Many movies and television programs are also designed specifically for children. These have all been a great boon for the conveyance of children's literature; however, the children still have their own world of games, songs, and stories.

What about cultures that did not develop the concepts of reading and writing early in their history? Are these societies without literature? Are these people to be considered uncultivated? Until recently most, if not all, Polynesian societies have flourished without the benefit of the written page.

With the intrusion of the explorers and the missionaries from the west into the Pacific Basin came a great transition. For the most part the Polynesians were considered illiterate and pagan by the western interlopers. In their zeal to convert the heathen to the "truth" and teach them the proper way to behave, these outsiders neglected to observe the profound and complex body of knowledge and story that already existed. The problem was that the sum of Polynesian culture was not recorded in a form that the westerners could understand, nor were the Polynesian methods of teaching and learning familiar.

As in early western societies, formal education in Polynesia was only for a select few. Large schools did not exist in the islands until after the European missionaries came; whether a child was selected for formal instruction often depended upon his family's standing or position in the community

Education for the great majority of children was conducted on a very informal basis, often resulting from watching older children. Since most Polynesian societies had no written language, their stories, dances, songs, and chants were the actual means of conveying legends and myths from generation to generation.

In Polynesia, the family structure has been an important factor in determining how and what a child learns and receives as literature. The family has included not only the husband, wife, and children, but often the grandparents, aunts, uncles, and others. And as the younger adults would go to work in the taro patches, go fishing, or be engaged in other activities, the children would be left in the care of the older children or grandparents. The grandparents became the children's primary teachers. Stories, philosophies, and transferral of skills were integral to the daily interaction between grandparents and grandchildren. And the younger children would also learn much through observing and listening to the older children, who were often given the responsibility of caring for them and keeping them entertained and out of the way.

Children are fascinated by stories, especially the many stories for children which are filled with animal characters. It is generally believed that animal stories were told primarily, although not exclusively, to children. The oral tradition has been, and still is, a very prominent aspect of literature throughout Polynesia. Adults have often gathered in the evenings to "talk story." The storyteller in these communities has been a person very much revered as the purveyor of the traditions, beliefs, and entertainment of the society. His stories emphasized the basic needs of everyday life and gave explanations about how things came to be. And although these stories were meant for adults, the children would observe and listen, and thus learn them.

With the intrusion of western cultures into Polynesia, ways of living changed. Western-style public schools and books are now available to children. The isolation that was so much a part of island living has been canceled by the presence of television. Island tales are now available in print.

One must exercise caution while reading the stories of Polynesia, however, because they may not be accurate representations. For the most part, Polynesian literature was not written down by Polynesians but by western missionaries, anthropologists, travelers, and writers. As well-meaning as these people were, they distorted or neglected much of the original Polynesian literature because of the covert need to make it comfortable or palatable to western readers. The missionaries wanted to convert the pagans, as they perceived the Polynesian to be; so they often changed the interpretation and meaning of the stories, legends, and myths in order to reflect Christian ideals and traditions more closely.

Many of the stories told to children in Polynesia are already lost because they have been replaced by western school readers and stories. The art of storytelling has given way to the more hypnotic influence of television. Even though Polynesian literature for children may never be seen as a genre in the anthologies of folk literature, we need to encourage the collection and preservation of literature from the islands of the Pacific before it is totally obliterated.

Chapter 19

THE LEGEND OF PUNIA--
MORE THAN MEETS THE EAR?

Edna L. Hurd

The story of Punia's outwitting the sharks is popular
with storytellers in Hawaii. In brief, the boy Punia lives
with his mother in the village of Kohala on the coast of the
island of Hawai'i. His father has been killed by Kai'ale'ale,
king of the sharks, who, with ten underling sharks, now
guards the lobster cave and bay so that no villagers may swim
or fish there. Punia outwits the sharks by throwing stones
far out from the shore. The sharks rush to the place where
the stones hit the water, allowing Punia time to dive for the
lobsters. He does this ten times, each time praising another
shark for helping him. The other sharks devour the accused
shark until only Kai'ale'ale is left. Punia dives and allows
himself to be swallowed by Kai'ale'ale but props the shark's
jaws open with two iron-wood sticks and proceeds to light a
fire and cook his food in the shark's belly. Kai'ale'ale, in
great pain, dashes through the ocean for ten days until,
exhausted, he once more reaches the shore of the island of
Hawai'i and is trapped in the shallow waters off the beach.
Punia has outwitted the sharks but, because of being in the
belly of Kai'ale'ale for such a long time, emerges completely
bald.

The first printed version of this story seems to have
appeared in Fornander's Collection of Hawaiian Antiquities

and Folklore (Fornander, 1919, pp. 294-301), which was not
published until sometime between 1917 and 1919 although the
materials were collected from about the 1860s to the 1870s.
There are several available retellings of the story, many of
which are included in the bibliography of this paper.

The story of Punia is a popular one and is generally
classified in the genre of trickster story. One might think
no more about it save for the general knowledge that Hawaiian
legends are filled with hidden and double meanings, and one
might begin to wonder whether there might be hidden meanings
in the Punia story. In the Hawaiian Dictionary (Pukui, 1971,
p. 397) Punia is simply listed as the son of Hina of Kohala
who tricked the sharks. When we look up the individual
components of the word Pu-nia, a new idea begins to develop.
Now we find that "nia" means "smooth, round, bald" (ibid.,
p. 245). The Fornander version makes a great point of the
baldness, mentioning it twice on the same page (Fornander,
1919, p. 298).

"Pu" is translated in the same dictionary as a "general
name for a pumpkin or squash. Also called ipu-pu." (Pukui,
1971, p. 317). "Ipu" is translated as "the bottle gourd,"
"the watermelon," and "general name for vessel or container"
(ibid., p. 96).

We know that the true pumpkin was not introduced to
the islands until the time of Captain Cook (Handy, 1940, p.
207); but in a later publication (Handy, 1972, p. 214) we
also learn that "ipu" is a term applied to any round fruit.
Neal also tells us that the autumn and winter squashes were
called both "ipu-pu" or "pu" (Neal, 1965, p. 813). Since
both pumpkins and gourds belong to the same family, La-
genaria siceraria, and have a similar appearance and similarity
in Hawaiian names, the two terms could have been used interchangeably, especially by the time these stories were collected in the 1860s and 1870s.

We will proceed on the assumption that the two terms
may be used interchangeably. When it is discovered that one
meaning of "nia" is "bald" and that "pu" may be translated
as "gourd," a new idea begins to form. Perhaps this tale
could be categorized not only as a trickster tale but also as
a tale of origin, such as why the coconut has a face, why
the leopard has spots, why the gourd has no hair. When

Punia emerges from the belly of the shark he is not only bald but "ua holu ohe," without body hair, as a gourd would also be (Fornander, 1919, p. 298). And would not the gourd bear a striking resemblance to the cranium of a bald-headed man?

Place names mentioned by Fornander are Kohala, Kona, Alula, and Hi'iakanoho-lae. The first two are still well-known areas on the island of Hawai'i. In Place Names of Hawaii we are told that Aululu is a bay in North Kona (Pukui, 1974, p. 11), and that Hi'iaka-noho-lae is a "rock beyond the sea wall (between the Kona Inn and the end of the wall) at Kailua Village, Kona.... In one legend the stone is the shark form of a priest turned to stone in response to an enemy's prayer to Pele" (ibid., p. 45). The fact that this rock is mentioned by name, even though from another legend, helps to locate and verify boundaries of the Punia story.

With the location established, attention may now be turned to the matter of gourds. Handy's Hawaiian Planter (Handy, 1940) offers much pertinent information: "Gourds grew best on the hot shores and lowlands on leeward and southerly coast...." He continues, "Kau, Kona, Kawaihae, and Kohala were the gourd raising areas on Hawaii" (p. 211).

Also bearing on the location is William Ellis's description of Kailua: "Kailua, though healthy and populous, is destitute of fresh water" (Ellis, 1963, p. 29).

The picture becomes a little clearer. In such a dry locale the water gourd in particular would certainly assume great importance, and its personification could be nothing but a hero.

We know that the gourd was of vital importance to the early Hawaiians. Ernest S. Dodge (1978) summarizes the importance of the gourd by stating:

> A Polynesian, in the pre-European days, was probably more conscious of the gourd plant than any other human being on earth. The conditioning of the Hawaiian was particularly influenced by the presence of gourds, and countless were the manifestations of this plant on his life. He was brought up on the myth that the heavens were the top of an enormous

gourd, that the earth was the lower half, and the celestial bodies were the seeds and the pulp thereof. Throughout life he drank his water from gourd bottles, ate his food from gourd bowls, danced to the rhythm of gourd drums ... and at last, after death, his bones were perhaps cleaned and kept in an ossuary urn made of a gourd [pp. 2-3].

More pertinent information is forthcoming from Handy when he states, "The cleaning process for the bitter gourd consisted in cutting off the top and filling the gourd with sea water. The water was changed every day for ten days" (ibid., p. 210). It is interesting to note that Punia was also inside the shark for exactly ten days, during which he must have had his fair share of being washed by sea water. We know from Peter Buck that "The Hawaiians recognized a sweet gourd (hue Manalo) and a bitter gourd (hue 'awa'awa). The bitter gourd was not eaten but was made into utensils" (Buck 1964, "Food," pp. 34-35).

Again, referring to gourd cleaning, and quoting from the Kuokoa newspaper of March 24, 1922, Handy (1940) relates:

Care was taken not to let the water remain in it long lest it rot. At this time, when the water was poured out, scrapers were put in to clean it out. When all the pulp had been removed, then the cleaners were put to work.... Stones from the beach were the sand paper at that time. The cleaning was done in the evening, after eating, when one sat down to talk. As the mouth talked, the hands rubbed [p. 209].

The picture is purely speculative, of course, but what an excellent time for storytelling, appealing to both the auditory and tactile senses: the swishing of the water in the gourd as the shark dashes this way and that in the ocean; the scraping away of the innards as Punia scrapes the insides of the shark for food; the rubbing and rattling of the stones inside the gourd--a great aid to work.

In Handy (1940) we are told another story which links the gourd and the shark:

The deep sea fisherman always carried a number of

large gourds in his canoe. When he sighted a tiger
shark (niuhi) making for his canoe, he took a gourd
and threw it high out over the water, not toward
the shark, but to one side. The gourd landed in the
water with a sharp splash, and the niuhi, attracted
by this, turned from the canoe and rushed at it.
When his nose struck the gourd, it bobbed away, and
while the shark furiously attacked it, trying in vain
to get it into his mouth, the fisherman dashed for
shore [p. 211].

This paragraph is perhaps the most telling metaphor.
Punia is victorious in tricking the sharks in much the same
way as in the factual account.

At the end of the Punia legend, Punia is still inside
the belly of the beached shark when the people of the village
come down to the beach and begin to rain blows on the shark.
At this point Punia pipes up and says, "Do not hurt the man
inside" (Fornander, 1919, p. 298). This aspect of the story
is more difficult to substantiate, but we know that there were
in existence small drums made out of either coconuts or small
gourds and covered with the skin of a scaleless fish. William
Ellis (1963) mentions "a rustic little drum, formed of a calabash, beautifully stained and covered at the head with a piece
of shark skin" (p. 29). Of course, gourd drums of this
kind would probably not endure for long. There are almost
none in existence today. In Resource Units in Hawaiian Culture, Mitchell (1982) expands on the subject:

> Puniu-coconut knee drum. (Pu-container, niu-coco-
> nut) The top, or upper fourth, is removed from a
> large, polished coconut shell to form the resonance
> chamber of this drum.... The drum head, which
> tightly covers the opening, is traditionally from the
> durable skin of the kala, a scaleless fish.... Bishop
> Museum has a rare type of puniu which might be
> called a puipu since the resonance chamber is a gourd
> about the size of a coconut shell [p. 46].

The word "pepehi" used in Fornander's version may be translated as either "kill" or "beat" (Pukui, 1971, p. 299). One
could well conjecture that a personified gourd, covered by a
shark skin and being drummed upon, might indeed cry out
that, in striking the shark, the drummer should take care

not to hurt him. The remark seems much in keeping with the Hawaiian sense of humor.

Drumming and baldness are related in the Hawaiian proverb, "Ku ana ua ohule, Kani ana ka pahu." (There stood a bald head, the drum sounded.) This is translated as: "Rain follows a bald headed man" (Judd, 1930, p. 86).

In addition to the Fornander tale and the many retellings of it, another related story appears. In <u>Kona Legends</u>, Eliza Maguire tells us, "These few legends were told us when Huehue Ranch was started in 1886" (Maguire, 1966, preface). In one story, "The Catch of the Gods," we again meet our hero: "They decided to go to Puniaiki of Kohala, for he was a renowned destroyer of Akua..." (ibid., p. 35). The reference to destroyer of Akua (evil spirits) is a reference to the second part of the Punia story in Fornander. Puniaiki tells them "to call him Kalepeamoa, cock's comb on account of his bald head" (ibid., p. 36). One of the objects he takes with him to do the job is a hokea, a long gourd or calabash. So it seems that Punia is still a part of the oral tradition of the Kona coast.

At first glance the legend of Puniakaia (Fornander, 1918-1919, pp. 154-162) does not seem to be connected with the story of Punia. First, the locale is Kane'ohe, and its surroundings are wetlands noted for fishing and not as a gourd-growing area. Punia's parents are of the royal blood of Ko'olauloa and Ko'olaupoko, the names given to two districts in the area. The translation of Puniakaia given in Fornander (1918-1919) is "coveting fish, or given to fishing proclivities" (p. 154).

And yet the story has an interesting structure. The section headed "No Kaalaea" ("Relating to Kaalaea") seems not to fit with the rest of the story, as if it might be an insert, the combining of tales. In <u>Hawaiian Mythology</u>, Beckwith (1970) reminds us:

> The tendency is to be seen on the one hand of centering ... exploits about a single figure, on the other hand of a local detachment which gives rise to a district hero cycle on each island or even from district to district, hence a multiplication of trickster figures each with his own cycle of adventures, sometimes

borrowed from district to district. Most of the stories
on record are of wide distribution ... [p. 430].

Certainly there was constant communication between the islands, and a good story is, after all, a good story.

Early in the story Puniakaia is described in Fornander
(1918-1919) as "a very handsome man and had not a single
blemish from the top of his head to the bottom of his feet.
He was erect front and back, and so on the sides" (p. 154).
This might seem like a strange way of describing a person,
but perhaps not. The Hawaiians were very proud of perfection in form, especially in their chiefs.

There is a Hawaiian saying, "Haumanumanu ka ipu 'ino
ino." This is translated as "A misshapen gourd makes an
ugly container." Not only does this describe an ugly person,
but it is also used as a warning to a mother to mold the body
of her child so it will not be imperfect or ugly (Pukui, 1985,
p. 59). Body molding of children was commonly practiced in
Hawaii.

In yet another work, Pukui (1972) states:

> Infancy was the time to mold the bodies of favorite
> children.... If the baby was a chief's son, he was
> given an additional ... form of molding. This was
> the shaping of the head. The back of the head must
> be broad and rounded, rising to a rounded peak; the
> forehead should be low and sloping. Such was the
> ideal. To attain it, the infant's head was encased in
> a well-padded gourd [p. 32].

Here we have two instances of allusions to bodily perfection used in conjunction with gourds. The gourd itself
was carefully tended as it developed. Handy (1940) tells us,
"... the gourd required careful handling in every stage of
growth and preparation after picking" (p. 209).

> As the gourd grew big, a little prop or frame ...
> was made with three sticks, set so that the gourd
> hung suspended between them: this made the fruit
> symmetrical. Stones and pebbles were removed from
> beneath the gourd, and a "platform" of grass or
> leaves ... was laid out under the gourd [p. 210].

Even in the planting, care must be taken, says Handy. "It was believed that a pot bellied man should plant gourds, and that before he planted he should eat a large meal, so that his gourds would fill out like his stomach" (ibid., p. 209).

So it would seem that the perfect gourd might be described as very handsome and without a single blemish from top to bottom. It should be erect front and back, and so on the sides, as Puniakaia was described.

Puniakaia's mate Kaalaea is also described as "a very beautiful woman ... she was just like Puniakaia [very pleasant] to look upon" (Fornander, 1918-1919, p. 154). The entire section "Relating to Kaalaea" has a delightful tongue-in-cheek quality. When the canoes of the fishermen landed, "Kaalaea went up on the sand and sat down and did not go about from place to place; but just looked on as the men and women helped themselves to fish" (ibid., p. 156).

Puniakaia likes her "quiet demeanor, not at all like the other women," and his mother agrees that "they are alike in looks and behavior" (ibid.). Puniakaia tells the girl, "When we get to my mother, don't be backward but go and sit on her lap" (ibid.).

Of course the behavior of sitting on a lap to gain privilege or rights was not an uncommon human procedure in Hawaiian society. The chief Umi, for instance, claimed his kingly birthright by sitting down in the lap of his father, Liloa. Still, the proper place for a gourd bowl might also be on the lap.

In a subsequent passage, after Puniakaia has accompanied his wife to her home, the story continues: "At meal times it was customary with the brothers-in-law of Puniakaia to prepare the meal, then send for Puniakaia and make him sit on their laps while they fed him" (ibid.). This would surely be somewhat strange treatment toward a grown man.

One day Kaalaea's aunt visits and finds Puniakaia and his wife in bed. She scolds in this peculiar manner: "'Wake up, Puniakaia, and let us go crabbing.... What do you do, anyway? Just sleep, and when you get up clean your eyes and catch flies and eat?'" (ibid.).

Certainly one might feel like addressing a recalcitrant young chief, or a gourd, like this, but in either case it would be a mistake. Every living and growing thing had its own spirit which must be courteously and encouragingly addressed. One writer points out, "... the guardian spirit of the tree or bush may hear you talking about it, and will stop the flow of its vital essence ..." (Wichman, 1931, p. 40).

Puniakaia is naturally displeased by the speech and does nothing but sleep and eat for twenty more days, refusing to get up and work.

Puniakaia hears the aunt through the soft mantle that covers him and Kaalea. The Hawaiian word used is kalukalu, which is defined as either "a kind of rush or grass" or a "fine gauze-like tapa ... reserved for chiefs" (Pukui, 1971, p. 115). Such a definition would fit either of our heroes.

Handy (1940) would have cautioned the aunt on this matter:

> A gourd vine should not be planted where the shadows of people walking back and forth will strike the flower, because the gourd is the body of ... Lono, the rain god. For the same reason a gourd vine should never be touched by a menstruating woman [p. 209].

No wonder the aunt's punishment is severe. She is sentenced to death by the brothers-in-law. This might certainly have been the punishment for breaking the kapu in ancient Hawaii.

At this point in the story Puniakaia abruptly leaves his wife's home and a new episode begins with the hero's departure for his fish-attracting work on the island of Kaua'i.

Although the inferences in the Puniakaia story cannot be traced as can the elements in the Punia tale, the knowledge of the latter gives rise to speculation about the meaning of the former.

In her biography on the life of Abraham Fornander, Davis (1979) tells of how he collected these original tales:

> Fornander realized that he could not rescue them

[stories] singlehandedly, and also that some would
never be confided to a foreigner. So he hired two,
and sometimes three, intelligent and educated Hawaii
whom he paid for several years to travel throughout
the islands, taking down from the lips of elders, in
their exact words, all they could remember of the
past [p. 199].

An important phrase in this paragraph is: "some woulc
never be confided to a foreigner." There is still a tendency
among Hawaiians to let the obscure remain hidden, and unde
standably so. Much of their culture has been taken from th
Hawaiian people, and perhaps what is left may better be
guarded. On the other hand, much of the richness of Hawaiian tales is unknown to today's younger generation of
Hawaiians and, indeed, even to their parents.

Again, Davis (ibid.) suggests:

Perhaps one day, before the subtle nuances of the
language are completely lost, (if that day has not
already passed) a Hawaiian scholar will do for all th
narratives what has so far been done for only a few
They cry out for translation not only uncensored bu
done in a manner that will reveal the poetic narratio
the subtle word play and hidden meanings, the fres
beauty of metaphor, which is found in many of them
[p. 276].

Punia, and its related stories, might well be one of
them. In addition to being an excellent trickster story on
its simplest level, it is also a very complex and integrated
composition combining lore, humor, and elements of daily lif
in highly entertaining ways and providing a rich experience
for the descendents of those early tellers-of-tales.

REFERENCES

Beckwith, Martha Warren. Hawaiian Mythology. Honolulu:
University of Hawaii Press, 1970.

Buck, Peter H. (Te Rangi Hiroa). Arts and Crafts of Hawa
section: "Food." Bernice Pauahi Bishop Museum Special
Publication 45, 1957. Reprinted, Honolulu: Bishop Muse
Press, 1964.

Davis, Eleanor Harmon. Abraham Fornander: a Biography. Honolulu: University of Hawaii Press, 1979.

Dodge, Ernest S. Hawaiian and Other Polynesian Gourds. Honolulu: Topgallant, 1978.

Ellis, William. Journal of William Ellis. Honolulu: Advertiser Publishing Company, 1963.

Fornander, Alexander. Fornander's Collection of Hawaiian Antiquities and Folklore. Memoirs of the Bernice Pauahi Bishop Museum, vol. 5, pt. 1. Honolulu: Bishop Museum Press, 1918-1919.

_____. Fornander's Collection of Hawaiian Antiquities and Folklore. Memoirs of the Bernice Pauahi Bishop Museum, vol. 5, part 2. Honolulu: Bishop Museum Press, 1919.

Handy, E. S. Craighill. The Hawaiian Planter, vol. 1; His Plants, Methods and Areas of Cultivation. Bernice Pauahi Bishop Museum Bulletin 161. 1940. Reprinted, New York: Kraus, 1971.

Handy, E. S. Craighill and Craighill, Elizabeth Green. Native Planters in Old Hawaii; Their Life, Lore, and Environment. Bernice P. Bishop Museum Bulletin 233. Honolulu: Bishop Museum Press, 1972.

Judd, Henry P. Hawaiian Proverbs and Riddles. Bernice Pauahi Bishop Museum Bulletin 77. 1930. Reprinted, New York: Kraus, 1974.

Maguire, Eliza D. Kona Legends. Hilo: The Petroglyph Press, 1966.

Mitchell, Donald D. Kilolani. Resource Units in Hawaiian Culture, rev. and expanded ed. Honolulu: The Kamehameha Schools Press, 1982.

Neal, Marie C. In Gardens of Hawaii. Bernice Pauahi Bishop Museum special publication 40, rev. ed. Honolulu: Bishop Museum Press, 1965.

Pukui, Mary Kawena and Elbert, Samuel H. Hawaiian Dictionary. Honolulu: University Press of Hawaii, 1971.

Pukui, Mary Kawena. 'Olelo No'eau: Hawaiian Proverbs and Poetical Sayings. Bernice Pauahi Bishop Museum special publication 71. Honolulu: Bishop Museum Press, 1985.

Pukui, Mary Kawena, et al. Nana i ke Kumu (Look to the Source), vol. 2. Honolulu: Hui Hanai, 1972.

Pukui, Mary Kawena; Elbert, Samuel H.; and Mookini, Esther T. Place Names of Hawaii, rev. ed. Honolulu: University of Hawaii Press, 1974.

Wichman, Juliet Rice. Hawaiian Planting Traditions. Honolulu: Honolulu Star Bulletin, 1931.

BIBLIOGRAPHY

Colum, Padraic. Legends of Hawaii. New Haven: Yale University Press, 1937.

Dolch, Edward W. and Dolch, Marguerite P. Stories From Hawaii. Champaign: Garrard, 1960.

Luca, Lois. Plants of Old Hawaii. Honolulu: The Bess Press, 1982.

Mohan, Beverly. Punia and the King of the Sharks. Chicago: Follett, 1964.

Pukui, Mary Kawena, collector, and Curtis, Caroline, reteller Piloi and Other Legends of the Islands of Hawai'i. Honolulu: The Kamehameha Schools Press, 1949.

Taylor, Clarice B. Little Blond Shark. Honolulu: Tongg, 1969.

Thompson, Vivian L. Hawaiian Legends of Tricksters and Riddlers. New York: Holiday House, 1969.

Wheeler, Post. Hawaiian Wonder Tales. New York: Beechhurst Press, 1953.

PART VII:

OF THE WRITER'S AND EDITOR'S CRAFT

Victor Kelleher reflects upon the complex life of the children's author in Australia.   Charlotte Zolotow reveals the pleasures and commitments of someone who is both editor and author.

Chapter 20

WRITING FOR CHILDREN IN AUSTRALIA TODAY

Victor Kelleher

I should like to address myself to some of the problems and challenges facing any Australian who is currently writing for children. Although, inevitably, I shall make critical comments about the situation in my country, I shall not be writing only as a critic. I shall also try to give a writer's point of view which, while it may not be wholly objective, will have the merit of being wholeheartedly felt.

One of the main handicaps of being an Australian children's writer is the size of the home market. I'm not of course suggesting that the average author is overly preoccupied with the unseen audience. Many authors write largely for themselves, others attempt to forget about audiences during the actual stages of composition. Nonetheless, sooner or later writers have to glance over their shoulders at the readers hopefully waiting "out there." And when Australian writers do this, they find a total home population of only fifteen million people and a considerably smaller audience of children.

What this means, in practical terms, is that the Australian market alone cannot, except in rare cases, support the writer financially. And to anyone like me, who has to put in a full day's employment before sitting down to work on the current book, this is a very considerable factor in his writing life. There is an enormous difference between being financially

213

free to give the best hours of each day to writing, and being forced to cram one's creative life into those "free" hours following fulltime employment. Any full-time writing that falls to most of us is usually the result not of local publishing success (which rarely adds up to more than a substandard wage), but of the generosity of the Literature Board of the Australia Council which awards periodic fellowships to writers of proven success.

The smallness of our market also creates other problems. In the case of an American writer, for instance, the acceptance of a manuscript by a reputable publisher (which is one of the main hurdles any writer has to face) opens up a potential market of more than two hundred million people. For the Australian writer (and I fully appreciate that this applies to many other countries represented at this conference), that acceptance hurdle has to be jumped over again and again, because all a modest success in Australia achieves, in wider terms, is a slightly improved chance of interesting publishers overseas. In other words, we have to "crack the market," as it were, repeatedly. And this is no easy thing to do, especially in the world of publishing, which is frequently and notoriously astray in its judgments.

The results of trying repeatedly to clear this publishing hurdle are often rather bizarre. In my own case, my books have sold throughout the Commonwealth and have been successfully translated into German and Swedish; yet so far I've been unable to find a U.S. publisher. Nor is this at all unusual. When Australian writers try to reach an American audience, they are constantly knocked back on the grounds that the American market is highly specialized and idiosyncratic. Unfortunately, these same arguments seem to be largely forgotten when it comes to exporting American books to Australia. And this should not be construed as a jibe at our American hosts. It is just a fact of life and therefore has to be stated. To a lesser extent the same point could be made about the British market.

One of the claims constantly made by overseas publishers is that they are looking for "typically Australian" literature. But what is meant by this? Judging by their sales, a children's book like Walkabout (originally published, I believe, under the title, The Children) and an adult book like The Thorn Birds are widely regarded outside Australia as typically

Australian. Yet are they? Anyone exposed to discussion of
The Thorn Birds within Australia might have serious doubts
about this. As for James Vance Marshall's Walkabout, perhaps it would be better to give not my opinion, but that of
a group of my postgraduate students. They all felt that its
treatment of racial issues was oddly out of keeping with contemporary attitudes. And they were merely amused by the
book's natural history, which they regarded as something of
a travesty of outback Australia.

Of course the problem of what constitutes typically
Australian children's literature is not only faced by overseas
publishers. It is also a problem within Australia, because
like any other young country mine has been going through
something of an identity crisis for some time.

This crisis is to some extent apparent in our earlier
children's literature, in which at least two major trends can
be discerned. On the one hand, a body of work was produced
which more or less accords to traditional views of Australia.
And here I have in mind such works as Turner's Seven Little
Australians and Lindsay's The Magic Pudding. On the other
hand, there are a great many books which are distinctly
English in feel--books which are influenced as much by English conventions as by their Australian setting. Quite often,
in fact, one feels that their setting is beside the point and
that what we're dealing with is a summer holiday adventure
on the English model which just happens to be set in vaguely
foreign climes. Much as I admire the more recent work of
Patricia Wrightson, I must confess that I put even some of
her early books in this latter category. Anyone who has
been thrilled by The Nargun and the Stars or The Ice Is
Coming should not turn to early works like The Bunyip Hole
expecting to discover the same peculiarly Australian ethos.
For what The Bunyip Hole gives us, above all, is a Ransome-
type adventure which, for me at any rate, is only incidentally
Australian.

For previous generations of Australians, then, there
have been at least two views of our society, one quite distinctly "English," the other quite uniquely itself. And this is
not to suggest that the English view is somehow wrong or a
falsehood. Australia, traditionally, has been both a highly
individual place (as our idiosyncratic development of the English
language should make clear) and also a place quite English in

its orientation. How, precisely, these two disparate elements mixed or co-existed is a problem--a problem inherent in the writing process and mirrored in the very different kinds of children's books which Australians produced.

Indeed, this is still a problem facing the Australian writer, but one which has been made far more complex by postwar developments.

For instance, recent years have seen a strong reaction against what we term cultural cringe: the notion that overseas ideas and attitudes (particularly English ones) are automatically superior to our own. But even as we have begun abandoning our supposed English-ness, we have simultaneously been bringing into question traditional notions of what constitutes our uniquely Australian culture. In particular, we have been exposing as myths (in the worst sense) what formerly we regarded as truths. Take the myth of the bush as an example. For a long time now, many Australian and overseas readers have assumed that Australian children's books will be set either in the bush or in small country towns. Yet the fact is (and it has been a fact for many, many years), most Australian kids don't live anywhere near the bush. We are one of the most urbanized societies on earth. Something like 80 percent of our population is concentrated in about five cities. Most of Australia is so barren that it is barely populated at all; and the coastal strip, which can be farmed, is hardly teeming with people. In addition, even the small portion of our population which does live in the bush is not secure in its way of life. As a recent nationwide drought sadly demonstrated, living in the country, for many, can last only as long as good seasonal rain.

Undeniable as these facts may be, it would be well-nigh impossible to derive them from a survey of either children's or adult Australian literature over the past fifty years. Again and again writers have clung to the myth of the bush as the heartland of Australia rather than mirroring the larger truths of our society.

Nor is the myth of the bush an isolated example. The plight of Aboriginals, in both the past and the present, is also ignored by much Australian writing of yesteryear. Writers haven't so much lied about Aboriginals as evaded the issue. Again a single example must suffice. Nan Chauncy, in her

children's novel, They Found a Cave, raises the question of
what happened to the Aboriginals in Tasmania. The closest
we get to the truth is when one of the children informs the
others that the Aboriginals simply died out. The truth is
far more grisly: all full-blood Aboriginals were ruthlessly
wiped out by white settlers. Let me emphasize at this point
that I'm not simply "having a go" at Nan Chauncy, a writer
whom in many respects I admire. What she does in this book
is reflect the attitudes of her society which preferred until
recently to cling to a convenient myth rather than tell children
the plain and undeniable truth.

Of course Australia is not alone in clinging to myths.
As we all know, American society in the twentieth century
has been bedeviled by notions of the American Dream, an
elusive and potentially destructive myth which continues to
claim its share of tragic victims--and the recent death of
Richard Brautigan comes immediately to mind. In Australia,
however, the drive to expose our myths is much more recent
and therefore much more of a pressing issue in the life of a
contemporary writer. For the exposure of myths is synonymous
with the exposure of a set of unacknowledged values. To
bring into question our view of ourselves is equally to bring
into question those values by which we have lived.

It is this questioning process which, in my opinion, has
tended to dim the reputations of some of our more established
writers. As an example, take Ivan Southall, a man who has
enjoyed enormous success at home and abroad. His work is
still what it has always been--highly original and linguistical-
ly skillful. So why the relative loss of popularity? The answer, I think, lies in the image of Australia which his books
project. For me, his attitudes toward ideas of class, sexual
role-playing, leadership, Christian ethics, all point towards
the Australia of the late thirties. I simply don't find the
modern world (not my modern world, anyway) depicted in
most of his books. This, of course, is not to damn his work.
It is, for me, a way of placing his novels in a context which
will make sense of them. After all, he is a child of the thirties,
and like many children's writers he turns instinctively and un-
erringly to the world of his own childhood. Were more Australian reviewers to take this into consideration, I fancy he
would receive kinder reviews within Australia.

But to return to the central issue, the fact remains that

for many of our contemporary writers, Australia is a confusing place, a place in which myths about ourselves and our often superficial value systems are being given close scrutiny.

One of the factors which precipitated this self-analysis was the massive immigration program implemented in Australia shortly after the war. The thousands upon thousands of Greeks, Italians, UK citizens, Lebanese, Vietnamese, etc., who have made Australia their home have had an almost immeasurable effect upon our society. Naturally, Australia has changed these immigrants, but they in turn have changed Australia. Our food, our homes, our way of living, our values, have all been radically altered. Whether we like it or not, we are now the second most multi-cultural society on earth.

It must be pointed out, however, that being a multi-cultural society is not the same as acting like one. To see and think of ourselves in multi-cultural terms is something which many Australians find difficult. And again this difficulty impacts upon the writer.

For one thing, many overseas publishers are interested only in books which recapture older, surer, more easily recognizable images of Australia--e.g., blond-haired, sun-tanned kids who pursue their adventures in an ever-sunny, ever-summery, dusty Aussie outback. Perhaps I exaggerate, but still the tendency is there. It is a tendency even among some Australian publishers. As I've discovered from talking to other Australian writers, I'm not the only author who has seen an editor visibly wince on discovering that my next novel will have a non-Australian setting.

In fairness to writers and editors alike, it is extraordinarily difficult to write about the "real" Australia when there are so many "real" Australias to choose from. Were I, for example, to try to write a book which somehow represents the life of the inner-city suburb of Sydney where I live, I'd be completely stumped. The old Victorian terraced houses in my immediate vicinity are inhabited by a bewildering mixture of people, ranging from old Aussie diggers at one extreme to young trendies at the other. If I walk a mile to the south of my house, I find myself in an area which is so Italian that many of the shops don't include any English on their hoardings; while a similar walk to the north takes me into Chinatown

Only slightly longer walks bring me into contact with predominantly Vietnamese, Greek, and Turkish communities--communities which, through their Australian-born children, are having an ever-growing influence on the country at large.

This is hardly the popular, Paul Hogan-type image of Australia which is accepted abroad. Indeed, it is an image from which many Australians turn their eyes. Yet it is a reality, far more of a reality, I would contend, than the spurious image of a predominantly Anglo-Saxon rural community.

Fortunately, some of our writers have addressed themselves to this newer, more bewildering Australia and have tried to make fictional sense of it. Probably the best known amongst such writers is Patricia Wrightson. Abandoning unacceptable myths about her own people and her own land, she has reverted to older, more enduring myths. Rejecting European folklore because it is ludicrously out of place in the great southern land, she has replaced it with Aboriginal folklore which is not only endemic to Australia, but has a lineage so old that it leaves most of us breathless. This rejecting process has not been an academic exercise on her part; it is something that justice demands of her. Anyone who reads The Nargun and the Stars knows immediately that the rich heritage of Aboriginal legend and its close identification with the land are very real and very dear to her. Equally, she has turned from European ideas of ownership and materialism and tried to recreate, in her fiction, what it feels like to belong to that wider spiritual community which lies at the core of traditional Aboriginal culture.

Other writers have discovered their Australia, not by scrutinizing the very distant past, but by grappling with the growing pluralism of Australian life--a pluralism which probably had its inception in the gold rush days of the 1850s. David Martin, a much underrated author, has written a fine series of books in which he highlights the role of the Chinese, the Sikhs, and the Aboriginals in Australia's social, political, and historical life. He has also made repeated assaults on the myth that white Australia is essentially a comfortable, lower-middle-class society. In books like The Chinese Boy, The Man in the Red Turban, Hughie, and The Cabby's Daughter, he gives children a sympathetic glimpse of the grinding poverty and hardship, as well as the violence and racism, which form part of our immediate history.

As a new Australian, I need hardly add that such fictional attempts at redefinition are dear to my heart, though in my own case I face a further problem. As with many new Australians, I brought more with me to Australia than a suitcase. I also carried with me a vast store of memories and experiences of my years in Africa and Europe. When, some nine or ten years ago, I started to write both adult and children's novels, it was that weight of memory and experience which I had to unload first. The result was a series of books which, on the face of it, were most un-Australian--European-type fantasies and realistic novels and stories set in Africa and England. The response of overseas publishers was one of bewilderment. How could they "sell" me when I didn't fit into any category of Australian writer? Many Australian publishers were equally bewildered. Didn't I perhaps fit in overseas? Where I belonged was only part of the problem. My books, or so some would have me believe, didn't rightly belong anywhere. Yet when we look at the facts of Australian society, my predicament is hardly unique. Many Australians share my kind of background. Australia, like Israel, contains numbers of people whose spiritual selves are scattered halfway across the globe. And to this extent at least I've always contended that my books are Australian in a very true sense, in that they mirror that diversity of experience which is an essential feature of any multi-cultural society.

While this is a straightforward truth about our lives that many Australians have come to accept, there are still, sadly, those who reject it. My earliest books, for instance, were not entered for any literary awards, presumably because it was assumed that either the books or the author or both were self-evidently non-Australian. And even after I had won the Australian Children's Book of the Year Award with Master of the Grove, I found that reviewers persisted in referring to me as an English writer, notwithstanding the fact that I had made a permanent departure from England more than thirty years ago. I'm happy to say now that at long last, after much complaining and bludgeoning, nearly all reviewers (though not, alas, all editors) accept and assert the Australian status of my fiction.

Thus far, and then only cursorily, I have dealt with the

problems attendant upon being a writer in Australia. But
over and above what I would call such regional problems,
Australian children's writers also have to face the widespread
prejudices and misconceptions which plague children's fiction
at every level and have to be coped with by authors throughout the world. All I can do here is refer, more or less in
passing, to what I consider some of the worst of these prejudices and misconceptions.

One of the first differences I discovered between the
world of adult fiction and the world of children's fiction is
that the latter is strewn with well-meaning adults who possess
a fixed image of the child and who use this image to modify
or temper any judgments they make about children's literature.
When, for example, I am interviewed about my adult work, I
am rarely asked how I feel about adults, or whether or not
I like people as such, or whether I think my books are moral-
ly acceptable to my audience. By contrast, when I am interviewed about my children's work, these and associated questions continually arise. Do I like children? Do I spend time
with children? What do I like about children? What do I
dislike about them? Do I feel any moral responsibility to my
audience? And so forth. Apart from anything else, such
questions demonstrate an astonishing insensitivity to the variousness of children. They are only one step removed from
the old racist and gender-based questions: How do you feel
about Black people? How do you feel about Asians? What is
your opinion of women? The classic answer, of course, is:
Which particular Black people/Asians/women do you have in
mind? And much the same answer applies to misplaced questions about kids. There is no magic formula or sweeping
generalization which encompasses all children.

Most of us, I fancy, know this well enough. Nevertheless, the questions drone on. And even when they are not
put explicitly, they are often implicit to any discussion of
children's fiction. What I find so disturbing about them is
that they imply a form of censorship. I often suspect that
many kids' books, including my own, are not discussed for
what they are but rather are measured against what they
should be. And that "should," that hidden imperative, is
too frequently a corollary of fixed modes of thought; i.e.,
given the specific needs or nature of the young audience,
children's books, if they are to be significant, must do this
or that.

The deadening effect of this approach (as prevalent among editors as among teachers, librarians, and reviewers) need hardly be emphasized. At its worst, it must tend to produce either stereotypes or veiled forms of moral tales for the young. What it overlooks is that good work, in any area of fiction, is seldom dependent upon the writer's views of his or her audience. Thus Shakespeare gives every evidence of holding an abysmally low opinion of humanity when writing plays like Macbeth, Twelfth Night, Troilus and Cressida, and Timon of Athens. Later in life, when writing, say A Winter's Tale, he gives equally clear evidence of having forgiven humanity its heinous faults and foibles. Yet this gentler view doesn't necessarily make A Winter's Tale a better or more watchable play than Macbeth. It simply makes it different. And it is this difference, this variousness (which finds an unmistakable parallel in the larger audience of any artistic production), which we must guard as jealously in children's fiction as in any other area of the arts. Finally, what I think of kids, or how I visualize them, isn't in itself of any great importance. What matters is the kind of fiction I write and whether it produces any meaningful response in my youthful audience.

And by "meaningful response" I don't mean just popularity. Good fiction is not necessarily popular. Which brings us to another widely held misconception about kids' books: namely, that in order to be good, they must have a wide appeal. It is perhaps understandable (though not excusable) that editors often confuse these two ideas. Popular books, after all, pay editors' salaries. What is more alarming is the extent to which this same confusion flourishes among libraria Some years ago, for instance, I discovered a group of Willian Mayne's books on the reject/for sale shelf in a local library. They were in good condition and had been acquired comparatively recently, and so I asked the librarian why they were being sold off. The kids never look at them, I was told. They were just cluttering up the shelves. I didn't argue at the time--I was only too pleased to acquire some 20¢ copies of William Mayne's books. I wasn't even shocked, mainly because it's an attitude which is all too prevalent. Many of my graduate students have exhibited the selfsame attitude. "Th kids can't bear it" is frequently used to justify their judgme of a particular children's text. Similarly, reviewers often us the same criterion, even when it is grotesquely out of place. Thus, several years ago, when a book of mine won a nationa

award, many reviewers praised the judges for at last choosing
a novel which was popular among young readers. Now while
it was gratifying for me to see that stated in print, it was
also oddly distressing, because the particular award (as everyone involved in children's books knew full well) was given not
for popularity, but for literary merit. Many reviewers over-
looked this important point, not because they were forgetful
or stupid, but because the kind of confusion I am referring
to is an indelible feature of children's literature.

It does not flourish nearly so well in the realm of adult
fiction. I shouldn't imagine that many people assume that the
vast popularity of, say, Barbara Cartland, is in itself an in-
diction of the worth of her books. Conversely, the fact that,
say, Milton's Paradise Lost is not available at airline terminals
is in no sense a proof of its non-relevance. Adult publishers
and readers, for the most part, make a simple distinction between popularity and worth.

This is not to say that popular kids' books needn't be
good. In America, S. E. Hinton, in fine novels like Rumble
Fish, has shown us how to produce work whose mass appeal
is balanced only by its value, while in Australia, Colin Thiele
has performed the same enviable trick.

Nor am I inferring that we should force onto young
readers a host of books which they may find boring and then
justify our action on the grounds that such books are "good
for the young." All I'm saying is that everyone involved in
children's literature, including the children themselves, should
be far more aware that a healthy literary scene must include
not only novels which are widely read, but also those which
appeal to only a minority taste. Books like Alan Garner's
Red Shift may well be too difficult for the majority of young
readers (and perhaps even for most adult readers), but that
does not detract from their value. I for one find Red Shift
an astonishing novel and would consider children's fiction very
much poorer if it ceased to exist. Books of that caliber are
more than justified if only a tiny minority of young people
derive pleasure or profit from them.

While I'm talking about qualitative judgments, I should
perhaps also complain of some misconceptions about types of
children's fiction. For instance, in Commonwealth countries
at least, there is a whole body of opinion which automatically

equates fantasy with poor or escapist fiction. Over the year
I have discovered from numerous reviewers that fantasy is a
very poor horse for a serious writer to ride; that it can do
little more than divert us; that it is a literary cliché we
would be better off without; that an interest in fantasy is,
alas, a stage which some children (especially boys!) have to
go through; that, ho-hum, here we have another alternate
fantasy world for those who feel they're not yet ready to
grapple with the real world; and so on.

Similar "put-down" attitudes are often adopted for science fiction writing. In the minds of some it is inconceivable
that a science fiction novel can be anything more than a
"good read," while in English journals and newspapers especially, I have detected a distinct antipathy to any children
novel which falls within the category of fast-moving adventure
"Another 'Boy's Own' adventure story" is a not uncommon
critical reaction.

The absurdity of this type of blanket response can
hardly be too strongly emphasized. In the case of fantasy,
in particular, it makes no sense at all. Fantasy, arguably,
is the oldest of all literary modes and includes the work of
Homer, Chaucer, Shakespeare, Milton--and so I could go on.
Of course fantasy, like any literary mode, can be used to produce worthless books. But as Chaucer demonstrated so con-
vincingly, any literary mode can also be employed in the pro
duction of good work. To mention Barbara Cartland once
again, any dissatisfaction we may feel with her novels should
not taint our attitude to the romance as such. Jane Austen
we might recall, also dabbled a little in the business of writing fictional romances.

I have mentioned adult writers here with a purpose,
because the point I'm making affects adult and children's
literature alike. Both suffer from this order of prejudice
from critics who believe that a book can be dismissed simply
by placing it in a particular category. This is more than jus
lazy or slipshod thinking--more, even, than just bigotry. It
also bespeaks an implicit belief in a mainstream culture, a be
lief that certain perspectives on life are, per se, correct, an
that others are integrally inadequate. Many middle-class Vic
torians, as we all know, clung long and valiantly to such an
attitude. God, they were inclined to believe, was in His
heaven and all was right with the world. Given that view,

it was reasonable to assume that there was a correct, Trol-
lopean approach even to the writing of novels.

One hundred years later we may not be much wiser,
but we should be able to see a little more clearly--clearly
enough, anyway, to perceive that all literary modes are highly
artificial, that they can all be used either as escapist tools
or as a means of examining the world we all inhabit.

Such observations, one might imagine, are so obvious
as almost to be truisms. Yet unfortunately that is not the
case. If you doubt me, go into any large bookstore, go to
the science fiction shelves, and try to find the following works:
Orwell's 1984; Huxley's Brave New World; Lessing's Briefing
for a Descent into Hell; Golding's The Inheritors; and Hoban's
Riddley Walker. Unless I'm very much mistaken, you won't
find them among the science fiction, even though they are all,
self-evidently, books written in that mode. You'll find them
instead among the supposedly mainstream novels. You see,
they've made it: they've all been taken seriously as works of
literature. Which means that for many people, including
many serious-minded academics, they no longer have any
place on the science fiction shelves.

Some may see this relocation process as merely an act
of convenience. I must confess that for me it has a more sin-
ister undertone. Consider how much easier it is to rubbish
science fiction if its ranks have already been denuded of the
most outstanding works.

The same point can be applied to Gothic fiction. Like
many students I was taught that the Gothic novel was a
minor form that flourished mainly in the nineteenth century.
What no one taught me, what I had to discover for myself,
is that Wuthering Heights is a marvellous example of what
can be done with the Gothic novel. That silence again!

Or take the wealth of fantasy writing which enriches
our culture. Throughout the whole of my undergraduate
days nobody mentioned to me the very obvious fact that
Shakespeare chose fantasy as the vehicle of his last great
phase. Yet many of those same academics, who remained so
obdurately silent on that issue, are quite prepared to dismiss Tolkien slightingly as mere fantasy. I, too, am not a
total devotee of Tolkien, but not because of the fantastic

element in his books. What disappoints me about his work is
the looseness and wordiness to which his language is too
often prone. But that is the kind of criticism one can level
at any fiction.

Again I must apologize for taking my examples mainly
from the adult ranks. I've done so because (if I can direct
your attention to your local bookstore once again) the distinction I'm making is more clearly illustrated in the way the
shelves devoted to adult fiction are arranged. Children's
fiction is usually all lumped together. On a single bank of
shelves we might well discover the science fiction of John
Christopher, the social realism of Vera and Bill Cleaver, the
disaster novels of Ivan Southall, the fantasy of C. S. Lewis,
the quasi-religious adventures of Peter Dickinson, or the up-
to-the-minute teenage dramas of Paul Zindel. On the face of
it, children's fiction enjoys a democracy of spirit denied to its
adult counterpart. But don't be fooled, dear reader! Kids'
books are crammed together because in the minds of many
they constitute no more than a minor sub-form, an insignificant branch of the great body of literature. This is driven
home to me whenever my academic colleagues casually enquire
whether I've written any "kiddies' stories" lately. Or as one
of my close colleagues so aptly put it: "Is your next novel a
real book or for children?"

Yet insofar as children's literature is taken seriously,
my overall complaint still holds. I would go so far as to say
that the immediate readiness of many adult readers to dismiss
fantasy or to laud the God-given merits of psychological realis
is even more apparent when children's books are the point at
issue. Why am I so convinced of this? Because I read my
fair share of reviews. And an inability to make simple distinctions is just one of the myriad criticisms that can be lev-
elled at much (though of course not all) of the reviewing of
children's books.

Having raised the specter of such reviewing, I can
hardly pass it by. For of all the many burdens that the
children's writer (and any serious reader of children's fiction)
must labor under, none surely is quite so irksome and depressing as the paucity and lowly standard of reviewing. In
Australia many children's books get no notice whatsoever in
major newspapers or journals. When they are mentioned, it
is more often than not in a group showing in which each book

enjoys no more than a brief paragraph.   And even when the
reviews are longer (as in educational or library journals),
the writer is not much better off, because all too often the
standard of reviewing is appalling.   That rigor of mind, which
we at least look for in adult reviewing, is seldom applied to
kids' books.   Given that many reviewers in Australia can
barely rise above retelling the story of a novel (usually badly
and sometimes by lifting it straight from the blurb), it is no
wonder that when it comes to making judgments, many of them
casually dismiss any type of fiction they happen not to care
for or fault books without giving a single example of what they
consider weak or wrong with them.

It must be conceded that writers have always complained
about their reviewers.   I recall reading one of Joseph Conrad's letters in which he cries out in desperation to a friend,
on the subject of reviewers, "Who are these people?   Where
do they come from?"   But how much worse off is the children's
writer or the children's librarian who, in seeking a critical
assessment of any work, stands a more than even chance of
encountering either silence or a standard of discussion that
wouldn't merit a pass mark at first-year college level.

In such a dimly lit critical atmosphere, it is hardly sur-
prising that prejudices, bigotries, and misconceptions should
flourish as they do.   And I assure you that they do flourish.
Even as our kids are increasingly exposed to gratuitous violence and the glorification of war on children's TV programs,
so editors and reviewers are insisting that the intelligent
treatment of such subject matter is not suitable for children's
books.   What I would term a "cute" treatment of teenage
problems is acceptable, as is a close examination of strained
interpersonal relationships.   But a glimpse of the darker,
more frightening side of an ever more violent society sends
lots of editors and reviewers running in panic.   For many of
those involved in children's literature, the unwritten rule is,
don't be pessimistic.   Don't present certain disturbing aspects
of reality because they may prove to be depressing.   And for
this reason the young person's novel is for the most part
still afflicted by a bad case of late-Romanticism, a kind of
let's-fiddle-while-Rome-burns mentality.

It must also be conceded that children's literature is
not alone in this regard.   The adult novel is similarly afflicted.
For although the adult book world tolerates and even welcomes

a great deal of sex and violence, it gives short shrift to
writers who allow such violence to darken their viewpoint
and to lead them to a gloomy vision of the world. The watch-
word is, "celebrate." Criticize human beings, by all means;
go ahead and present their less lovely side; but ultimately,
continue to celebrate them.

It was, I suspect, William Golding's obdurate refusal
to wallow in such celebration which led to the widespread out-
cry at his winning the Nobel Prize. His skills, his output,
his intellectuality, were attacked on the flimsiest of grounds.
Yet what really irked his critics, I feel sure, was his unwillin-
ness to glorify humanity at large. He doesn't give evidence
of hating human beings in the manner of Swift--rather he dis-
approves of facets of their basic nature. And he shows us
why, quite truthfully, in book after book.

Critical opposition to writers' telling us unpalatable
truths is not something new. It will be recalled that Dr.
Johnson criticized Shakespeare for overstepping the bounds
of propriety. He felt that the death of Desdemona in Othello
and the putting out of Gloucester's eyes in King Lear go too
far: they are too painful to behold. I applaud Dr. Johnson's
unfailing compassion; but for all his great genius, I question
his judgment. The scenes he refers to are deeply disturbing;
the violence perpetrated there is close to unforgivable and
fills us with profound dismay. But if I can invoke Aristotle
briefly, these scenes are also cathartic: the terrible truths
Shakespeare reveals about human beings purge away our il-
lusions and leave us, if not uplifted, at least clear-eyed. We
emerge from Othello not elated, not ready to celebrate the human spirit, but sane, and better able to cope with a less than
perfect world.

So why should we wish on our children anything less?
If the book is to counter the gratuitous violence of TV, it
must meet this problem head on and give to this undeniable
area of our lives the kind of intelligent treatment that so
many television producers seem incapable of. I'm glad to
say there are such children's writers around. S. E. Hinton
and John Christopher are two novelists who don't flinch from
presenting kids with some very disturbing ideas about our
world and about human beings in general. I can't help thinking, however, that these authors are the exceptions rather
than the rule. Their writings run counter to the critical

climate which, as I see it, suffers from the same faded romanticism that afflicts many children's books. And this is worrying. For if Matthew Arnold is right--if we require a sound critical climate in order to produce great fiction--then children's fiction has an uncertain future despite the plethora of self-congratulation that presently characterizes the industry. Certainly a healthy critical climate is much more likely to attract, and to retain, the very best writers. A children's book, after all, requires just as much effort to write as an adult book. So why bother to make that effort if there is such a large possibility of its going unappreciated or of its being misunderstood?

Now I'm fully aware that I've been indulging in what my grandmother would have called a good old moan. Moreover, in spite of my disclaimer at the start of this paper, I've been tending to speak more as a critic than as a writer. (Though I'm sure you'd agree that the creative and the critical selves can never really function separately.) It's only fair, therefore, that I should round out this paper by attempting to right the balance somewhat by revealing some of my responses, as writer, to the larger world of children's literature.

How, for instance, do I survive in that world? Why do I choose to remain a part of it? Why did I enter it in the first place?

It must be said at the outset that when I came to write my first children's book I had no idea of what I was letting myself in for. I had little or no conception of the young reading public, and I knew absolutely nothing about children's books. Because of my lower-working-class upbringing in southeast London, I didn't read at all as a child. My only contact with children's stories came through comics and through hearing traditional tales in the classroom. And when I did start reading in my mid-teens, I'd already grown beyond the stage (or so I thought) of wanting to read even basic texts like Treasure Island and Wind in the Willows. I emerged into adulthood, then, completely ignorant of a tradition that many children know intimately.

So when I sat down to write my first children's book, some eight or nine years ago, I came rather as a lamb to the slaughter. I wasn't even drawn to the task by later catch-up reading. It was conversations with my ten-year-old son, and

listening to his complaints about what he was reading, which
first attracted me. Basically, he complained about two things:
the failure of so many books to sustain interest or suspense,
and/or their failure to resolve situations satisfactorily. Well
insulated by my own ignorance, I thought to myself: surely
I could write a novel for young people which sustained interest and brought about a satisfactory resolution!

And so I tried, only to run into the first major problem:
what to write about. Working on the assumption that I'd
only ever known one child very well--a boy called Victor
Kelleher who'd grown up in London nearly forty years earlier--
I did something I've continued to do ever since: I locked myself away in my study and tried to re-remember, as it were,
the kinds of things which excited and interested that same
young boy. I won't say I became him again. In certain respects that's a nonsense. I'm an adult, he's a child, and a
very real gulf will always remain between us. But I did manage to dredge up some of the images that moved and inspired
him; and even more important, I did recapture the sense of
magic, of potency, that once clung to those images. Even
now, many books later, I still subject any prospective ideas
or themes or situations to that same re-remembering process.
I still sit down alone with them for some time to test them
out, to see if they stir in me that sense of youthful excitement which was once so natural and immediate.

I tell you this not in order to lay bare the processes
by which I work, but in order to indicate why I was so surprised and disconcerted when I later discovered the sorts of
critical assumption that infuse the world of children's books.
I'd be the first to admit that I was highly naïve. (To discover an appropriate length for a children's novel, for instance, I had to do spot checks on novels in the children's
section of the local library.) Yet the subsequent fate of that
first book, Forbidden Paths of Thual, has shown that my in-
stincts were not wholly astray. To write a reasonably successful children's novel, it was not necessary to have a clear-
cut vision of what children are like or to work from a theory
of the child's reading needs. The then current attitudes
toward fantasy and the adventure story were equally beside
the point. In spite of my ignorance, I did at least one thing
correctly. Like any serious author, I wrote directly from my
own experience, without regard to the supposed needs or re-
quirements of the marketplace. As a child I was fascinated

by forests, so I wrote about a great forest called Thual. As both child and adult, I've been obsessed with the idea of the journey, so I wrote a book about a long and hazardous journey. And to my amazement, I found that kids forty years on responded to these ideas and images much as I had done.

Naturally my naiveté couldn't survive for long. Inevitably, I had to enter Blake's world of experience. I did so in two quite distinct stages.

The first and more productive of these stages occurred during the actual writing of Forbidden Paths. To finish that book to my own satisfaction, I had to learn lots of things about myself as a writer and about writing for children generally. Here are some of those lessons:

1. That if a fantasy is not to be escapist, it must engage genuine social and moral dilemmas, albeit in a symbolic form.

2. That the story of a journey is not in itself significant unless that journey becomes a quest. But how is this transformation from journey to quest achieved? Only through a series of conflicts which force upon the hero or heroine a reassessment of everything he or she formerly believed in.

3. That I couldn't turn to children's books for light relief. The same drive which inspires my adult work--namely, the need to create a subtle and complex sub-text--also had to be present in my children's work if it was to be interesting and challenging to me. But how could I marry a complex, deeper pattern of meaning to a fast-moving, much simpler surface story? There's no glib answer to that. It has to be done, that's all. And it parallels, in some respects, the difficulty of somehow writing for my childhood self while at the same time retaining my adult sensibility. (To some extent, it is this order of difficulty which both fascinates me and keeps me writing for children.)

4. That story, conceived as an "and then ... and then" process, is about as interesting as a box of tintacks. Story, if it is to be fulfilling, must carry a burden of meaning. As with fairy tales, it must add up to something worthwhile even in the absence of clear characterization and setting.

5. That action, similarly, must be taken far beyond the level of the traditional "Boy's Own" adventure yarn. At its best (reviewers please note), the page-by-page action must be an essential aspect of story. It, too, must carry a symbolic weight of meaning. Any details that fail to do this should be dropped.

6. That a children's book doesn't have to be uplifting, educational, optimistic, or anything else. It must answer to its own internal logic. If the situation depicted is basically sad, then sad it must be; if chastening, then it must chasten; if glad, then it must gladden. And if (horror of horrors!) it is not conducive to the celebration of the maturing, growing up process, then that is how it must be. In children's novels as in adult fiction, consistency is all. For consistency, in large measure, is what transforms a fiction into a strange form of truth.

I could, if I tried, go on with this list, but I hope I've said enough to make it plain that the business of writing for children is for me an immensely personal as well as challenging task. It not only engages me professionally, testing my skills as a writer, it also forces me to reassess both myself as adult and myself as the child who fathered that adult. Above all, it puts me in a position where I owe allegiance to two masters: the serious writer who seeks to create significant patterns of meaning, and the remembered child who craved excitement, adventure, action.

I don't want to give the impression that I'm totally shackled to that child. Like many writers in my situation, I try to get out into schools to meet and talk to young people. I derive ideas from a host of adult experiences--from my dreams, from images that come to me out of the blue, conversations, arguments, and so on. And also I like to experiment with different kinds of books. From my early fantasy novels, in which I deliberately blended elements of the horror story or of the thriller or of the traditional adventure, I have moved on to novels like Papio, which is a present-day drama set in Africa; The Green Piper, which is set in Europe and is a modern retelling and reinterpretation of the Pied Piper myth; and Taronga, which affords a futuristic glimpse of Australia. Yet throughout all these experiments, my remembered childhood response remains a major touchstone. The waters may change, but the compass remains the same.

But this brings me to the second stage of my education: my entrance into the world of publishers, reviewers, librarians, and real live kids who tell me precisely what they think of my books. I won't say I haven't found aspects of that world exhilarating and informative. As I have tried to indicate, however, some of the current attitudes have both disappointed and frustrated me. I would go further and say that they are quite at variance with what I am seeking to achieve as a writer. In fact, the whole of this paper (its major thrust, anyway) can be seen as an illustration of the conflict which, in my view, exists between many writers and the world of children's books.

There's nothing new in such an assertion. Writing, in essence, is a revolutionary activity. It always has been. Didn't Dickens and Thackeray inveigh against their society on every conceivable issue? Didn't Melville somewhere describe Moby Dick as a very wicked book? Didn't Conrad, in one of his most famous prefaces, claim that his task above all was to make us see things as they really are? Didn't novelists as diverse as Faulkner and Lawrence emphasize the discomfiture which is invariably associated with good fiction?

And again, why should children's fiction be essentially different? As with the rest of us, kids like (if that is the right word) being frightened by horror stories. They enjoy being made to laugh. They respond well to being challenged and disturbed. They even share that strange human need to be hurt and distressed by visions of what is undeniably out there in the world. To cry hurtful and bitter tears is as much a part of growing up as are laughter and blue skies.

I'd be the last person to assert that my own fiction achieves all of these ends. I'm quite sure, though, that many overprotective and closed attitudes within the current critical climate are inimical to the child's achieving a fullness of experience through reading fiction. I dream of waking up one day and discovering a society full of editors and reviewers who don't claim to know what kids are really like; who don't claim to know what the market can really bear; or to know that we're living through a renaissance period of children's literature; or to know what kids need or enjoy. Of course, were that to happen, were I to awake to such a sunrise, writers would have to lift their game as well. And that's another story. Too long a story for me to pursue here.

I see I've moved far from the specific problems associated with writing in Australia today. Much of this paper has dealt with the perennial and universal problems, faced by all authors, of creating fictions that will explore, mirror, and challenge the experience of a diverse, not always friendly, not always well-informed or receptive audience. Given the nature of this conference, I feel I need make no apology for that shift in emphasis. Today, more than ever before, I'm sure that the Australian writer's main tasks and difficulties are not so very different from everyone else's.

CHILDREN'S BOOKS MENTIONED

Chauncey, Nan. They Found a Cave. London: Oxford Univ. Press, 1958.

Garner, Alan. The Red Shift. New York: Macmillan, 1973.

Grahame, Kenneth. The Wind in the Willows. (Various eds. in various countries).

Hinton, S. E. Rumble Fish. New York: Delacorte, 1975.

Kelleher, Victor. Forbidden Paths of Thual. London: Kestrel, 1982.

_____. The Green Piper. London: Viking/Kestrel, 1984.

_____. Master of the Grove. London: Kestrel, 1982.

_____. Papio. London: Kestrel, 1984.

_____. Taronga. Ringwood, Victoria: Viking, 1986.

Lindsay, Norman. The Magic Pudding; Being the Adventures of Bunyip and His Friends, Bill Barnacle and Sam Sawnoff. Sydney: Angus and Robertson, 1918.

Marshall, James Vance. Walkabout (orig. pub. as The Childre London: Puffin, 1959.

Martin, David. The Cabby's Daughter. Hornsby, New South Wales: Hodder & Stoughton, in assoc. with Brockhampton Press, 1974.

_____. The Chinese Boy. Hornsby, New South Wales: Hodder & Stoughton, in assoc. with Brockhampton Press, 1973.

_____. Hughie. Melbourne: Thomas Nelson, 1971.

_____. The Man in the Red Turban. Hawthorn, Australia: Century Hutchinson, 1978.

Stevenson, Robert Louis. Treasure Island. (various eds. in various countries).

Turner, Ethel Sybil. Seven Little Australians. Sydney and New York: Landsdowne, 1983.

Wrightson, Patricia. The Bunyip Hole. London: Hutchinson, 1983.

_____. The Ice Is Coming. New York: Atheneum, 1976. (A Margaret McElderry Book).

_____. The Nargun and the Stars. New York: Atheneum, 1974 (A Margaret McElderry Book).

_____. They Found a Cave. London: Oxford Univ. Press, 1958.

Chapter 21

PASSION IN PUBLISHING

Charlotte Zolotow

As the time for this conference neared I was still not sure what, of all the things there are to talk and write about in this extraordinary world of books for the young, would be the one this conference wanted to hear. In answer to my frantic letter, Joan Blumenstein replied: "How about the way in which you discern the warmth and quality of an author and help develop the manuscript into the finished, coherent, telling, and sensitive book that is delivered into the hands of the child?"

Fine, I thought, I can do that. Then she went on: "You are a writer yourself and know fully well the other side, so would you touch, too, on how the author feels about delivering her work into the hands of an editor and publisher? Our attendees would want you to express yourself as an author as well."

So I will try to write a bit about myself as a writer, too. But being an author and being an editor are opposite ends of the pole. Being an editor means shutting out your personal opinions, emotions and preferences, it means being completely receptive to the opinions, emotions and preferences of someone else. Being an author means shutting out all external voices and listening to your internal voice, feelings, responses. One can't do both at the same time!

I'll open then with the editorial side of my life. But please understand I am speaking only for my own philosophy of publishing and writing. All editors and writers have different ways of working, different visions of what writing and publishing are about. After forty-eight years of experience at Harpers, I have reached very personal conclusions. Many have shifted through the years, much the way all my theories about bringing up children changed when I had children to bring up. But my original love for publishing, though it has altered, has not abated, any more than love for children abates when your theories on how to bring them up change.

I still hold that good publishing is a passion. I still hold a utopian idea that publishing and writing are not a business, but a way of life. Harsh realities often push me into a corner where my beliefs have to stretch and adapt with the changes in time. E. M. Hartley says: "The past is a foreign country. They do things differently there."

They do. And now I'll say they did, for I am in the present, 1986. But when I first started working in the Junior Book Department at Harpers it was that foreign country, the past. It was 1938 and there were three of us in the department. Now there are seventy. Ursula Nordstrom, one of the great pioneers of children's publishing, was head of the department, and the three of us sat in one small section of the office with identical desks and standup phones and old-fashioned Smith Corona typewriters and carbon paper without any tissue attached. We used the same carbon over and over until no ink was left on the page. Computers were not dreamed of. And when the phone rang whoever was nearest answered. If Ursula was busy she would sing out by the second ring, "Hurry! Answer! It may be Mark Twain!"

It seldom was, or is today, but I am still unhappy when I see staff members in our department pass a ringing phone. True, it is probably not for them, but they could find the person for whom it is. True, it may be a nuisance call, it may be a routine inquiry, it may be a wrong number. But it also may be an author, a writer, and the voice reaching out from Harpers' phone should be eager and receptive and welcoming because people of talent are the ones on whose labors the whole publishing world will always, fundamentally, rest. To quote Arthur Miller, "Attention must be paid." Respect is due.

For without the writer there would be no editors, no marketing departments, no budget centers, no management, no salesmen; for there would be nothing to edit, to market, to budget, to manage, or to sell--nothing to keep a publishe in existence. The writer is the core, the heart of this whol gigantic industry in which every one of us must keep remem bering that in the beginning was the word!

It was easier to do this once when it was all smaller and more personal, in that foreign country, the past. But although one alters and adapts and realizes we should be thankful for the new commercial push that can be set in motion once there is a book in hand, it is still the writer withc whom the vast business machinery of publishing could not g on.

Love and passion are a large part of being an editor; not love of the individual person who is writing, but love of his talent, his writing, which an editor must respect, must allow to grow. Every manuscript that comes in should be read and reacted to with understanding. Until you do so, you can't tell whether you have something wonderful or wea some. This is why the Harper Junior Book Group reads eve manuscript that comes to us, solicited or unsolicited. Some of our finest authors have come "over the transom" or walke off the elevator into our lives. Some manuscripts come to u because the author's first one was returned with an encouraging word for the potential in the early attempt.

A manuscript came to me last week that I have accepte The author's letter said I had written her kindly fourteen years ago when she sent her first work to me, so now that she has a manuscript she thinks is good, she wanted me to see it first. This is a continuity, a reaching out from one life, the editor's, to another, the writer's, that makes what we do vital, makes it more than business and bottom line. I had long since forgotten her first manuscript, but there was a warmth and lyric quality in the recent one that must have been stirring in the earlier work. This is one of the ways it is harder to be an editor these days, because the volume of manuscripts we receive is so enormous that it is difficult to send a personal word to everyone whose submission shows promise. We still try to do it. We should, because (and th is my private philosophy of publishing and I am unhappy when I don't fulfill it) it is the duty of the publisher to

encourage not only the authors whom we do publish, but anyone who has some spark that burns underneath even the unsuccessful attempts.

Joan asked, in her letter, about "the way in which you
discern the warmth and quality of an author...." It is done
intuitively, much like meeting strangers. Some you don't
respond to at all. Some have a beguiling sense of humor.
Some have feelings about life that are tremendously moving.
Some have compassion and sensitivity. But often, along with
the good things, are others--a tone of voice that is remote,
a too obvious attempt at style, a self-consciousness that is
obtrusive. The editor tries to see whether the appealing
qualities outweigh those that are not; tries to separate his
own thoughts and feelings from what the author wants him
to think and feel.

I have always wondered at theatre critics who are able
to write a review after rushing from the play to their typewriters the second the curtain goes down. For I find sometimes that an engrossing, well-written book which seems strong
and publishable may, a week later, have faded in my mind.
But other books which seemed flawed as I read them continue
to haunt me. Weeks later, scenes or characters from it, or
a phrase, or some insight or mood, springs into my mind
while I'm on the bus or in my bath or talking to someone
else. There was something in the book that took hold, and
these small aftershocks are important. I go back to the manuscript again, see what its secret was, see what didn't work
despite its strength, and then try to find out by phone or
letter or in person what the author thought he had done in
the places where it did not work. I ask questions, drawing
the author out if I can, almost the way one does in a game
of charades, until we both see what he was after, what still
has to be done.

Of the two books, the one that seemed perfect and has
faded, and the one that seemed flawed but keeps running
through my mind, it is often the latter that is stronger, for
it is coming from some inner place in the author's own world
that he is working through in the book. If it can be brought
to fruition, it may be a lasting book, surviving trends and
market conditions of the moment, because it comes from some
eternally human experience the author has reached us with.

There are of course glorious occasions when the excite
ment of the first reading holds. You remember the book
clearly and with the original responses to it, and weeks
later the writing, the sound and flow of the words, the imagery or vividness or atmosphere, the emotion and character
and motivations are still powerful and complete. There is no
need to change it at all, and in editing as in life, the cliché
holds: if it works, don't change it! Meddling is not editing

But some of the finest writers are so close to, so involved in what they write, that they need, not a critique or
directive, but a participatory exchange with someone else
about their books.

"How," asked Joan, "do you help develop the manuscript into the finished, coherent, telling, and sensitive boo
that is delivered into the hands of the child?" How, indeed
Differently with every author and differently from book to
book with each author. But the editor must always respect
the author's vision, his piece of life and the way he feels
about it, not--and I emphasize this because when I talk abo
myself as a writer it will be from the opposite end of this se
saw--not the editor's piece of life or the editor's way of
seeing it.

A good editor is a good listener, and he listens for
what is between the lines as well as for the way the lines
themselves fall upon the inner ear.

Like most editors, I usually make notes in the margin
of the manuscript, sometimes asking "Why?" or saying, "Is
this true to her character?" or "Doesn't he reply to her say
ing this?" And along with pointing out these little unfulfille
spots or places where the transition goes on too long, one
also spontaneously finds oneself reacting with, "Great!" or
"Good bit, this!" or "Wonderful!" But, as that wonderful
writer Adrienne Jones can tell you, my handwriting is terrible, and I have to be very careful when I write my marginal comments. Recently Barbara Wersba was following all
my marginal scrawls with her usual care but kept finding on
that mystified her. She showed it to her friend.

"What do you suppose Charlotte means by writing 'bur
ny' all through?" she asked. Zoie took the manuscript and
studied my writing.

"Not <u>bunny</u>," she said. "<u>Funny!</u>"

So now I've contributed to their household exchange: "There's a bunny show on TV tonight," or "a very bunny movie downtown!"

Bill Morris, who is head of our library promotion department, reads every manuscript for catalog copy. Sometimes it befalls him to get a manuscript with the editor's reactions to a revision still in the margins. Some of these read, to anyone who hasn't seen the first version of the story, as though the editor is out of her mind. For instance, Bill asked me once why next to a line that said, "He opened the door," I had written "absolutely wonderful" in the margin.

"What on earth is so great about that?" he asked.

And I explained that what was absolutely wonderful was not the line itself, but that the author had used that one simple line to replace three pages in the earlier version of a long, introspective bit which had no purpose other than to get the character through the house, up the stairs, down a hall and into the room, pages that slowed up the story, contributed nothing, and lost the readers' interest on the way. It is the author's mastery of his craft that leads to such exultant comments, but no outside reader could understand or guess that the simplicity of the result--"He opened the door"--came out of a long participatory exchange.

Editing is an emotional investment. You enter the author's world, his mind, philosophy, and feelings; and often they are so different from your own that they bring you a new world, an extra dimension to something you've never before seen from this point of view.

Some writers change the color of the world by their own extraordinary way of looking at it. Let me take the lovely example of Patricia MacLachlan, author of this year's moving Newbery Award winner, <u>Sarah, Plain and Tall</u>.

This was her eighth book for us. The first came in a series of small poetic images about a little boy trying to experience things around him in the way his grandfather, who is blind, does. Each image had tenderness and sensitivity

and a heightened sensory quality that was beautiful. But
there was no form or shape, the incidents were like scatter-
shot, no structure, just bits caught on the wing like a butte
fly in a garden. They did not make a book.

I knew nothing about Patty or how she worked, but
there was no doubt that a sensibility and childlike quality
were strong in her. So I wrote first saying what an extreme
talent she did have, but that in order to make these fragments into a book we needed a structure, whether it might
be a seasonal structure, an indoor-outdoor structure, or a
structure by the senses: smell, touch, hearing--and she
understood! Slowly the book changed shape, took the form
of one complete day; but always the initial tenderness betwee
the little boy and the grandfather remained strong, and the
final version was the book I hope you all know, called
Through Grandpa's Eyes.

That was seven years ago. Since then Patty and I
have met. Patty has done many books for us, and with each
she has strengthened her craft so that she needs very little
if any, editorial guidance. She did picture books and books
for the middle-grades group. We got to recognize the themes
in life she lived and wrote about and were able to understand
better all she wanted to get into each book. Sometimes she
would have so much to say that it crowded the book with
riches, and she learned to back away, extract what didn't
belong in that book and use it in her next.

Then Sarah, Plain and Tall came in. Hints of this
story are in several of her earlier books. First go, it was
something that one became completely absorbed in, a world
we entered and lived in. But as I said earlier, it is often
the aftertake that tells us the most. It was a lovely, publish
able book, and as my mind kept returning to it, I was drawn
more deeply into the world she had created. It was as thou
these were people I had known myself, she had made them so
warm and true and real. But in that first version the book
opened with the children waiting on the front porch of their
prairie home for the carriage to come with their father and
his mail-order bride. Their hopes and fears were so strong
that I found myself wanting to know, wondering what their
own mother had been like, what they had lost that made ther
await this new mother so intensely.

I told Patty I thought we needed a few bits about the first mother, the mother who died when Caleb was born. Patty agreed. All I said was that I'd like to know a bit more about what it had been like when the first mother was alive.

The book no longer opens as it first did, with the children on the front porch waiting for Sarah. Here is how it now begins:

> "Did Mama sing every day?" asked Caleb, "Every-single-day?" He sat close to the fire, his chin in his hand. It was dusk, and the dogs lay beside him on the warm hearthstones.
> "Every-single-day," I told him for the second time this week. For the twentieth time this month. The hundredth time this year? ...
> "And did Papa sing, too?"
> "Yes, Papa sang, too." ...
> "Well, Papa doesn't sing anymore," said Caleb softly....

Patty had made a beautiful book into a small masterpiece.

An editor has to enter the author's world. An editor has to listen to the way an author writes, to the sound of the words as well as their content. He has to listen to the writer's heartbeat. An editor has to love blue with the writer, even if the editor's favorite color is red. An editor has to feel what the author is feeling, otherwise one or both of them are failing the work itself. There has to be passion for the book from them both!

This is why a good book seldom comes out of some-one else's idea. Perhaps in nonfiction this is not true, but in fiction so much is the synthesis of the writer's own feelings and philosophy and his own senses that any outside idea about what he is to write doesn't work, for it doesn't come the way a dream comes, as part of the person, part of every-thing he has seen or done or been.

I had a powerful demonstration of this which underlies both my being an editor and my being a writer. It happened long ago in those days at Harpers when Ursula Nordstrom was the head of the department and there were only three of us in that one office space.

"Tell us something of yourself as an author," Joan says. One of our stars was Margaret Wise Brown, whose Goodnight Moon and many other works are true classics for children. Margaret had a child's vision of things, and a poet's magic, and she was the writer I most admired in the children's book world. She was the Katherine Mansfield of children's writing.

She came in often to see Ursula, her golden hair curling to her shoulders, her big dogs--poodles--pulling her along as she swept in with her newest manuscript. At that time I lived near Washington Square Park, and the cycle of life there, the change in who came to the park at what hour, the whole shifting nature of it, twenty-four hours around, fascinated me. Knowing Margaret's sensory response to the mood and atmosphere of places, I thought this would be a lovely idea to use in her next book. (I was very young, and very new in publishing.) I told Ursula my idea. She listened with a slight irritation and said she didn't understand what I was saying and to write it down.

It wasn't like Ursula not to understand, and I was anxious to show her just what I did mean about the park, so I drafted a longer than usual memorandum to her. I mentioned the sounds in the park. "What sounds?" she asked. So I put in some of the sounds, the shoeshine man calling, the balloon man, the water fountain. And left it on her desk.

Next day she came over to me. "You have the beginning of your first book for us here," she said. "Take it home, work on it." It was The Park Book, published back in 1944. Ursula had underscored a lesson that has colored both the writing and the editorial side of my life. Along with giving me the joy of having my first book accepted, she articulated a piece of wisdom it might have taken many more years to find on my own. For she told me, after we had celebrated my joy, that Margaret Wise Brown would never write a book someone else had conceived. Books come from the writer's own subconscious, from his own perceptions and reactions and feelings. Margaret, and all good writers, start from some inner place in themselves. "You," Ursula told me, "have put your own emotions into this, your personal point of view. It is your book, not Margaret's. You are the author!"

And ever after, my life was divided. To be an editor

and a writer too is to be professionally schizophrenic. An editor has to turn herself off completely, has to become another person and see and feel in another person's way; a writer has to turn off everyone else's way of thinking and feeling, and listen only to something deep within himself, his own personality and response to life.

"We want to know about you as an author," Joan said. There are many kinds of books for the very young child that as an editor, a mother, a former child, I cherish. There are stories with plots, stories slapstick-funny enough to make any reader laugh out loud, there are fairy tales and fantasies and an infinite variety of books that are not the kind I am able to write; so what I say applies to my own work as a writer.

I'll talk about the sort of book I write myself, what it is, how it puts itself together out of bits of memory and the past, as well as whatever place in the present I happen to be. For most of my books spring from personal relationships, friend with friend, brother with sister, sisters with each other, parents with children; in other words, my books are usually about interpersonal relationships and the emotions they engender--hate, jealousy, anger, joy, fear, tenderness, love.

These are the emotions we as adults experience over and over. Harry Stack Sullivan said, "We are all more human than otherwise," meaning that no matter what our ethnic background, nationality, sex, religion, or politics, our feelings, the emotions, are the same. As adults, we often forget that this is true, too, of children. A child's emotions and an adult's emotions are the same. Adults have better disguises than kids. We learn to develop various kinds of protective coating: religion, or cynicism or humor or playing it cool, or anything that will keep us from the vulnerability that belongs to the openness of childhood. But under this camouflage the same intensities, the same passions are hidden and ready to spring up when we are off guard. Being caught off guard is being plunged into our childhood self, and it is a direct line to one's childhood that makes one writer write for children and another writer write about them. Children's book writers are those who write for children because they are really writing for themselves, for that unresolved child in each of us living still in that time of life without whatever protective philosophy and experience we've since found as adults.

This doesn't mean that in our writing we ignore the knowledge we have acquired as we grew up. But it is that very knowledge carried back to the child we were, and in a sense still are, that makes a funny or reassuring book for those who are not yet grown. It is that knowledge that shapes the book; for it is out of bits and pieces of our entire life, present and past, that we put together the books that are for our childhood self, before we knew all the adult stuff that could have helped us then and that we call on to help us now, adults though we are. For, I repeat, children and adults are more alike than they are different from each other.

When I write it is because an adult emotion has reawakened the childhood one. For example, The Hating Book. It starts, "I hate hate hated my friend. When her point broke in arithmetic and I passed her my pencil, she took Peter's instead." It goes through events an adult might think very small but which to a child are very large. Children who read this book identify not only with the events but with the hatred they engender. They recognize it in all its force, as letters I get from them prove. Kids ask me whether I have a daughter and was it she and her friend I was writing about. "I had a fight just like it," one little girl wrote. And another asked, "How did you know about me?"

But the real event behind that particular story was not out of my daughter's life but my own. And the quarrel with my friend took place when my friend and I were both in our mid-fifties. It was my adult rage and hate and hurt in the book, made stronger by its familiarity from my own childhood. The equation in children's symbols--the pencil, the blackboard, etc.--came simply from memories of long ago.

The more I try to analyze children's books or children's minds, or the fusion of feelings and events that go into writing for them, the more I realize what a mystery children's thoughts are and what a mystery the whole process of writing for them is. Part of it is imagery and events and feelings that are completely individual; part of it is the deep mystery that underlies the flow of life and memory, the dreamlike, almost Jungian merging of thoughts, feelings, fantasies and desires that are universal.

I had a friend with two grown sons, and she was on

the brink of divorce, of starting out on a life of her own.
She told me that night after night she dreamed she opened a
door in the house where they had lived for thirty years and
discovered a room she had never known was there. Her
dream haunted me. Years later I used it in a book called
Someday, where a little girl is dreaming of lovely things she
would like to have come true. Someday was published in
1965.

Recently, a small girl who lives on my street rang my
bell and asked if she could go through my house. "I haven't
been upstairs in a long time," she said. She climbed the
stairs, humming under her breath, and disappeared until her
mother, a pretty young lawyer, came to collect her a few
minutes later. "She's upstairs," I told Mrs. Miller. "She
said she wanted to look at my house again." Andrea's mother began to laugh. "Ever since we read Andrea Someday she's
been searching for a new room in our house. I guess she
thinks since you wrote the book maybe she'll find it here."

Now what a fusion here! Of my friend Dee, and her
unconscious telling of new and unknown things ahead,
of the way the dream haunted me after she told me of it, of
its turning up without my realizing it years later when writing
Someday, and then its effect on this little girl who wasn't
born when Dee first dreamed her dream. There's a continuity,
a flow of something unexplainable, a lovely, slow, rich mystery
that lies at the core of life. We are all looking for that room.

It is this mystery that flows through much writing for
young children, although on the surface the stories may seem
to be about very ordinary things. Great writers such as
Sendak and Andersen and Grimm work with the dream material itself. Some writers deal with wild and funny exag-
gerations or extraordinary and fantastic events. My writing
is about ordinary daily common events, ordinary relationships,
and the infinite variety of personal encounters out of which
emotions rise--emotions, feelings that don't change from childhood to maturity. A child's emotions are the same as those
an adult experiences. We are all the same except that adults
have found a way to buffer themselves against the full-blown
intensity a child's emotions have, emotions that can be aroused
by the most ordinary daily situations. Along with the camouflage adults have learned, adults have knowledge and memory
to help them, to protect them from the full impact of what they

are feeling, for they have felt everything before as children. As a child there is no way of understanding that sad, sad eternal truth, "This too shall pass." But it is a truth that comforts, and there are ways to have that comfort brought to children experiencing feelings they don't understand.

So how do I write for the very young? For me it is an emotional déjà vu. My adult loss or anger or jealousy or love is intensified by its familiarity. It has happened to me before. I have felt this way before. I remember not only the childhood events but the feelings those events gave me, which are the same feelings I experience now, as an adult, from adult circumstances that evoke those same emotions. I remember the events of childhood, the simple (to an adult), trivial, or even funny circumstances that gave me grief or pleasure. I can see that these same sorts of events set off grief or pleasure in the children around me now. The events in my books are therefore images young readers recognize and understand and identify with. The emotions these events release are there because I, now, as an adult writing, am actually reexperiencing those emotions.

A grown person's unrequited love evokes misery similar to a child's misery when someone he wants to be with goes off without him. The loss of a coveted job can stir the same sense of unfairness a child feels when his friend is allowed to do something he is not allowed to do. And when someone we love dies, the sense of loss is the same sense of loss a child feels when his best friend moves away. We are not different, we adults, from the children we were, only more experienced, more philosophical, more defensive, and better able to disguise our feelings from others, if not ourselves.

To remember this is to empathize and reexperience, to respect a child's feelings in a way that leads, I hope, to this child's growing up with a self-knowledge that will help him better face the world.

In the hundreds of letters I've gotten over the years from children and parents, two comments please me most. One I quoted earlier from the child who wrote, "How do you know me?" The other is from any parent who complains that when he finishes reading the book out loud, the child turns to the front and asks to hear it again.

The reason a child thinks the book is about himself, or wants to hear it over again, is that he is facing or feeling or trying to clarify something he recognizes in that particular book. For young children this is often the most compelling search of all. They are trying to understand themselves. They want to know that their experiences have happened to other people too. They want to know they are not alone in this inexplicable world.

This year Harpers reissued The Park Book, that first book of mine published in 1944. I am happy that now in 1986 many of my books written in the forties, fifties, sixties, and seventies are being reissued. Sometimes the drawings are dated and have to be changed, but the emotions in the text are still accessible to children. Children of the forties, fifties, sixties, and seventies feel the same way the children of the eighties feel when they are lonely or frightened or jealous or angry or happy. Events change from period to period, in both history and our personal lives, but feelings remain the same. And trying to understand these, trying to understand ourselves, helps us understand one another.

A little boy wrote me, "I like the way I feel when I read your books." I liked the way I felt when I read his letter. For as a writer I am happy to put down my feelings so that someone else feels them too. I am happy to have the reader understand that whatever our nationality, religion, or age might be, adult or child alike, the search for understanding ourselves leads to our understanding others; for we are all more human than otherwise.

"How do you know about me?" the children ask.

I don't.

I am trying to find out about myself.

PART VIII:

A PLEA FOR THE WRITTEN WORD AND FOR CHILDREN

Dorothy Butler challenges all of us to keep children in touch with story, and thus in touch with themselves and their world.

Chapter 22

WHAT HAPPENED THEN? THE NEED FOR
NARRATIVE IN CHILDHOOD

Dorothy Butler

In this presentation, I'm going to mount a few of my favorite hobby horses and canter about, indulge in a little gentle nostalgia, tell you a story--or part of one--and even shake you up a little.

When asked, some months ago, for a title for this paper, I produced my present one, "What Happened Then? The Need for Narrative in Childhood," without hesitation. I was at that time absorbed by a thought which, while always present on the outskirts of my consciousness, had never before seemed as significant to me as it suddenly did. This was that children will attend to narrative prose with a concentration they seldom give to dramatic performance. Or, more precisely, that the narrative speech of the storyteller--whether oral or through the written word--appears to nourish the human condition with a directness which is facilitated by the very nature of the human mind and spirit. My observation of children from birth has convinced me that this is so; that "storytelling" is part of all our lives, from the earliest moments of consciousness of self; that we cannot make sense of our lives except by devising narratives to explain and construct, to reflect on the past, consider the present and speculate on the future, and that our dreams and daydreams reflect, reinforce, modify and are part of this purpose. This view presents "storying" as a primary function of mind.

It has been commonly believed--and is still believed by many people, not all of whom can be excused as unintelligent--that as maturity advances in the individual, so reality replaces fantasy in inner life. We need only look honestly at ourselves to know that this is not so. Einstein's remark, made late in his life, that "the gift of fantasy has meant mor to me than my gift for absorbing positive knowledge," gives some insight into the potential for achievement open to that rare person who recognizes the true nature and need of the human mind and spirit while finding fascination and opportunity in an area of scientific study.

It has always seemed self-evident to me that the spontaneous fantasies of early childhood exceed in horror anything the mere storyteller can invent and that one of the fun tions of storytelling and reading aloud must be to give form to the nameless and to substitute the acceptable for the unbearable. The more successfully we stock children's minds with stories which can become the raw material of invention and expression, the firmer their feet will tread the earth, the quicker will be their response, the more ready their laughter, the deeper their understanding.

It has been gratifying to discover that there is some professional support for this view. The Jungian psychologis James Hillman, has written:

> To have had story of any sort in childhood--and her
> I mean oral story, those told or read (for reading
> has an oral aspect even if one reads to oneself) rath
> er than watching story on screen--puts a person int
> a basic recognition of, and familiarity with, the legit
> mate reality of story per se. It is given with life,
> with speech and communication and is not something
> later that comes with learning and literature. Comin
> early with life, it is already a perspective to life.

Earlier in the same paper he says:

> From my perspective as depth psychologist I see that
> those who have a connection with story are in better
> shape and have a better prognosis than those to who
> story must be introduced.... To have "story-aware-
> ness" is psychologically therapeutic. It is good for
> the soul.

From the field of literature comes this comment from
Barbara Hardy:

> I take for granted the ways in which storytelling en-
> gages our interest, curiosity, fear, tensions, expecta-
> tion, and sense of order. What concerns me here are
> the qualities which fictional narrative shares with that
> inner and outer storytelling that plays a major role
> in our sleeping and waking lives.... In order to
> really live, we make up stories about ourselves and
> others, about the personal as well as the social past
> and future.

Of course, ordinary people have always known this.
Conversation--whether gossip around the village pump or
scholarly disputation in halls of learning--has always taken
story form. How can we doubt that storying is natural to
the human condition when we consider that our earliest forebears related their own activities, feats and fantasies around
the tribal fire before the dawn of recorded time? The benefit is clearly to the teller as well as to the listener; now as
then we all eagerly await our turn to contribute an anecdote,
offer an illustration, give our version of how, why or when it
happened. News is, after all, true "story," and everyone
wants to know what is going on, and why. If someone were
to fling open the door of this room, this minute, and shout:
"Guess what just happened to me!" no one would want to
listen to this address any longer--and I would be as anxious
as anyone to hear the tale in all its embellishment!

It is unlikely that anyone listening to or reading this
doubts the truth of these things; but what, by implication,
is our responsibility in practical terms? I suggest that our
concern, as people who care about children and books and the
ways in which they interact, could be reflected in our answers
to the following questions: How well does our society cater
to every child's need for story? Do we recognize our obligation, as informed and professional people, to represent this
need to those in authority to establish standards and to work
for their support? And is this where our responsibilities
end?

It is reasonable to expect those countries which have
the highest material standards of living to be achieving a
high standard of care for their children in this field. After

all, books cost money, professional expertise is more readily available in developed countries than in those that are less affluent, the public is better educated and easier to reach. Does the achievement of such countries in fact reflect their advantages? Another question we might ask is: What factor or conditions in any society work against its chances of providing children with the storying that is their right? And here, of course, the answers will be as diverse as the countries represented.

In the case of so-called advanced societies, the counter indications are clear. We live in an electronic world. Human functions have been assumed by machines. And machines dazzle. Humankind has always given its highest respect, reserved its greatest awe, for those things it understands least; and how many people understand a television set or a computer screen, except in the gross function of button-pressing for instant result?

But surely, you are entitled to say, children attend to television programs--which are, after all, presented in dramatic rather than story form. Does this not tend to refute the theory that narration is of primary importance to children, that story will engage their attention in a way dramatic action does not?

Certainly, the television screen has a unique capacity for engaging human "attention." We all know that children will gaze compulsively at a flickering screen even if there is no picture there at all. This is, of course, for reasons that have nothing to do with the narrative versus the dramatic; it has to do with the quality and behavior of light. Those who know about these things tell us that the only natural equivalent of television, in terms of the compulsion it exerts on the human eye, is real firelight--and this is something I can believe. I, along with most of my generation in appropriate climates, grew up with open fires which blazed, crackled, glowed, and finally settled down to lives of their own: ever-changing, ever-luring, full of mystery and magic and "the stuff that dreams are made on." My own perfect evening is still spent with a good fire, a good book, and the understanding I have with myself that a certain amount of fire-gazing is not only delicious, but positively restorative.

What television program allows the mind of a child to

wander at will, her spirit to wonder and yearn, as the fires of my childhood allowed me? My brother and I would often try to show one another our own pictures in the flames or embers, but it never worked. My own witches, sailing ships or castles were not his, nor were his visions my own. And, unlike the children of the eighties whose television heroes are shared by their schoolfellows and millions beyond, we went off to bed night after night with our own stories rolling around in our heads. And fearful and wonderful tales they were! An amalgam of the people and things we knew, our beloved books and comics, and the infinitely various creatures and plots of our own imaginations.

My mother was a natural storyteller. She and her brothers and sister had been brought up in the old gold mining town of Thames; their parents had been real pioneers. My mother's tales of their everyday lives, before the days of cars, telephones, radio, or electricity, held endless fascination for us. Her family had boasted--as well as the usual complement of cats, dogs, fowls and horses--a monkey, and Jacko was our Pooh Bear and Peter Rabbit rolled into one. We each had our favorite story and would sit on after a meal, listening, as my mother brought these days alive for us.

My Uncle George out-Finned Huckleberry by far--and my mother's younger sister, after whom I was named, must surely have been the original Ramona! My mother, revealed in fading photographs as a thin, serious child with an inquiring expression, was surely Alice: never afraid to question and criticize hypocrisy and lack of what she called "gumption." A good cook and dressmaker, she was a less-than-fussy housekeeper, and I have often since blessed her for this. My brother and sister and I would usually find her lying on the old kitchen sofa with a book when we came in from school. "Goodness," she would say. "Is it really four o'clock? I must put the kettle on!"

Could we doubt that reading was fun? And books were always packed into bags along with the food and swimming gear when we set off on foot for one of the picnics my mother so loved to organize. I have realised only in latter years that both my parents enjoyed their children, and that this gave us all an incomparable base from which to step off into life. Loved children are fortunate, but children who are enjoyed as well are doubly blessed.

We were working-class children of sturdy pioneering stock; our parents had both left school at twelve years of age--and for the whole of their lives considered themselves educated, read enthusiastically, and wrote letters in immaculate, copy-book script, correctly spelled and punctuated. Their generation, born as one century turned into another, had somehow survived a world war and plunged into a bleak depression which, finally fading, revealed the clear intention of the distant European world to repeat the performance. And there we were, dangling off the righthand bottom corner of the map (sometimes not even getting in), attached to string held firmly by unknown masters in the north so that every tweak had us jangling. Hadn't our forebears braved the unimaginable journey in tiny sailing ships to get away from all that nonsense? my astute mother used to ask.

It has taken us a long time to start believing that we New Zealanders may perhaps exist in our own right; but I believe we are making headway at last. Unfortunately, we are also prey to every modern malaise and, as far as our children are concerned, one of the worst of these is undeniably television. And its evil is, I believe, understood only dimly, if at all, by those whose lives are engulfed by it. This is not the place to examine in depth the effects of television on children's lives. But it is relevant, I believe, to make several points and suggest that we reflect on their implications for children.

The first is the finding of recent research that watching the lighted screen slows down brain activity regardless of the quality of the program. (This is, of course, what makes television a useful tool for overtired and overworked adults late at night.) Remembering that the early years of life are a time of unparalleled mental activity, can we continue to accept a situation in which a prized product of the twentieth century, marketed and promoted with government support all over the so-called civilized world, actually depresses our children's intelligence?

My second point is television's invasion of children's lives in terms of time: not only time to read, but time to play, time to do nothing, time to experiment with objects and ideas, to lie and look at the sky, to reflect, to forge relationships, time to live. For many children, one suspects, the flickering screen has become the reality, real life the dream.

As each year rolls by, many millions of children have increasingly less chance of experiencing story through books. The reason hardly needs stating: to become an efficient and responsive reader, one must read.

Reading is, after all, just like swimming, skating, sewing or playing tennis. It is easy enough to teach anyone the rudiments; smooth, effective performance emerges only as the learner, having accepted perfection of the art as desirable, commits himself or herself to the business of mastering the skills involved. And this means practice. Practice, in turn, involves an investment of intellectual energy and a deferment of gratification.

Does modern life encourage these qualities in our children? Evidence reveals that many children are sadly lacking in such capacities. It is not that children are born without energy of every sort. It is just that the game needs to be worth the candle. Modern children, surrounded as they are by diversions and amusements which arrive unbidden and assail them on all sides, are to be forgiven for not struggling with a skill which must not only be mastered, but refined, if it is to avail them anything. How can they know that the ultimate state--in which meaning pours from the page to the mind--is worth working for? How many people in the average child's life derive obvious pleasure from long, silent hours of immersion in books of solid print?

And what of the quality of language children need if they are to read with fluency and response? For there is ample evidence that most "nonreaders" or "retarded readers" or merely poor readers suffer from a poverty of resource rather than any incapacity to master basic skills: poverty of vocabulary, concept, imagination, confidence.

If, somehow, storying could begin to play a prominent role in such children's lives, I believe that we would start to see a change. Listening would of course have to have first place, and rightly so. The child who is listening expertly is employing the senses and techniques that the mature reader uses; he is well on the way to reading. This child is able to accept and mentally process a stream of language to order the ideas presented, selecting the dominant, retaining the supportive and suppressing the irrelevant, relegating all to positions appropriate for maximum understanding of the author's message.

If we can bring children to listen in this way--and we can if we attend to the quality and the appeal of the story we are reading, to our own delivery of it, and last but by no means least, to our own relationship with these listening children--if we can induce this sort of response to stories read aloud, then we may start to hope that we will produce readers. For children must learn to tap the resources of the book if they are to begin to meet their own needs for narrative.

And surely we want them to use their own language, whatever this may be, in all its richness and vitality. "Get while you are young, the gift of English words," said Eleanor Farjeon; and her advice might carry over into any one of the world's languages, for its children's attention. For there can be no doubt that language is the strongest of all forces in the development of the human intellect. Only the most rudimentary thought is possible without language. In the long run, quality of thought, reason and imagination will depend upon quality of language. Humankind neglects this fact at its peril, yet it is neglected every day by those who seek to substitute electronic appliances for the literature of their language.

Increasingly, we hear of books being cast aside as inefficient vehicles for supplying students and others with the facts they need. "Education," we are assured by the supporters of bookless libraries, "is basically an information transfer process." Facts are what matter, it seems, and the most efficient way of turning up the relevant one is to press the appropriate button. "Knowledge" is increasingly unacceptable as a concept; "wisdom" is presumably an anachronism. The concern of philosphers, poets and scientists for thousands of years, wisdom is discovered in the eighties not to matter after all. Wisdom takes time, and in the eighties, speed is all.

Words are finely-tuned instruments of communication which must be encountered early if their shades of meaning are to serve the emerging intelligence. Edward Thomas, himself a master of their simple but dexterous use, said in his poem, "Words":

> I know you:
> You are light as dreams,

Tough as oak,
Precious as gold
As poppies and corn,
Or an old cloak:
Sweet as our birds
To the ear.

Young as our streams
After rain:
And as dear
As the earth which you prove
That we love.

We are depriving children of their heritage if we do
not make an effort to stir their awareness of words and the
power they have to represent not only things, but ideas,
hopes, fears, the whole range of human emotion and aspira-
tion.

Thomas finished his poem:

Let me sometimes dance
With you,
Or climb
Or stand perchance
In ecstacy,
Fixed and free
In a rhyme,
As poets do....

And I suggest to you that we can help our children to do
these things wherever, whenever and at whatever level we
find them if we care enough.

Recently, I spent a week in Fiji. It had been a hastily
arranged trip, and I was not quite sure what my hosts, the
Library Association, expected of me. I soon found out! Instead of the parents, teachers and librarians whom I had expected to address--or rather, as well as--they had organized
groups of four- to seven-year-olds for me to tell and read
stories to--on one day, six groups of thirty children each,
in a row! These children begin to learn English at school
entry, and I certainly could not speak their language!

Poetry and the age-old, universal tales saved the day.
The appeal of,

Bubble said the kettle
Bubble said the pot
Bubble bubble bubble
We are getting very hot!

Shall I take you off the fire?
No, you need not trouble
This is just the way we talk
Bubble, bubble, bubble!

carried me through, along with "The Gingerbread Man," "The Three Billy Goats Gruff," and several of their friends. Never has the power of narrative or the evocative strength of "the best words in the best order" been demonstrated more strongly to me. Those engaging, receptive children would have listened all day--or until I finally collapsed!

Let me give you another example of the power of narrative to move the human child--in this case, to action, as well as to rapt attention.

Several years ago a friend who had taken a post as librarian at a private school for boys in Auckland complained to me that the focus of the school seemed to be on nonfiction. She lamented this fact and wondered if I would be prepared to address both boys and parents at a coming function on the subject of "the value of reading novels." At first, I refused; this was a highly privileged school and my real interest lay in more needy areas. But my friend insisted, and I demurred and was ultimately lost.

Then I thought: This is impossible; I am obliged to talk to a whole hall full of boys aged five to thirteen, and their parents. What can I say to make any impact at all on such a diverse audience?

And then it struck me: I would read them a compelling incident from a novel. As an introduction, I would talk to the parents, briefly, about the advantage which might come to their children intellectually, imaginatively and emotionally from the habit of daily reading aloud. I would aim the actual reading at the ten-to-thirteens, assuming that this group would be derisive if the story were too young for them. I chose to believe that a dramatic performance would hold the little boys' attention but could not really arrange for this-- only hope.

On the night--horrors! Also present were the boys'
sisters (from an exclusive, adjacent girls' school) and their
smaller siblings too. In fact, there were babies crawling in
the aisles and a fair sprinkling of grey heads which had to
belong to grandparents. There was also, thank heaven, an
excellent sound system which worked.

Clearly, the exhortation bit had to be short, and I
made it so. Then I explained that the novel I would read
from was set in the late 1700s, in Gloucestershire, England,
and that it concerned a boy, Francis Place, who witnessed
a terrible deed and subsequently became involved in a series
of extraordinary adventures. I could have told the parents
that this book, Scarf Jack, by P. J. Kavanagh, might also
leave their children with the beginnings of understanding of
the root of present-day troubles in Northern Ireland, but I
did not. I merely explained that in the extract, Francis is
returning one winter evening to the lonely cottage where he
lives with his mother. A storm is brewing. Then he hears
a group of mounted men approaching. This is an unusual
occurrence, but the troubles in Ireland have made everyone
in this close-to-the-coast region apprehensive, and on impulse Francis hides beneath a hedge. From this vantage point
he looks directly into the eyes of a trussed man who, borne
to the spot across the back of a horse, is roughly dropped
to the ground. It is clearly the intention of his captors to
hang him. At this point, the storm breaks, the men carry
out their plan, and they hastily depart. Francis has by this
time moved to a safer hiding place in an adjacent hollow oak
tree. This is what I read:

> I knelt inside the oak and almost buried my face
> on the dry powdery stuff on the floor, sniffing its
> familiar smell for comfort, half-believing that if I hid
> my face I would make myself even more invisible.
> I need not have feared. They clearly did not
> want to linger round their crime and the rain made
> them more than ever anxious to be gone. They
> climbed on to their horses, leading away with them
> the now unburdened pack-horse, and quickly made
> their way in single file towards the gate more silently
> than they had come.
> Before they left the field they moved out of my
> sight so I waited a few moments until I could hear
> no sound but the rain. Then, cautiously, I put my

head out of the base of the old oak and saw, as well as was possible, in the teeming darkness, that the field was empty. With great difficulty I squeezed the rest of me out into the rain. It was as though my wet clothes had swollen on my body and for a moment I thought I might have to stay inside the tree until they dried, while the man swung on the end of his rope a few feet from me. I had a hope he might still be alive. The job had been done hastily, in the dark, and I had heard tales of men hanged who had lived on to old age and of other poor wretches who had survived the drop only to have to climb their gallows again to allow the executioner a second try.

As soon as I was out of the tree I ran to the side where he swung and climbed the branches behind him. I had a knife in my pocket that I used for splitting the pegs of my snares and I set to work on the rope above his head.

It was taut with his weight, and wet, so I had to saw at it, fearful my knife would blunt before the last strands snapped. The palm of my hand rubbed raw with the effort of it until at last, closing my eyes, I gave a last desperate saw to the hemp and the rope parted. My shut eyes could not prevent me hearing the sucking splash as the big body fell, helpless as a sack, to the ground below. When I looked down I saw he had sprawled half-forward, half-sideways, and I prayed the rain-soaked ground had made the drop easier for him, if he was still in this world. He had hit the ground hard three times that night to my knowledge.

As fast as I could I was down and forced myself to look at his face. I turned it gently away from the mud, pushing at his shoulder so that in the end he toppled on to his back. It cost me much to do this because, if alive, his bones might be broken and I might be doing him a worse injury than any he had yet received. But I liked his face, which had seemed a peaceful one, and I could not bear to see it lying in the mud.

The knot of the rope stuck out from his windpipe like a cravat but because it was a noose I was able to loosen it with my fingers, with difficulty as it was wet, but in the end I managed it, and felt the terrible welt where it had bitten into the flesh.

There seemed no life in him, no breath, and I
knelt on his chest to see if I could make the bellows
of his lungs work. I could no longer worry about
whether his ribs were broken, his neck or his back,
for if he did not breathe soon he would have no use
for any of them.

It was hard to know if I did any good because
although I was a large enough boy my knees seemed
very small on his huge thick coat and I could not
feel his rib-cage move. But perhaps what I did was
useful or perhaps it was never necessary because to
my great joy his lips parted and a moan came from
between them. My friend (for so I already thought
of him) had escaped his captors as somehow I had
always felt in my bones that he would.

Even the babies seemed to be listening as I finished,
and a great sigh swept around the hall, like the swell of a
summer wave. A pause, and then a clamour: Would I repeat the title, spell the author's name...? I did, many times,
for the audience later surrounded me, bearing pieces of paper
they had begged from their neighbors, to get the details
down. I was not in my bookshop the following morning, but
when I arrived in the early afternoon, I was met with accu-
sations: "Whatever did you say last night to cause half of
Auckland to ring up or come for Scarf Jack? Why didn't
you warn us--Penguin has sold out their stock too, to shops
on the other side of Auckland!" Six months later Scarf Jack
appeared, serialized, on television. To capitalize on this
event, Penguin issued a new edition with a photograph from
the film on the cover. We duly ordered this edition; it is an
excellent book. However, to the whole of Auckland, with its
nearly one million people, we sold a mere fraction of the number of copies snatched up six months before by that hall full
of assorted age groups. The power of narrative, you see!
Those people listening became the boy, Francis, terrified but
determined, closing his eyes but still hearing "the sucking
splash as the big body fell," forcing himself to look at the
hanged man's face, loosening the noose "with difficulty, as it
was wet," kneeling on the man's chest to see if he could "make
the bellows of his lungs work." And think of the humanizing
effect, in the midst of all this horror, of Francis' explanation:
"I liked his face, which had seemed a peaceful one, and I
could not bear to see it lying in the mud."

How much of this do you imagine the child watching television would receive from the mere action on the screen? Very little, I suspect. No, if our children are to examine cause and effect, reflect on human motivation, learn about the way the world works and how its people laugh and suffer, they must have their stories in narrative form, in language that is vigorous and honest, its words arranged by craftsmen. And they can, if we will only keep our vision clear and strengthen our resolution to help.

And along with our dedication must go a healthy suspicion that we are doing no more than merely scratching the surface. Carmen Garcia-Moreno told us movingly, but simply and factually, of the difficulties she and her colleagues experience in Mexico, difficulties which most of us here cannot even imagine. I found myself, to my shame, almost not wanting to know, when there seemed so little I could do. But we must know; we must avoid the complacency, the self-indulgence with which our work as professionals can be flavored when the product we handle is as alive and attractive as the good book. We must remind ourselves, daily, that the children are more imortant than the books. Unless we reach the children, our craft is an empty, passionless thing. And we must reach them in their homes, for that is where changes in their lives can be made, not in seats of government or halls of learning. We need campaigns which bypass schools and libraries while drawing these institutions in and using all their resources. We need people of good heart and strong determination to give parents of new babies confidence in themselves as the best possible people to meet these babies' needs. They need to know that their influence will surpass that of schools, libraries and all other institutions; that institutions have a duty towards them, and that most of them are more than willing to help. Are we doing this?

* * *

The world's greatest resource is its children. In a very real sense, children constitute the world's only true resource. Certainly, if we cease to produce children, the world as we know it will come to an end. Humankind's only hope in these desperate days is that the next generation will manage to bring order and sanity to a world which its forebears have all but destroyed. Our children are our only hope. And they offer us, in abundance and against all reason, the qualities the world needs now, not only for survival, but for triumphant survival: courage, honesty, a scornful eye on hypocrisy, humor, an infinite capacity for love, loyalty and forgiveness, and a fascination with the world itself and the way it works.

Can we preserve these qualities? We must, if we are to survive. I will not accept a charge of over-simplification when I say that the habit and expectation of communication, of relationship, entrenched in the earliest days, months and years is the only answer. I hope you will believe me when I say that binding children to books that are good and true, with all the laughter and wonder that such books have to offer, is a simple, enjoyable and infinitely valuable contribution to a cause which is not only good, but desperately urgent.

Appropriate poetry seems to have surfaced at key points during this conference. As I lay in bed this morning, these well-known words of David McCord's came into my mind:

> Blessèd Lord, what it is to be young:
> To be of, to be for, be among--
>   Be enchanted, enthralled,
>   Be the caller, the called,
> The singer, the song and the sung.

Let's try to make it like this for all children, not just the favored ones.

REFERENCES

Hillman, James. "A Note on Story." Children's Literature in Education 3 (1975).

Hardy, Barbara. "Narrative as a Primary Act of Mind," in The Cool Web: The Pattern of Children's Reading. Margaret Meek, Aidan Warlow, and Griselda Braton, eds. New York: Atheneum, 1978, c.1977.

Kavanagh, Patrick Joseph. Scarf Jack. London: The Bodley Head, n.d.

McCord, David. "Blessèd Lord," in his One at a Time: His Collected Poems for the Young. Boston: Little Brown, 1974.

Thomas, Edward. <u>The Collected Poems</u>. R. George Thomas,
ed. London: Oxford University Press, 1978.

PART IX:

L'ENVOI

Arne Nixon reflects upon the conference and adds his own appreciation of children and their literature.

Chapter 23

CONFERENCE SUMMARY

Arne Nixon

This conference now draws to a close, and now comes the moment of truth which I cannot avoid any longer. My worthy colleagues on the Conference Planning Committee have instructed me: "Summarize!" I have worried, my friends, about my adequacy to fulfill this mandate. I have worried. Last evening, those worries became chronic and acute, and I reached a point sufficiently desperate that I began to consider my plight prayerfully. But nothing seemed to come to any kind of closure. There has been so incredibly much to see and hear and consider during these wonderful days which now draw to a close.

I have worried. But the full, awesome impact of my charge did not really hit me until just now as I sat here listening to our wonderful friend, Ashley Bryan. I thought, "My Lord God Almighty! How can anyone possibly follow Ashley, first of all, and secondly, how can anyone possibly summarize in a few minutes all that we have experienced and heard--the richness, the excitement, and the wonder of these past five days?

Now, I must attempt that task. Where do I turn? What do I say? The moment has come. Not even Samuel Johnson's observation, "If a man is to be hanged in the morning, it concentrates his mind wonderfully," seems to offer much help.

It does not! Nothing seems to help, and my burden at this
moment is heavy. Even under the best conditions, summarie
are difficult. But this! To distil into a few moments so mu
which has been so wisely and eloquently offered! What is it
the child said when he complained about having to write a
book report and was asked, "What is a book report?" His
response was, "A book report is when a kid tells the story
worse than the guy who wrote it." So, I'm afraid, it is wit
summaries.

But I shall find some comfort during these next few
minutes which God and the Planning Committee have allocated
to me by taking refuge in the fact that I no longer can hear
very well. So, if you hear me reporting that which you did
not hear and understandings which you did not understand
and which reflect a different reality from that which you hav
it is because I did not hear very well what was said. In thi
summary, I shall conclude that if I had heard the speakers
more clearly, they undoubtedly would have been saying thes
things.

It has truly been a wonderful conference. We have
heard so much that has been interesting and insightful at th
major presentations and also in the smaller group sessions.
We carry away enough to occupy our thoughts for many day
to come.

Victor Kelleher reminded us so well that ours is an interesting and curious profession, those of us who are concerned with children and young people and their literature.
He is so correct, in my view, in his statement that somehow
life is seen in such different ways and through such differer
spectacles when it comes to writing for children. Good literature, many seem to think, is associated only with a brigh
and optimistic celebration of life, while literature which is no
so optimistic is thought somehow less worthy. There is considerable truth in that perception, I think. There is truth
also in his view that somehow those of us who labor in these
vineyards, whether as writers or critics or teachers of child
literature, are in some curious ways to be regarded as somewhat immature or unsophisticated or non-serious folk who da
ble in something called "kiddie lit."

But let us not be deceived. First of all, we need to
be sure that we are dealing with common currency as we

consider this important and interesting field in which we work. There are so many species of story and poetry confronting us, and not all of them are necessarily literature of much consequence. Nor do my views or yours as to the significance of so much of what we offer to the children necessarily coincide with the children's views.

Too, we find many adult interpretations of what that literature is or ought to be. There is, for example, that distressingly large population of folks who continue to regard children's stories as merely somewhat simplified versions of adult stories. It is true, to be sure, that good stories do cut across rigid lines of age and circumstances, and good stories continue to speak to us throughout our lives. But many factors of maturity and experience affect the abilities of children to bring understanding and meaning to that experience of literature.

There are also among us, I would suggest, those who do not understand that world of childhood, and they want to make that world and its stories conform to their own curious notions as to what those children and that world are. Some see the child as one who comes "trailing clouds of glory." And he does come to us that way. But that child comes also with a dark heart at times, and his literature ought to speak to that heart also. Among the many writers for young children who recognize that reality so well is Maurice Sendak.

One speaker was right when she reminded us that there really are no exclusively adult emotions. Children may confront such emotions on more primitive levels and on less sophisticated terms, but they need to be free to confront them honestly. Where better can they do this than through the experience of good literature? Children also know love and hate, fear and courage, and sorrow and joy. Someone has said (Was it P. L. Travers, I wonder?) that there is no such thing as an exclusively adult emotion. Children are not emotional mendicants. They need to know and to face emotions on their own levels of readiness and understanding. I would make only one stipulation, and I have heard it repeated here by various speakers and in various ways. That stipulation is that whatever the stories offer to children and wherever those stories lead the children, they should not leave them without hope. As was so well stated by one of the speakers, children pass through many stages of growth in understanding, and their

problems may be simpler ones than those of adults. But
children often cut to the heart of such problems with greater
precision than do many adults, and children can see with
greater clarity the distinctions between truth and falsehood
and between good and evil, even though perhaps not always
with the same applications as adults do.

This is why those old folktales and fairy tales and the
modern fantasies such as Peter Rabbit are such important fare
to offer to children. Peter Rabbit is much more than a story
about a naughty little boy in fur. If that is all he was, he
would and should have died an early and well-deserved death
But he lives! He is now well into his eighties. His is in
many ways a great love story, and I go back and reread it
quite often to make sure that it has not changed. Children
need Peter Rabbit, and they need Mike Mulligan and Ping and
Mrs. Mallard too. Children find insights and understandings
in these stories, which continue to speak also to the adult in
whom that child still lives. It is a road which leads surely
and truly from Peter Rabbit to Othello, Dr. Leland Jacobs
used to tell me, and Peter Rabbit and Othello are citizens of
the same kingdom.

The child who knows Mrs. Mallard and Ping and Peter
and Mike, and who knows also that somewhat retarded goose,
Petunia, and that equally retarded honey bear, Winnie, lives
with worthy companions of the journey. The child who knows
them not is a deprived child, whatever may be the other circumstances of his life. Yes, and he is doubly blessed if he
knows also the Cowardly Lion and Water Rat and Mole and
Johnny Tremain and Sarah, Plain and Tall. He needs to be
in that forest with the Tuck family and to catch a glimpse of
eternity, and he needs also to be with Scrooge in that dark
night of his agony. If he meets and knows these and so
many more, he will one day be ready for Othello. But they
are of no less importance even if he never meets Othello.
The stories may and should be, many of them, tough and sad
under appropriate circumstances, but they should never be
without hope.

Katherine Paterson, one of the giants of our time, state
this truth so well. She says in one of her essays--and I
hope I can paraphrase it adequately--that people are always
asking her why she keeps writing about burdened and rejected children; and they keep wanting to know when she is

going to write one with a happy ending. She reports that one librarian "gave it to me straight," saying, "'Every time I start to read one of your books, I try to figure out what you're going to do to ruin the ending.'" "Why," asks Paterson, "do I continue to inflict my own grief and sin on innocent children? Can't I allow the young a few short years free of the care of human experiences as we adults know them?" She goes on to say that "the answer is no. The children of their nation have been shot. They have seen increasing terrorism and senseless war. They know how hungry most of the world is. They have experienced the death of family and friends." Paterson says that children have always loved these tough old stories, including fairy tales and the unexpurgated Bible. Paterson reminds us that "the whole truth is seldom comfortable, but it is finally the strongest comfort." She says that she can only see through her one pair of eyes, but she does not have two truths, one for children and one for grownups.

Do you remember her great acceptance speech when she won the National Book Award? She recalled in that speech the story in the Old Book when Moses sent out the spies to scout the Promised Land which finally lay before the children of Israel--the land for which they had longed and searched. The spies returned and said it was indeed a land of milk and honey, a good land. But they reported also that it was powerfully fortified and defended by strong armies. It would be folly to enter it. But there was a man of hope among them who gave a minority report which said, "It is indeed a strongly fortified land, but we are well able to overcome it."

Paterson said in that speech, "I, too, want to be a spy like Caleb. I have crossed the river and tangled with a few giants, but I want to go back and say to those who hesitated, 'Don't be afraid to cross over. It is worth possessing, and we are not alone. I want to be a spy for hope.'"

Paterson's view has struck me so forcefully during these past several days which we have spent together. We have many "spies" here, I think. Sheila Egoff spoke of "faces turned lovingly toward each other"; Larry Yep walked with us through a labyrinth of childhood cross-cultural puzzlements and perplexities and visions and dreams; Charlotte Zolotow reminded us of the power of the word in bringing wonder and mystery to children, including the one who questioned, "How

did you know about me?" And Zolotow confessed, in her own
wisdom and humility, "I didn't. I was trying to find out
about myself."

I kept coming back during these days to the subject
of fantasy. What a powerful instrument it is for helping
children in gaining insight into some of life's deepest truths.
I think I cannot find adequate words to express the gratitude
which I feel toward the masters of this genre, such as our
own Eleanor Cameron, who has contributed so much richness
to the lives of millions of children and so much hope to so
many of us who have sat at her feet and listened also. Children turn to fantasy, that which is not real but which, if it
is good fantasy, deals with such deep truths. They turn to
it to find answers to their questions and, in a most profound
sense, to find peace. Isn't this the essence of Max's situation
when he goes to the land of the wild things, discharges his
anger, and returns again to find peace with his mother and
a meal which is still hot? Where the Wild Things Are is classified as a fantasy by adults, but it is not a fantasy to children
at all. It is a most basic expression of realism, isn't it? Oh,
yes! I have told that story to at least a hundred thousand
children, and I am certain that to them it is real. If things
were as they ought to be, my friends, that book would be
issued with each birth certificate, along with Goodnight
Moon and the Runaway Bunny. What precious expressions
they are of growing organisms reaching out toward independence and still needing to know that unqualified mother love
is there. I wish we had a month together to talk about the
implications of such stories. Fantasy? Go again, as I often
do, to Eleanor Cameron's book, The Green and Burning Tree,
to understand better fantasy's role in the lives of children.

I am so glad that Margaret Bush summoned us to be
concerned about the state of the literature for the middle
grades. It is true that there is a serious gap there. We
have great wealth in the stories and poetry which are available for younger children, and I think that the needs of the
older children are well served also; but I do worry about
those middle years. They need more than we are offering
them.

I have pondered a lot during these days also about
values and the role which they ought to play in children's
stories. Values, of course, undergird every human motivation

and action; but when we begin to speculate about how they ought to be expressed in young people's literature, the problem becomes complex. Certainly children need stories which have substance and strength.

I think it was Lloyd Alexander who spoke several years ago about a capacity to believe and a capacity to value. Values and beliefs may change, Lloyd said, capacity remains-- whether it is a capacity to believe in Santa Claus, Communism, the Prophet Elijah, or King Arthur. Certainly I understand and accept this. I believe, too, that such capacity begins to develop at an early age, and it continues to develop and grow in a soil which is rich and hospitable. Or it may be still- born or destined to wither or die under less generous circum- stances. Values are important, and we need to have a gentle and loving concern about them.

Speaking of values, I don't usually involve gadgets in my storytelling. But one morning, I was going to be telling stories to five-year-olds. I had chosen as one of those stories Margaret Wise Brown's Golden Egg Book. On impulse, I picked up a beautiful little toy, a cloth egg which could be unzipped--and out would come a beautiful yellow duck. When I finished the story with the children, I pulled the cloth egg out of my bag and displayed it dramatically to the children. I lied shamelessly about how I had found it by the roadside and how I had stopped and picked it up and brought it to them. "What," I inquired dramatically, "do you boys and girls think is inside the egg?" Thirty hands shot up. I selected one child to answer. It was not a happy choice. In- stead of telling me, he said in a tone of stern disapproval, "You shouldn't have taken it." "I'll take it back," I muttered. The thirty judges nodded somberly.

Oh, there is so much to say. But time has run out. Well, it's all right. Each one of us will and should make his own summary anyway. We will do just that in the days and years to come, and we will in our own quiet moments and places continue to identify those things which we found to be good and beautiful and true in what we experienced in this place. In such quiet moments, we will decide how these shall be served.

We who have this awesome stewardship to children and young people are privileged indeed. I stand with Mollie Hunter in her profoundly beautiful and powerful statement when she says, "No comment about childhood has moved me so deeply as Chesterton's poem, "The Nativity," in which he says:

> Have a myriad children been quickened,
> Have a myriad children grown cold?
> Grown gross and unloved and embittered,
> Grown cunning and savage and old?
> God abides in a terrible patience,
> Unangered and unworn.
> And again for the child that was squandered,
> A child is born.

Mollie Hunter says, "What a catalogue of blame, and what a note of grace at the end."

Alfred North Whitehead, American philosopher, wrote an essay many years ago which I read and reread each year. It is called "The Aims of Education." He declares that such aims are three: activity of thought, receptivity to beauty, and humane feelings. Where can these be better served than through good stories and poetry?

Because we are, and because we are here, and for so many reasons, may each child whose life we touch find in the dignity and richness of the reading experience that which will enable him, wherever he may be, to say with the ancient psalmist, "I will lift up mine eyes."

CONTRIBUTORS

DOROTHY ANDERSON, a Canadian by birth, wrote her dissertation on Mildred Batchelder. After public library experience and advanced studies, she came to teach at the Graduate School of Library and Information Science, University of California, Los Angeles, where she is now Assistant Dean.

MILDRED BATCHELDER served for 30 years as executive secretary of what is now called the Association for Library Service to Children of the American Library Association. Her awards include the Constance Lindsay Skinner and Grolier Awards. Ms. Batchelder's intense interest in the translation of children's books from abroad was honored by the establishment, in 1968, of the Mildred L. Batchelder Award, presented annually to a U.S. publisher of an outstanding children's book originally published elsewhere in a language other than English.

JOAN BROCKETT is senior lecturer at the Auckland College of Education, New Zealand, where she teaches children's literature. A particular interest is her encouragement of the writing and dissemination of literature concerned with Maori children, who have had, until recently, sparse representation in the children's books of her country.

ASHLEY BRYAN has lived and traveled in many countries and has been a college art teacher. He is best known for his self-illustrated books of Black folklore, such as The Ox of the Wonderful Horns and The Cat's Purr, and Black spirituals. In 1981 he won the Coretta Scott King Award given by the American Library Association for his illustrations in Beat the

Story Drum, Pum-Pum. His moving readings from Black poetry, folklore, and spirituals are widely acclaimed.

MARGARET ANN BUSH has had a varied career in librarianship and is presently teaching children's literature at Simmons College. She has recently been president of the Association for Library Service to Children, American Library
Association, and was chair of the Advisory Committee for the
1986 edition of the Children's Catalog. She has written numerous articles for professional publications.

DOROTHY BUTLER has not only raised a large family but
has earned her degree, established a bookstore, written books,
and given lectures while doing so. Her advocacy for reading
aloud to children at an early age is well known through
Cushla and Her Books and Babies Need Books. In 1982 she
was honored by being named the May Hill Arbuthnot Lecturer
in the United States.

ELEANOR CAMERON writes both fantasy and realistic fiction
for young readers as well as highly-regarded criticism. Some
of her titles are The Wonderful Flight to the Mushroom Planet,
To the Green Mountains, The Court of the Stone Children,
for which she won the National Book Award, Children's Category, in 1974, and Julia and the Hand of God, for which she
won the FOCAL (Friends of Children and Literature, Los
Angeles Public Library) Award in 1985. The Green and Burning Tree is a gathering of her critical essays.

JEWELL REINHART COBURN is a college teacher, lecturer,
and author who has won awards for her trio of Southeast
Asian folktales, Beyond the East Wind, Khmers, Tigers and
Talismans, and Encircled Kingdom. She has traveled and
worked in Southeast Asia and Africa and has special interests
in international understanding and mental health. Her book,
Unlocking the Stories Within You, resulted from teaching
creative writing at the college level.

SHEILA EGOFF was the organizer of the First Pacific Rim
Conference in 1976. She is past professor, School of Librarian
ship, University of British Columbia, and has written widely
in the fields of children's literature and children's librarianship. Only Connect and Thursday's Child: Trends and Patterns in Contemporary Children's Literature are two of the
titles she has written or edited. In 1979 Ms. Egoff was chosen
as the May Hill Arbuthnot Honor Lecturer.

CARMEN GARCIA-MORENO has influenced the development of children's literature and children's librarianship throughout Hispanic America. In Mexico, her native country, she has produced international conferences in children's literature and established an annual children's book award, as well as appearing regularly on radio in behalf of children's books.

SHANTA HERZOG, formerly head of the Children's Film Society in India, is executive director of the Children's Film and Television Center of America, headquartered at the University of Southern California. She promotes creative use of film and television among teachers and librarians and has interacted with many groups of children, often introducing films made from books. Ms. Herzog has directed both national and international film festivals.

EDNA L. HURD is on the staff of the Kamehameha Schools / Bishop Estate. Her particular interest is research into the history and beginnings of the tales which Polynesians have handed down as metaphors of their cultures.

RONALD S. JACKSON is chairman of the Division of Education, Brigham Young University, Hawaii Campus. His research into the tales, games, and dances of the Polynesians has resulted in a videotape of children and adults engaging in folk activities common in Samoa, Tonga, New Zealand, and Hawaii.

VICTOR KELLEHER was born in London, traveled widely in central and southern Africa, and settled in Australia, where he now teaches college courses and writes. He received the West Australian Young Reader's Book Award in 1982 for Forbidden Paths of Thual and in 1983 for The Hunting of Shadroth. His Master of the Grove won the Australian Children's Book of the Year Award in 1983. The Beast of Heaven brought him the 1984 Australian Science Fiction Achievement Award.

MYRA COHN LIVINGSTON is a poet, anthologist, lecturer, and critic who also spends much time with children in schools. She is the author or anthologist of such books as The Malibu and Other Poems, A Tune Beyond Us, Four-Way Stop and Other Poems, and Sky Songs. Among her many awards are the Commonwealth Award, presented to a California author for excellence in writing, two Texas Institute of Letters Awards, and the National Council of Teachers of English Award for excellence in poetry. The Child As Poet: Myth or Reality is among her contributions to criticism.

ELIZABETH MILLER is young people's librarian at the Invercargill Public Library, New Zealand. She is a well-known storyteller, specializing in Maori folklore, and speaks frequent ly in behalf of her profession. She adapts techniques discovered in her travels to her own successful work.

OKIKO MIYAKE is professor of children's literature at Baika Women's College, in Japan. In addition she is an author, translator of children's books, and critic. She has authored or co-authored such books as English and American Children's Literature and The First Step to Children's Literature, and a forthcoming title on the history of St. Nicholas Magazine. Australian children's literature is another specialty. She has translated Colin Thiele, Charlotte Zolotow, the Hurds, Virginia Hamilton, and Eleanor Cameron.

ARNE NIXON teaches in the School of Education and Human Development at California State University, Fresno. He is known nationally as a storyteller and for his many conferences on children's literature. He is constantly traveling in the United States and elsewhere lecturing, giving workshops on children's literature to teachers and librarians, and visiting schools.

S. SHELLEY QUEZADA is a former children's librarian whose present position is consultant for library services to the unserved for the Massachusetts Board of Library Commissioners. She also reviews books in Spanish for Horn Book Magazine because her knowledge of these books ranges over publications in the United States, Mexico, Central and South America, and Spain.

JANE RICKETTS teaches in the School of Humanities, University of the South Pacific, Suva, Fiji. This university serves the students of eleven island nations, and she incorporates the folktales of these nations into her courses on children's literature. She has also launched a program of videotaping storytellers from the various islands in order to preserve a possibly vanishing art.

SPENCER SHAW is professor emeritus, Graduate School of Library and Information Science, Unversity of Washington.

Prior to that he had a distinguished career as a children's librarian, and he has an international reputation as a story-teller. Mr. Shaw has lectured and told stories in Canada, Hawaii, Australia, and New Zealand. Among his many awards and honors is the Grolier Award, presented for his contribution to his profession by the American Library Association.

GARY STRONG began work in public libraries and later became deputy state librarian for the State of Washington. He is currently California state librarian and is particularly interested in establishing an information network spanning the Pacific Ocean. His support for children's work is evident in the State Library's co-sponsorship of this conference and its grant to help finance it.

CHARLOTTE ZOLOTOW has retired from her position as head of Harper Junior Books, but she retains her own imprint with that company. Her long and distinguished career as editor is matched by her extraordinary list of charming and sensitive picture books, including <u>My Grandson Lew</u>, <u>The Hating Book</u>, and <u>Mr. Rabbit and the Lovely Present</u>.

INDEX

EDUCATION